The Grand

Rivers of Michigan Series

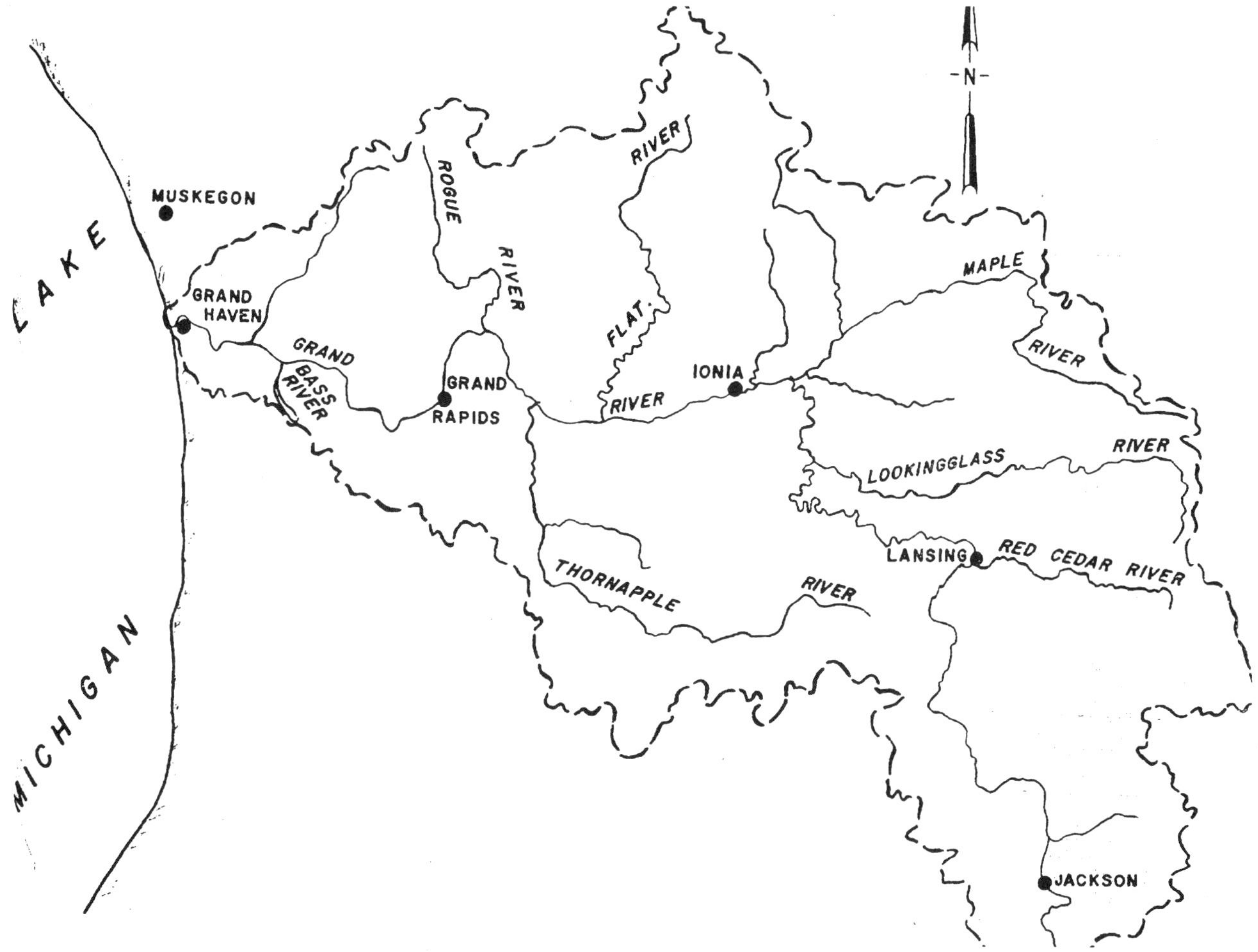

by Kit Lane

Pavilion Press
P. O. Box 250
Douglas, Michigan

Copyright 2007

by Pavilion Press

All Rights Reserved

International Standard Book Number
978-1-877703-39-3

Front Cover: Top, the Michigan Power Company dam at Lansing about 1909. Bottom, the steamer Lizzie Walsh passing by Dewey Hill on the way from Grand Haven to Spring Lake.

Back Cover: A 21st Century trip down the Grand River from Grandville to Fruitport on Spring Lake aboard the sternwheel excursion boat Grand Lady. The moveable gangway, which allows the boat to land on any stable point, extends from the bow at right.

Table of Contents

The River 5

Natives and Early Visitors. 10

Fur Traders and Missionaries. 14

Villages Spring Up. 20

Planning Canal Connectors 23

Navigation on the River. 26

Turning on the Lights 35

High Water on the Grand 40

Ecological Future 49

From Beginning to End 57

      The Sources 58

      Jackson to Eaton Rapids 66

      Eaton Rapids to Lansing 73

      Lansing to Ionia 81

      Ionia to Grand Rapids 102

      Grand Rapids to Lake Michigan 114

Bibliography 145

Index 149

Photo Credits and Acknowledgements 159

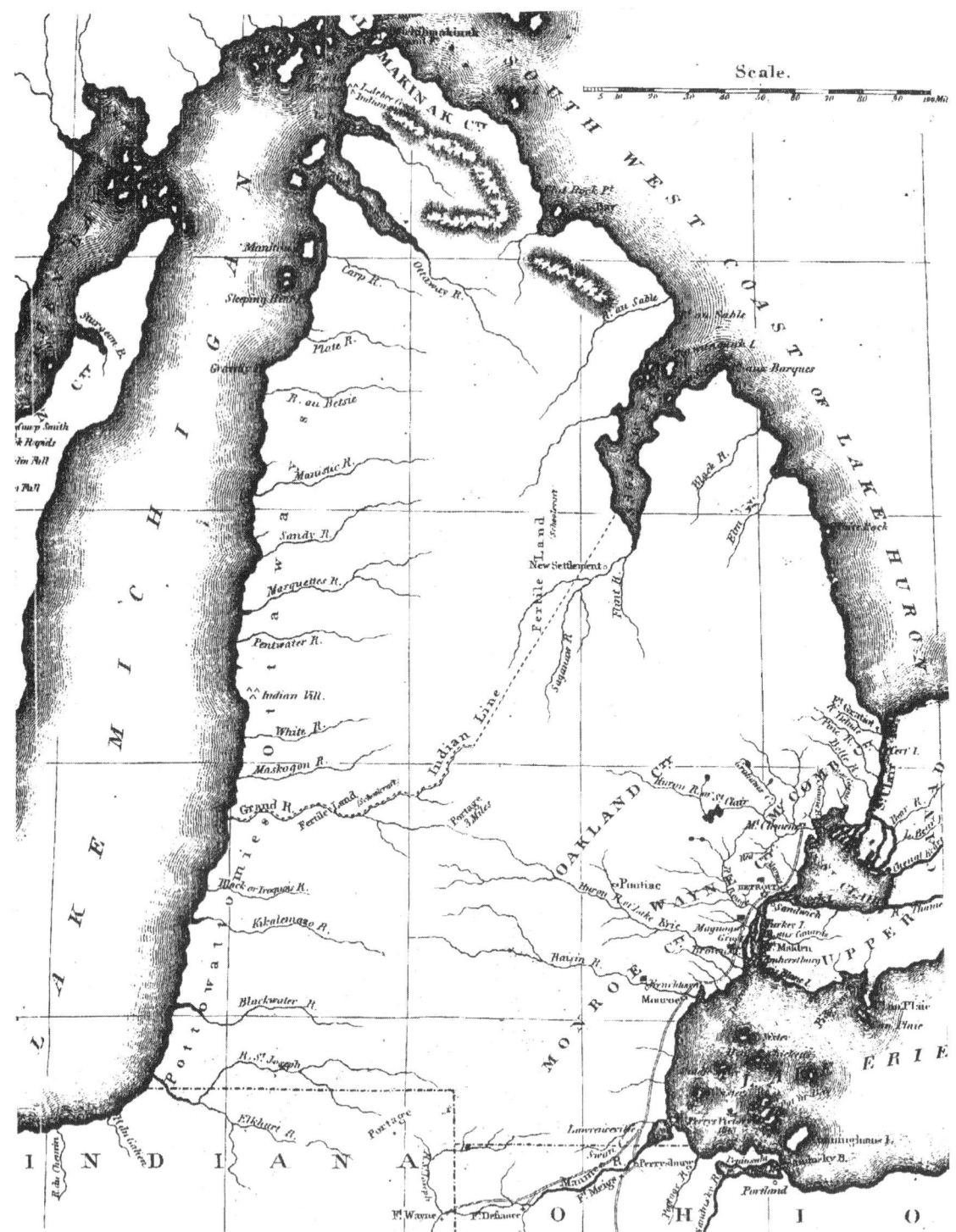

This 1829 map of Michigan Territory shows the Grand River part of an "Indian Line," marking the northern limits of the land ceded by treaty with the Native Americans and indicates that there might be a connection by portage into Saginaw Bay. It also clearly marks a three mile portage between the Grand River and the Huron River,, which would make a connection into Lake Erie south of Detroit. On this map the mouth of the Maumee, where Toledo was later built, was still part of Michigan.

The River

According to a 1926 federal survey, the Grand River is the largest stream in Michigan. It has a drainage area of 5,572 square miles. The survey gives it a total length of "about 300 miles." This would be taking into full account every bend of the river – and there are thousands. An actual measurement of the main channel today, taking a direct path through the lakes and other wide spots, would be over 250 miles from the source to Lake Michigan, but probably less than 300.

Two Branches Form a Single River

A *Gazetteer of the State of Michigan* published in 1838 by John T. Blois describes its beginnings:

> *Grand River.* – (Indian name *Washtenong*) . . . At its source are two tributaries – the East and South branches. The former takes rise on the western confines of Sharon township, in Washtenaw county, and the South branch on the northern border of Wheatland township, Hillsdale county. They both unite in Jackson county, a little above the village of Jackson. [1]

The total fall over the entire course of the river is just over 400 feet, depending on the level of Lake Michigan, with most of the changes in elevation occurring before the flow reaches Grand Rapids. The last 40 miles, from Grand Rapids to Grand Haven, there is a fall of only six feet, with half of that in the upper six miles

In addition to the main river there are a number of tributaries which are themselves each more than 50 miles long, and supported considerable commerce and mill activity in years past. They include the Thornapple which comes into the Grand at Ada, the Maple which joins the main flow near Muir, the Looking Glass at Portland, the Red Cedar at Lansing, the Rogue at Grand Rapids, the Flat at Lowell and the Portage near Jackson..

The entire river system watershed includes all or parts of 18 counties. The watershed is oval in shape and is bounded by the North Muskegon and Saginaw watersheds on the north, and the Kalamazoo watershed to the south. (See map on title page.)

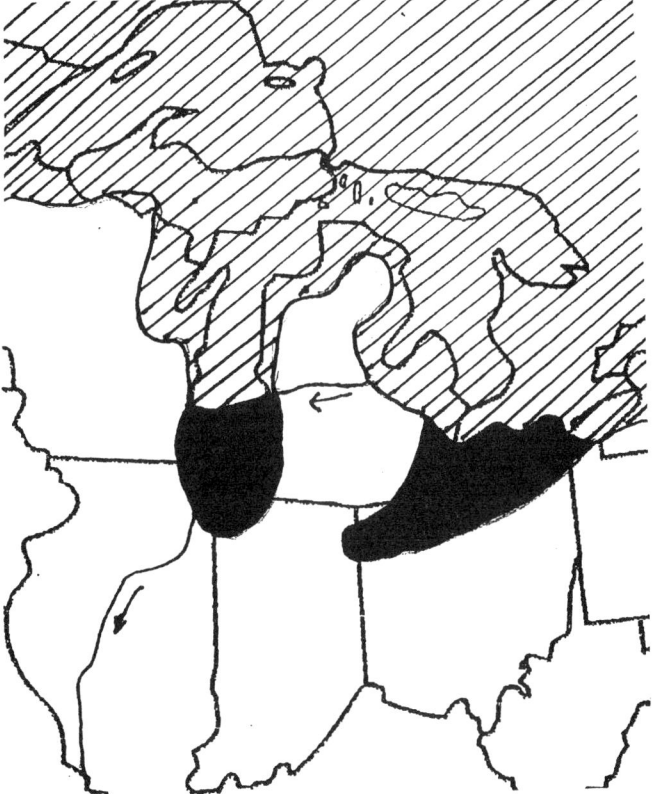

The glacier receding formed two lobes with the ancient Grand River as a connecting link. Water from the melting glacier (hatchmarked areas) entered the ocean through the Mississippi River.

The Mighty Grand River in Antiquity

About 14,000 years ago the Grand River, or at least its ancestor, was one of the deepest and most important rivers in North America. As the glaciers began to recede from what would become Michigan, they didn't melt evenly. The ice was deeper in the gouged-out areas which would become the Great Lakes. The ice tended to melt first where it was not so thick, over the future land area of lower Michigan. When the glacier formed the Lake Michigan lobe and the Saginaw Bay lobe (the two areas of ice which covered what would become Lake Michigan and what would become Lake Huron) were separate at first. Then they collided and joined in western Michigan – near Grand Rapids.

When the glacier began to recede the two lobes split apart in about the same place until they were two peninsulas of ice with land in the middle. When that happened a channel formed between the two lobes of ice to carry water from the melting glacier. This ancient channel followed the Maple River to the Grand River as it flowed westward. Some geologists claim that the European mapmakers got it wrong, and that the Maple River should be the dominant stream, with the Grand River, east of Muir, as the tributary.

The river was very deep, in places over 100 feet; however, at first, because the ice remained to the north and west, the flow turned southward through Hudsonville and out the Black River channel exiting into Lake Chicago (the earliest configuration of what would become Lake Michigan) near modern-day Holland. The water then flowed south through the Illinois River and into the Mississippi River.

Later, after the ice retreated farther north, the Grand found a shorter route to the lake by continuing westerly at Jenison in the direction of Lamont. When this channel first formed, the site of present-day Allendale was its western terminus. Over the centuries a 100-square-mile delta formed from Allendale to Grand Haven. When the glacier retreated far enough to the north, the water began to flow around the top of the peninsula, at the Straits of Mackinac, and the role of the Grand River was diminished to that of a local river.

This 1744 French map shows a portage from "la Grande Riviere" to Saginaw Bay.

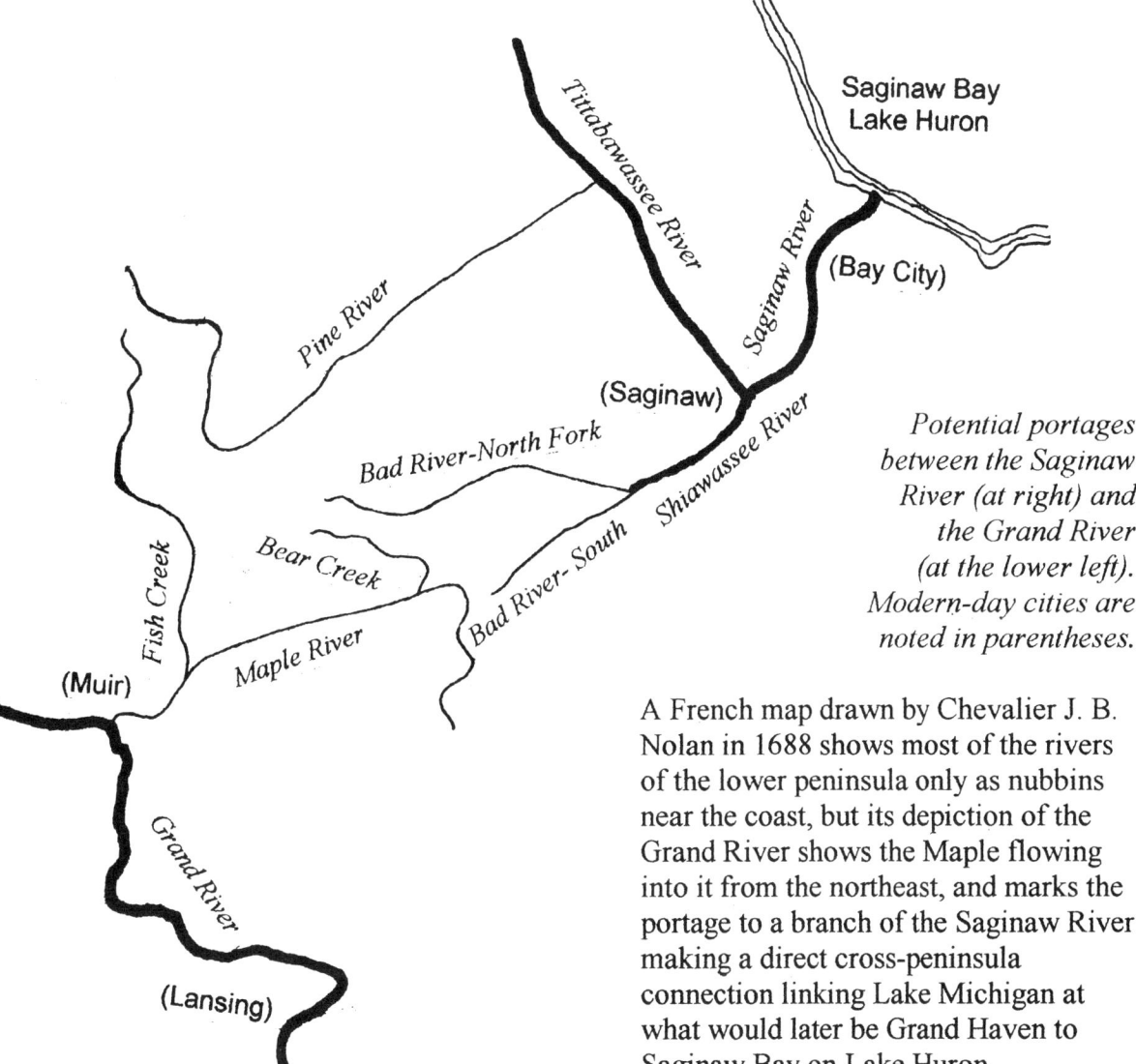

Potential portages between the Saginaw River (at right) and the Grand River (at the lower left). Modern-day cities are noted in parentheses.

Early Maps Show Indian Portages

However, even after the glaciers had retreated out of sight and memory, the first inhabitants of the area could span the lower peninsula with their canoes and shallow draft boats by several different routes. These routes were well known to the Native Americans living in the area when the first missionaries and fur traders arrived, and the locals were not reticent to share some of their knowledge with the newcomers.

A French map drawn by Chevalier J. B. Nolan in 1688 shows most of the rivers of the lower peninsula only as nubbins near the coast, but its depiction of the Grand River shows the Maple flowing into it from the northeast, and marks the portage to a branch of the Saginaw River making a direct cross-peninsula connection linking Lake Michigan at what would later be Grand Haven to Saginaw Bay on Lake Huron.

A map drawn by Jacques Nicola Bellin in 1844 clearly marks the portage from *"La Grande Riviere"* to a branch of a stream entering *"B. de Saguinam."*

Cross-Peninsula Routes

This connection could be established in several different ways. The "superhighway" of cross-peninsula traffic was a route from Saginaw Bay on Lake Huron up the Saginaw River to the Shiawassee to the south fork of the Bad River near

Saginaw, followed by a short portage into the Maple.

This route is still in use. At the portage the terrain is flat and sandy, and drainage ditches in the area have brought the two streams to within a half a mile of each other. The biggest obstacle to the canoeist is getting stuck in a culvert.

Another route that was sometimes used was to leave Lake Huron on the Saginaw River, turn north up the Tittabawassee, and then southwest up the Pine to Fish Creek, then a portage over to the Maple River, and into the Grand. This route was longer but handier for travelers from the north country, or those headed that way.

Some maps show another, apparently less used, possibility to travel cross-peninsula using the Grand River. A slightly longer portage would allow a traveler to go directly from the headwaters of the Shiawassee into the Looking Glass River, entering the Grand River at Portland.

From Lake Erie to Grand Haven

An 1829 map of Michigan Territory drawn by J. Finlayson and engraved by Young & Delleker only suggests the possible portage into the Saginaw River, but states that the connection between the Grand and the Huron River, which would provide a route from Lake Michigan to Lake Erie, was only three miles. (See map on page 4.)

This route, too, had two different connections. Both involved entering the Huron River at its mouth in the southeastern corner of Wayne County and paddling west through Flat Rock, Ypsilanti and Ann Arbor. The main route was a portage into Portage Lake Swamp in northeastern Jackson County, through the Portage Lakes, then down the Portage River to the Grand north of Jackson.

The other route moved northward into Portage Creek (note: one route moves on Portage *River*, the second on Portage *Creek*) in the southwestern corner of Livingston County. Portage Creek flows north to Lowe Lake (formerly called Portage Lake), then there is a second portage into Doan Creek southeast of Dansville, then north paddling into the Red Cedar River just west of Williamston. The Red Cedar River flows into the Grand River at Lansing, then it's a straight shot to Grand Haven and Lake Michigan.

Naming a River

According to early settlers the Native Americans called the Grand River the Owashtenong meaning "far-flowing water" or "far into the interior" or more literally "far-off land river." The natives gave it that name because it went places.

The white men, trying to translate the Indian language phonetically, spelled the word a variety of ways including Owashtenong, Onatanon, Achentnon, and Ionachetanon. An old French spelling puts a symbol that looks like a figure 8 in the first syllable, said to be an old French equivalent of a "We" or "W" sound, and makes the word look like I-8-achtenon. An old letter from Fr. D. La Richarde dated at Detroit in December of 1741 was addressed to Fr. DuJaunay "at the river d'8Achetnon." By 1744 maps had begun using the French name for the river, calling it the

"*Grande*" or "Grand." This appellation, French for "large," applied to both the size of its mouth at Lake Michigan, and its known length. The Indian name Gabaguoache, meaning "big mouth," is sometimes applied to the river itself, and sometimes to an early settlement at Grand Haven near the mouth.

The riverbanks were settled first in the places where there was enough fall to harness for power. The names of some of the new towns reflect this geographic feature: Eaton Rapids, where the dam on the Grand River would provide power first for the lumber and the grist needed by the settlers, then for a world-renown woolen industry, and Grand Rapids, the city which would specialize in furniture. There was Jackson at its headwaters and Grand Haven at its end. The settlement of Lansing was given impetus when it was named state capital in 1847.

And there were other smaller gatherings along the river. Some of these,

Wyoming, Walker, Comstock Park, Ada, Grandville and Jenison, drew strength from nearby Grand Rapids. Grand Haven, Ferrysburg and Spring Lake grew up as a conglomerate settlement. Others grew into more isolated self-sustaining cities including Grand Ledge, Ionia, Lowell, and Portland.

Others along the river: Lyons, Dimondale, Saranac, Onondaga, Lamont, Eastmanville, and Delta Mills, remained small. Still other communities flourished for a while and then all-but-vanished. These include Kinneville, Berryville, Petrieville, Columbia, Waverly Park, Austerlitz, Tallmadge, Charleston, Ottawa Centre, Millett, Spoonville, and Pottamie.

(Below) A 1703 French map shows the newly founded "le Detroit" at the right and "la Grande Riviere" at left. "Marameg" is an old name for the Kalamazoo River.

Natives and Early Visitors

According to archaeologists there have been human beings in the area which later became Michigan for at least 12,000 years.

Pre-Historic Native Inhabitants

During the Paleo-Indian period, 10,000 BC to 8000 BC, the natives began the use of primitive flint tools. The few sites of this period in Michigan tend to be in the north. During the Archaic period, 8000 BC to 1000 BC, better tools were developed, and copper began to be utilized. Evidence is that the Indians adapted well to forest life. Sites of these civilizations have been uncovered along the St. Joseph River in southern Michigan, and in the Saginaw River valley.

It was during the Woodland period, 1000 BC to 1650 AD, that the concentration of natives along the Grand River began. During this period of development the Indians engaged in the creation of pottery, and began to domesticate plants in an early form of agriculture. Burial rites were well developed. It was during this period that burial mounds in the city of Grand Rapids, known as the Converse site and destroyed during the development of the city, and the Norton Mounds, near Grandville, were constructed.

The Norton Mounds, so named because they were on the farm property of Captain Anson N. Norton, were on the banks of the Grand River about 38 miles from the mouth, and three miles east of the city of Grand Rapids. In addition to the destruction that came with the settling of the lands, and the curiosity of small boys who lived nearby, the mounds were first "scientifically" excavated in 1875 by Wright L. Coffinberry, under the auspices of the Kent Scientific Institute. Items removed included decorated pottery, conch shell beads and containers, engraved turtle shell dishes, copper awls, axes and rolled copper beads. Nearby were sheet mica mirrors, carved pipes and the teeth and jaws of wolves and bears.

Artifacts in Ottawa County

Another site at Spoonville near Crockery Creek was, according to early histories, destroyed during the construction of the first mill. However, a portion of the old site, or a new one nearby, was excavated by students and archaeologists from Grand Valley State University from 1962 to 1991. The project uncovered evidence of several Indian villages and mounds from the period 10 B.C. to 400 A.D. near the junction of the creek and the Grand River.

At a site on private property near Crockery Creek the Grand Valley team uncovered artifacts that dated from 100 B.C. to 1400 A.D., nearly historic times. The 1991 archaeological team uncovered a rare "Hi-Lo" projectile point which was very old; preliminary carbon dating showed dates from 8000 to 10,000 B.C. Smaller groups of mounds and some artifacts were also recovered from sites near Tallmadge and Ferrysburg in Ottawa County.

None of the historic Indians encountered by the settlers had any knowledge of the building of the ancient burial mounds. They revered the mounds, occasionally adding their own dead to further confuse archaeologists, but told the white men that the mounds were already in place when they arrived. During the exploration of the Norton Mounds in 1870, trees on top of the mounds were found to be more than 250 years old, lending credence to the idea that the mound builders had been gone many years before the historic Indians arrived.

Native Villages Along the Grand

The earliest arriving white settlers noted that there were Indian villages along the Grand River at the future sites of Portland, Lyons, Ionia, Lowell, Ada, Grandville, Crockery Creek, Battle Point (near Spring Lake) and two villages at Grand Rapids, one at the head and one at the food of the rapids.[2]

The Grand River was the southern boundary for members of the Odawa in historic times more commonly rendered Ottawa) group. The Odawa, along with the Ojibway (sometimes called Chippewa) to the north, and the Potawatomi to the south, make up the "People of the Three Fires." The three tribes were all Algonquin speaking and, although there were disagreements between them, had similar cultures and needs, occasionally forming loose alliances in the face of a common enemy.

In the early days of settlement the Native Americans and the newcomers lived in relative harmony. The white men learned many things from the Indians including how to grow corn, hunt in the forest, and construct canoes and dugouts which were much coveted as a quick way to travel on the river.

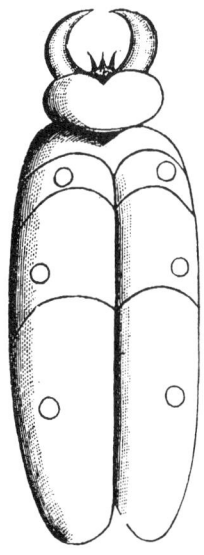

An insect-shaped relic found in the mounds in Court Street, Grand Rapids, about 1880.

LaSalle First European to Cross Peninsula

Fur traders and other Frenchmen traversing the Great Lakes and running about in the woods must have stumbled on the Grand River shortly after they arrived in the territory, but no one wrote about it until Robert Cavelier, Sieur de La Salle, passed that way in 1680 as part of his efforts to expand French fur trade in the New World.

He sailed into Lake Michigan in August of 1679, on a large sailing vessel called **Griffon**. He sent the boat back with a load of furs, and went with some men down the shore of Lake Michigan to the mouth of the St. Joseph where they had established a fort. Anxious to hear from the boat, in March of 1680, La Salle and five men started out across the lower peninsula on foot.

They traveled through Van Buren, Kalamazoo, Calhoun, Jackson and Washtenaw counties, He wrote in his journal, "through the woods which was so interlaced with thorns and brambles that . . . our clothes were all torn and our faces so covered with blood that we hardly knew each other."

In an entry in early April La Salle wrote that they had paused to thaw their frozen clothes and the fire brought them to the attention of a Mascouten war party, but the Indians were prevented from molesting them because of a "rather deep stream which they could not cross, because the ice which had formed in the night was not strong enough to bear them."

Historians who have studied both the journal and maps of the area have concluded that the "rather deep stream" was the Grand River north of Jackson in Jackson County.

After an unsuccessful attempt to go down the Huron River, La Salle completed his walk to what would be the site of Detroit, rafted across the Detroit River and went on to Niagara where he learned that the Griffon had not been heard from. It never was.

The British Visit during the Revolutionary War

The mouth of the Grand River was described in January of 1779 when the British Navy toured the Great Lakes attempting to "reconnoitre the different bays and creeks in lake Michigan" and to gather what Indians they could find to assist with the military offense at Detroit. They found "about 80" on the Grand River, but most declined to participate on such short notice.

Later in 1779, on the pretext of looking for rebels around the Grand River, **H.M.S. Felicity**, a sloop in the Royal Navy, sailed down the east coast of Lake Michigan. The log of that expedition is still in the British Museum and includes an entry dated October 31, 1779: [3]

> At daylight this morning we weigh'd anchor & stood for the grand River SSE a wind from the East; at 10 A.M. we cam in the river about 2 cabbel lengths & mored her with the anchor on the shoar the Bank being steep too so that we stept from the vessels gunwale on the shoar; th narrowest part of the river at the entrance is about 70 or 80 yard wide 3 & 4 fathoms deep, upon the barr there is 2 fathoms. I imeaditly sent Mr. Gaulty with 3 hands in the boat up 4 Leauges to the first indean *[Indian]* village to see if it was possible to get canoes to fetch down the corn.

There was no news the next day, but the following day:

> At 12 this day a fresh Breeze from the N.W. At 12 this night Mr. Gautly returned but saw no indeans although he was 6 leauges up the River, therefore saw it was truth which the indeans at Mishigon *[probably Muskegon River]* had told us that they had all left the lake side upon account of some distemper of which a great many had died; the negro at the river Mishigon also told me that, none of the tradders had yet passed for the grand River nor the Kikanamasa *[Kalamazoo]*.

Hugh Heward Crosses Michigan by Canoe

After the Revolutionary War, the area of Michigan was surrendered to the newly-formed government of the United States in the Treaty of 1783 and Great Britain agreed to withdraw all its garrisons from the territory. This was not done, however, and Michigan remained essentially under British rule until 1796.

Hugh Heward, a British fur trader who had declared his intention to remain a British citizen, [4] left Detroit with seven French-Canadian "engages" and started up the mouth of the Huron on March 28, 1790. Taking on an Indian guide they finally found the portage into the Portage River and on April 22 were told by the Indians at a local lodge that they had, indeed, found the Grand River.

On April 24, having just left behind a group of Indians, "an ill looking Band of about 12 who seem to be refugees from the Otaways & peutowatomas, strong fat vagabonds," they set out from Onondaga in Ingham County. The April 24 entry in the journal notes:

Refited our Cannots (*canoes*) with Gum and set off. Passed a Rapid in about an hour after which high broken Land some pine Trees the Banks of Red Land from thence came to a River from the East & a little lower two Cabins from Sagana *(North Lansing)* . . . another Island about Mid Day *(Delta Mills)* came to another Island afterwards three Small Islands & some pine Trees on each side of the River & high rocks on the North & a small Run of Water from the South *(Grand Ledge)*[5]

The little band, in two canoes, paddled almost 50 miles that day, a feat that is re-enacted, occasionally, as the Hugh Heward Challenge by Jackson area canoeists.

Heward and his men reached the mouth of the Grand River on April 27, 1790, where he was greeted by fur trader Charles Langlade.

Cadette Everett Fitch
Grand Rapids History & Special Collections
Grand Rapids Public Library

Fur Traders and Missionaries

Arrival of Fur Traders.

Old French records put the first fur trader, Charles Langlade or his representatives, on the banks of the Grand River as early as 1742. Especially under the French these traders moved in and out of areas, paying little attention to boundary lines and franchises. They left little behind to show they had visited. Later missionaries wrote that they often felt that the traders "tainted" the natives by offering them alcoholic beverages, when it would get them the best deal, and caring little for their welfare.

The British had a tighter rein on fur traffic, but it was largely in the hands of John Askin and others who controlled the purse strings. After the government of the United States of America finally got around to taking control of the area west of the Appalachian mountains in 1896, the fur traders were required to be licensed and were held accountable for their actions, but even then abuses abounded. (See license on page 15)

Pierre Constant One of the First

Pierre Constant, with the British Fur Company, set out in 1810 to find new markets, and paddled up the Grand River to what is now Allendale Township, pausing at a creek now known as Trader's Creek. He built a cabin and cemented relations with his suppliers by marrying an Indian woman. They had six children including a daughter, Louisa or "Lisette," who became her father's clerk when she was 12 years old. When Lisette was 17 her father died, and she left the British Fur Company and became a trader with the American Fur Company for six years before marrying a fellow trader and moving to Wisconsin. In 1836, with the fur trade waning following a fashion trend in Europe away from beaver hats, the land where his trading post stood was sold to speculators who tried to establish the city of Charleston, but it never caught on.

A Lady Takes Over

Joseph la Framboise, a French fur trader with the American Fur Company, had established a post on the Grand River, below the mouth of the Flat River, before 1796. That year he was married to Madeline, described as half Indian, the daughter of a chief and a French woman. They lived a portion of each year at Mackinac Island, and eventually built a cabin where they stayed during the summer. On their way south in 1809 they encountered a group of Indians who demanded liquor, which they refused to furnish. An angry Indian stabbed Joseph, some accounts say as he knelt in prayer, killing him instantly.

Madame La Framboise gathered the remains of her husband and traveled on to the trading post, later disinterring the body and taking it back to Mackinac Island with her. She continued to trade on the Grand River until 1821 when she sold her posts to Rix Robinson and retired to the island. Her only daughter, Josette, was married in 1817 to Captain Benjamin K. Pierce, the head of the Fort Mackinac guard. Captain Pierce was the brother of Franklin Pierce, president of the United States from 1853 to 1857.

*Instructions to Louis Campau, this day licensed
to trade with the Indian nation at _____*

1. Your trade will be confined to the place to which you are licensed.

2. Your transactions with the Indians will be confined to fair and friendly trade.

3. You will attend no Councils held by the Indians, nor send them any talk or speech, accompanied by wampum.

4. You are forbidden to take any spirituous liquors of any kind into the Indian country; or to give, sell or dispose of any to the Indians.

5. Should any person attempt to trade in the Indian country without a license; or should any licensed traders carry any spirituous liquors into the Indian country; or give, sell or dispose of any to the Indians, the Indians are authorized to seize and take to their own use the goods of such traders and the owner shall have no claim on the Indians or the United States for the same.

6. Should you learn that there is any person in the Indian country trading without a license, you will immediately report the name of such person, and the place where he is trading, to some Indian agent.

7. You will take all proper occasions to inculcate upon the Indians the necessity of peace; and to state to them that it is the wish of their Great Father, the President, to live in harmony with them; and that they must shut their ears to any wild stories there may be in circulation.

Given under my hand, at the city of Detroit, this 15th day of November, 1822.

       William Woodbridge, Secretary,

and at present vested with the powers of Superintendent of Indian Affairs therein.

Fur Traders Become Settlers

Rix Robinson, in 1821, bought the posts which had been built by Mr. and Mrs. La Framboise including an existing French store about where Ada was later built, near the mouth of the Thornapple River. In addition he had a number of other posts on the Grand, Kalamazoo and Muskegon Rivers. Robinson married an Indian woman, Pee-miss-a-quot-o-quay or "Flying Cloud Woman." Later, after her death, he was married to Se-be-quay or "River Woman." In 1836 he retired from the trading business and took up farming, building the community of Ada as well as Grand Haven where he had pre-empted a tract. He was the first supervisor of Ada Township, served with the Michigan legislature, was an associate justice of the circuit court, and assisted the Michigan Indians in several different negotiations with the federal government. There was even talk of Rix Robinson for governor, but he begged off, saying that he felt his Indian wife was not up to the social responsibilities which went with the office.

Louis Campau was born in Detroit in 1791, a third-generation Detroit resident and the fourth generation of his family to be born in North America, his great-grandfather, Jacques, having arrived in Detroit from Montreal in 1708. As early as 1822 Louis Campau received a license to trade with the Indians. His first work was an effort to dispose of some outdated stock in the Saginaw area. In 1826 he arrived at the "grande rapids" as an independent trader with a working relationship with a New York merchant. He built two cabins on the west side of the river, one for himself; the second for the trading post. His brother, Toussaint, joined him in 1827. Both brothers decided to stay and were founders of what would eventually be the City of Grand Rapids.

Daniel Marsac, an 18-year-old Frenchman from Detroit, arrived near the confluence of the Flat and Grand rivers in 1829 to set up a trading post. In 1831 he built a small log cabin on the south bank of the Grand River. He married an Odawa girl named Jenute.

When the white settlers began moving in, Marsac was said to be ashamed of his Indian wife and went to Detroit and married a French woman, bringing her back to his cabin, a move that did not please the Indians who frequented his post. Marsac attempted to plat a settlement named Dansville, but it was not a success, so he sold his land and moved on.

Mr. and Mrs. Louis Campau

Missionaries

Earliest missionary efforts in Michigan were those of French priests who were in the New World as early as 1618, and in Michigan by 1641, beginning with a mission at Sault Ste. Marie and working slowly to the south. First came the friars of the Recollet order, followed in 1625 by the Jesuit missionaries, who traveled around the lakes contacting native tribes, baptizing and burying. These early missionaries included Pere (French for "Father") Jacques Marquette who would afterwards have a railroad named for him; Father Claude Allouez, who labored with both the Odawa and the Potawatomi from 1665 to his death in 1689; and Father Louis Hennepin, who explored the Great Lakes and the upper Mississippi, 1679-1680.

There is a tradition that Father Gabriel Richard, a Sulpician priest, visited the Indian villages on the Grand River at the rapids, about 1799 following a trip to Mackinac Island and the Odawas on Little Traverse Bay. Grand Rapids historian Albert Baxter writes, "There is very little of authentic record concerning the mission; but enough to give probability to the story." Father Richard became parish priest at St. Anne's, Detroit, in 1798 until his death in the cholera epidemic of 1832. He was also a representative to Congress, founded the first newspaper in Michigan, and was an early educator.[6]

Isaac McCoy and Thomas Mission

In Grand Rapids, where missionary fervor preceded settlement, it was the Baptists who arrived first. Isaac McCoy, a Baptist clergyman from Kentucky, established a mission on the St. Joseph River near what would become Niles, in 1822. The following year he called first at the Odawa Indian village located near the "*grande*" rapids, but his plans for establishing a new mission there were not well received by the natives. In 1824 a delegation of Indians from the rapids asked McCoy to return. He arrived on the banks of the Grand River to stay in 1826 and set up the Thomas Mission, named for a Baptist missionary to India, on the west bank of the river near present-day Bridge Street.

It was McCoy's feeling that there was no hope of creating a Christian civilization among the natives as long as they were subjected to the bad influences of the fur traders and others on the frontier, who would furnish liquor and otherwise corrupt his efforts. In his memoirs he recorded after his first visit to Grand Rapids that he had formed a resolution to :

> . . . thenceforward keep steadily in view, and endeavour to

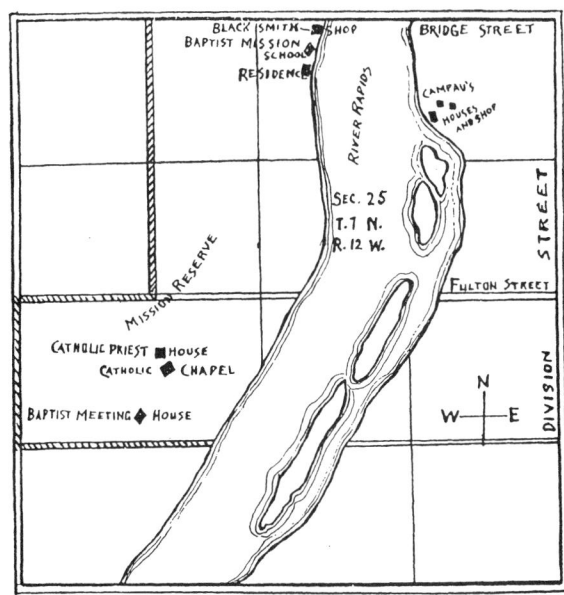

MISSION RESERVE—FROM SURVEY IN 1838.

The Baptists at the head of the rapids, the Catholics at the foot in 1838.

promote a plan for colonizing the natives in a country to be made forever theirs, west of the state of Missouri and from that time until the present I have considered the promotion of this design as the most important business of my life.

He arranged for a government-promised blacksmith, set up a school, delivered the farming equipment provided by the federal government and built a small building for worship. Lumber for these buildings was furnished by a water-powered mill. McCoy stayed only six months at the rapids before moving on to Kansas. He turned the work of Thomas Mission over to the Reverend Leonard Slater in 1827.

As Grand Rapids begin to develop Slater found it increasingly difficult to wield any influence over the natives in that setting. To gain a more isolated setting for his work, in 1836 Slater led about a third of the residents of the Grand Rapids Odawa village to a new mission in Barry County, not far from Gun Lake. The only improvement they took with them was the chapel, which was dismantled and re-erected near Gun Lake.

Father Baraga and the Catholics

In 1833 Father Frederic Baraga, born in Slovenia, came to the New World to convert the Indians to Roman Catholicism. He was assigned to the Indian village near the rapids. For a while he used a building offered by Louis Campau, but when the two disagreed, in October of 1833, he constructed a new chapel, partially funded by Austrian Catholics.

The two Indian villages at the rapids had different religious leanings. The northern one, near present-day Bridge Street, was headed by Nawequageezhig (known by the settlers as Chief Noonday) who was the brother-in-law of Rix Robinson, a fur trader at Ada and Grand Haven. He favored the Baptists. The south village, near today's Fulton Street, was headed by Kewaycooshcum (or Blackskin) who was friendly with local trader and later town founder Louis Campau. He favored the Catholics.

As the Indians moved onward, the Catholic mission at Grand Rapids gradually evolved into a white parish, the foundation of the Roman Catholic presence in Grand Rapids today. Father Baraga moved to the Upper Peninsula of Michigan, where he was founding bishop of the Diocese of Marquette.

Indians Lose Land and Move West

The lands along the Grand River were gradually ceded to the government of the United States by the Indian inhabitants, who had only a tenuous grasp of land "ownership" anyway. The headwaters area was ceded in the Treaty of Detroit of 1807 and the riverbanks from Jackson to about the Flat River at Lowell were ceded in the Treaty of Saginaw of 1819.

When west Michigan began to be opened to settlement, the Grand River was selected as the northern boundary line of land ceded in the Treaty of Chicago of 1821. For 15 years native people were encouraged to move to the north of the Grand River. Then in the Treaty of Washington in 1836 the northwestern portion of the lower peninsula, from the Grand River on the south to the Straits of Mackinac, was ceded. Beginning in the 1830s the Potawatomi Indians who occupied the rich agricultural land of southwestern Michigan were removed to reservations in the west, although some of the Odawa and Ojibway tribes in the more sparsely settled north, were allowed to remain. Many have since returned to the homeland, and there is a strong presence of all three tribes in Michigan, especially the Grand Rapids area, into the 21st Century.

VIEW FROM MONROE STREET TRAIL IN 1832.
A—Island No. 1.   B—Noonday's House.   C—Mission.
D—Indian Wigwams.   E—Trading Post.

A view of Grand Rapids in 1832 before the arrival of the first true settler. Marked B in the background is the house of Chief Noonday, in the foreground an Indian wigwam. Middle right, the house and trading post of Louis Campau, and marked C in the background the mission buildings.

Villages Spring Up

Rivers, which are now valued mainly for their scenic value, were of great practical use to the earliest settlers. The river was a source of water for household use, agricultural purposes and often important in industry. The power of running water drove the saws in the lumber mills, turned the grinding stones in the flour mills, and turned the lathes in the furniture factories. Later the river would provide the power for streetlights and interurban electric railroads. Even when steam power became popular, water from the river was an important ingredient.

In addition the river was used for transportation. Household goods and machinery were brought around the Great Lakes and then moved up the river by steamboat, sometimes as far as Grand Rapids, and, by barge or small boats, even farther inland. The river was also an avenue for moving timber from the forests to the mill, and the finished product, by raft, to markets downriver. Especially before the coming of the railroad, lumber and other wood products, and occasionally flour and other farm produce, were taken to Grand Haven where they were transferred to sail and steam vessels and sent on to eastern markets.

Although the fur traders, missionaries and a few other Europeans stayed for varying periods of time along the river as early as 1795, they are not usually counted as "settlers." The fur traders were there to turn a profit, to take the beaver furs that they bought from the Indians and send them to Europe where they could be turned into fashionable beaver hats. The missionaries were more interested in collecting souls.

Rapid Settlement in the 1830s

Settlement of the interior of Michigan, discouraged during French rule, and

The small cabin of the Guild family at Grand Rapids in 1833.

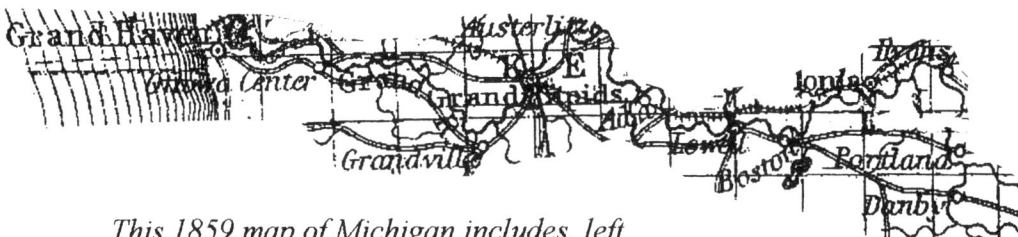

This 1859 map of Michigan includes, left to right, Grand Haven, Ottawa Center, Grandville, Grand Rapids, Austerlitz, Ada, Lowell, Boston (later Saranac), Ionia, Lyons, Portland, Danby, Grand Ledge, Lansing, Biddle City, Eaton Rapids and Jackson. Double lines are roads.

permitted but not encouraged by the British, could not truly begin until the early 1830s after the land was surveyed and opened for sale and settlement. When settlement began it continued rapidly the entire length of the river.

The Grand River at Jackson was an early starting place for pioneers and land speculators from Detroit to begin the exploration of areas west. Horace Blackman built a cabin near what would be Jackson in July of 1827. The town was platted in 1830, and became county seat in 1833.

A Real Settler at Grand Rapids

Although it had been an early site of both missionary work and fur trading, Grand Rapids can mark its beginnings as a settlement from 1831 when Louis Campau, a fur trader, purchased, for $90, land which would become the central business district. A post office was opened in 1832, and the settlement incorporated as a village three years later. The first actual intentional settlers, nine members of the Joel Guild family from Oneida County, New York, arrived in 1833.

In 1832 Luther Lincoln came down the river with others looking for a town site. Just below the "grand" rapids they found what they were looking for and remained in the area during the winter of 1832. The following spring they purchased the site and settled there. A post office opened in 1834. It was platted and registered as Grandville in 1835.

In the spring of 1833 Samuel Dexter led five families, and one single man, from Herkimer County, New York, to form the settlement which became Ionia. They bought a place where the Indians had a garden plot planted to corn to sustain them until they could sow their own crops.

The same year, 1833, fur trader Rix Robinson built a trading post at the site of Grand Haven, and the following year the Reverend William Ferry, Robert Stuart and Nathan M. White formed the New Haven Company to develop the area.

Also in 1833 Harry and Zine Steele founded Steele's Landing on the north bank of the river in Ottawa County. In 1855 Lamont Chubb offered to give the village a road scraper if they would name the village after him and it became Lamont.

The first white settlers, the Libhart family, arrived at the site of Lyons, in Ionia County near the mouth of the Maple River, in 1833. In February of 1836 Lucius Lyon, who would be one of Michigan's first U. S. senators, bought the town site and renamed it Lyons, convincing several of his relatives to move there from Vermont to help build the new settlement.

Onondaga in Ingham County was begun by Oliver Booth in 1834. The village of Saranac, Ionia County, was platted and registered and the first post office opened in 1839.

Eaton Rapids, at the rapids in Eaton County, was platted and received its first post office in 1838. Founders of the village included Amos and Pierpont E. Spicer, Benjamin Knight, Samuel Hamlin and C. C. Darling, all from Ohio.

Eastmanville, in Ottawa County, was settled in 1838. It was first called Scranton, then Polkton, and eventually Eastmanville after the large Eastman family which settled there.

The Second Decade of Settlement

By the end of the 1840s most other settlements along the river had begun: Dimondale, Eaton County, where the first dam was constructed in 1840; Delta Mills, where a post office opened in 1842; and the Kinnieville plat in Ingham County, which was recorded in 1849.

Now one of the largest municipalities on the river, Lansing had early beginnings in the paper town of Biddle City platted in 1836 near the confluence of the Red Cedar and the Grand, but no one actually lived in Biddle City. Development at Lansing did not begin in earnest until the area was selected as the site of the new state capital in 1847.

Tributary Towns

In addition to places on the Grand River itself, a number of towns were established on tributary streams, where the fall from the creek dropping into the Grand River valley could be used to power industry without building a dam on the big river which might hinder navigation. Lowell, in Kent County, was founded in 1847 at the site of a former fur trading post a half mile up the Flat River; Muir, in Ionia County, began three-quarters of a mile up the Maple River in 1854; downtown Ada developed a half mile up the Thornapple River, near Grand Rapids.

Other towns on tributary streams, but influenced by the proximity of the big river, include Leslie, in Ingham County, two and a half miles up Huntoon Creek which was founded in 1836; Rockford, settled in 1843, six miles up the Rogue River, north of Grand Rapids; and Spring Lake, on a bayou of the Grand River just east of Grand Haven, where a mill was built in 1837.

Planning Canal Connectors

The Erie Canal of New York State, linking the Hudson River with Lake Erie, opened in October of 1825 and was an immediate success, cutting the transportation costs along that section up to 95 percent and slashing travel time. To a place like Michigan, which was just a collection of peninsulas separating navigable waters, a canal seemed like the obvious solution.

The Bad River Canal

The first constitution, adopted in 1835 when the Territory of Michigan first applied for statehood, made it the duty of the government to encourage internal improvements, and provided the framework for obtaining the funds needed. The Bad River Canal was one of the first projects approved after Michigan finally became a state in January of 1837.

As drawn by state engineers the project would be the final link of a cross-state canal which would create a continuous waterway from Grand Haven on Lake Michigan eastward to the Maple River at Muir in Ionia County, up the Maple River in a northeastern direction into Gratiot County, where a canal would be dug northward to the Bad River south and just east of Ithaca. The Bad River flows eastward into the Shiawassee River near St. Charles in Saginaw County, which connects with the Saginaw River south of Saginaw and into Lake Huron.

Using funds from a loan negotiated by Governor Stevens T. Mason with New Jersey bankers, work was actually begun on the canal extending west from the forks of the Bad River early in the year 1839. The process was hampered because of the remoteness of the area, 10 miles from any white settlement, and the difficulty in transporting workers, supplies and equipment.

Work was pushed forward by a crew of Irish canal builders, many veterans of the Erie Canal in New York State, and continued until August or September when the New Jersey banking firm failed, and defaulted on the promised loan to the State of Michigan. The workers, who had not received the last installment of their wages when work was stopped, paraded in the streets of Saginaw demanding their money. But, according to an 1889 account, "after a proper explanation of the cause of the non-payment of their wages they left without doing any damage to anyone."[7]

When the economy settled down a little there was talk of renewing work on the Bad River Canal as well as a similar project which would connect the Kalamazoo and Clinton Rivers farther south on the Lower Peninsula, but nothing ever came of it.

The Holland Canal

Various schemes were tried to increase river traffic from Grand Haven to Grand Rapids. In 1889 the Board of Trade of Grand Rapids studied a number of proposals including a canal from Grand Rapids which would enter Lake Michigan at Holland. The October 2, 1889, *Grand Rapids Telegram-Herald* described the proposed route:

The project is to run the canal from the mouth of the Black river at Black lake, five miles from lake Michigan, at Holland in a northeasterly direction through what is known in tradition as the old bed of Grand river, now a low marsh extending to Hudsonville. From that point is more marsh land and Buck creek, which flows into Grand river at Jenison. From Jenison the remaining eight miles to the city can be covered by the river or a canal parallel to it.

On a map published in the Grand Rapids newspaper, the Holland men who drew it depict not only the connection at Jenison, but a short canal across a curve in the Black River which would bring traffic closer to Zeeland. Groups of businessmen from both Ottawa and Kent counties surveyed the project, first from the deck of the river steamer **Wm. H. Barrett**, and later by carriage along the route of the propose canal.

"Canal within the River"

At the same time the Grand Rapids Board of Trade had under consideration the proposal from Holland, there was another choice on the table. This was a plan to create "a canal within the Grand river" by dredging a navigable channel in the river itself. There was some hope that this plan would eventually extend at least as far inland as Lamont.

A portion of the plan had been attempted in 1881 when the people of Grand Rapids convinced the federal government to work on the shallow spots of the river, creating a four foot channel. Appropriations were approved for three years: $10,000 in 1881, $15,000 in 1882, and $25,000 in 1884. The work was only a partial success. The government report commented:

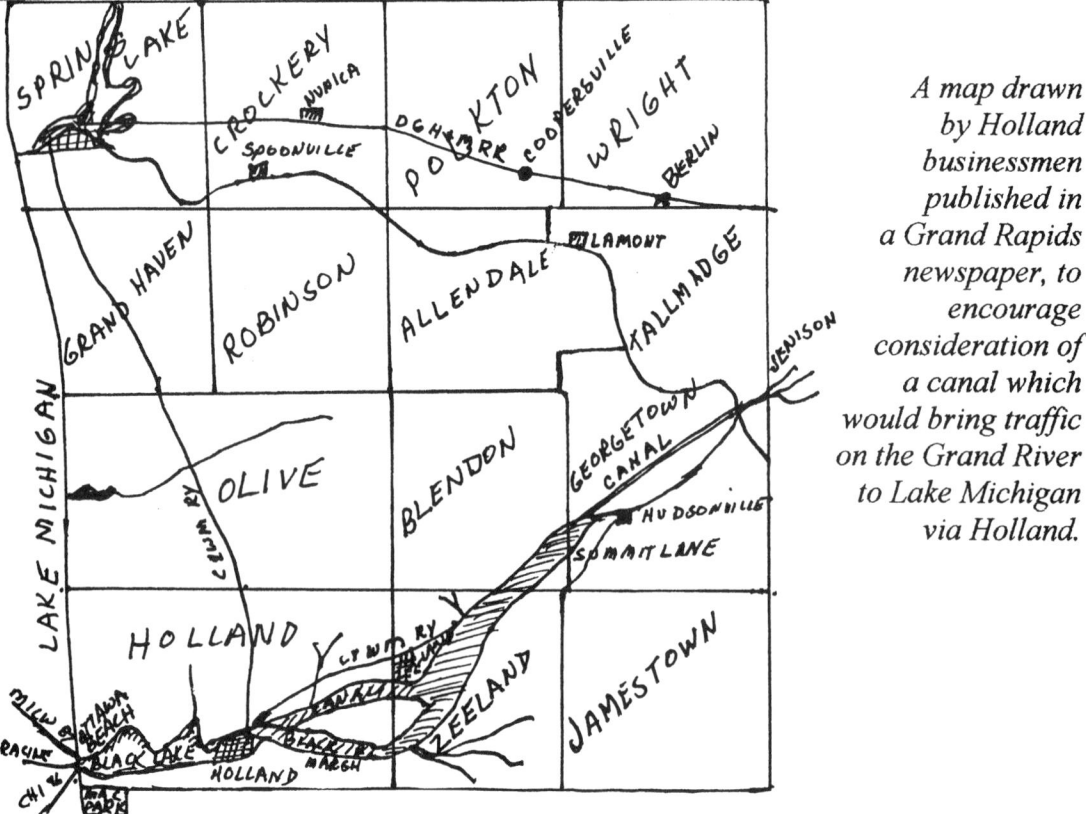

A map drawn by Holland businessmen published in a Grand Rapids newspaper, to encourage consideration of a canal which would bring traffic on the Grand River to Lake Michigan via Holland.

There still remain a number of places where the depth is less than 4 feet... Large appropriations would, beyond a doubt, properly applied, result in giving deeper water during the low water season, but I am not satisfied that the increase in the commerce of the stream would be commensurate with the outlay.

Despite the enthusiasm (but no offers of funds) from the Holland business community, the Grand Rapids men voted to pursue the "canal within the river" idea. Holland resident G. Van Schelven described all of the negative reports in previous government surveys and said that they were awaiting the results of the new survey which the Grand Rapids men had requested from the Corps of Engineers. He wrote in the November 23, 1889, issue of the *Holland City News*:

> Grand Rapids people have the right to take the route they prefer. . . [the Board of trade of Grand Rapids] is a body of high-minded gentlemen, representing great interests; and during the present cessation nothing should be said or done on our part, which will, in any way, embarrass an early resumption of the mutual consideration of the Holland route.

An 1893 State of Michigan publication noted, "Preliminary surveys and preparations have been made to deepen grand river from Grand Rapids to its mouth so as to make it navigable for lake vessels. Virtually making the city a seaport. The importance of this work could hardly be overestimated."[8]

However, federal engineers were not supportive, and neither project was ever accepted by a government agency willing to fund it.

Cross-Peninsula Idea Revived

Unable to get any action on either the Holland canal or the "canal within the river," Charles Sligh, a Grand Rapids furniture manufacturer who had been chairman of the committee on transportation for the Grand Rapids Board of Trade, renewed the idea of a canal across the Lower Peninsula and, in 1891, submitted the proposal to a joint legislative committee. He said a canal link connecting the navigable portions of the Grand River to the Saginaw River would:

> -- shorten the water transportation from the west to the east from 150 to 325 miles depending on the route taken.
>
> -- be a regulator on the railroads for all time.
>
> -- provide cheap internal transportation and assist in the development of "the unsurpassed resources with which the Peninsula State is endowed by nature."[9]

He concluded, "Such a system of water inter-communication would be, in the future, the highway of commerce for the entire west and Northwest and would convert the interior of our state into a hive of industry."

The idea was discussed favorably for a while, but no action was taken.

Navigation on the River

Navigation on the Grand River never fulfilled all of the dreams of the settlers and investors, but boats ran on a fairly steady basis from Grand Haven to Grand Rapids until about 1900, and then sporadically until 1917. Traffic in more recent years has been revived by excursion boats, some of them modeled on the old stern paddlewheel steamers which ply the Grand for the benefit of summer tourists.

Native Canoes and Pole Boats

The first boats on the river were those of the Native Americans. These included both types of Indian craft. The birchbark canoes, which were mainly constructed up north where birch trees grew of sufficient size, were used to make the major trek south on Lake Michigan and probably came at least a short distance up the river. The smaller dugout canoes, made from hollowed-out logs, were more suitable for transportation on the river itself, having great maneuverability and sturdier hulls which could ram a rock or a snag without breaking. Many of these craft were strictly one-man vessels. When Baptist missionary Isaac McCoy first arrived on the banks of the Grand River in 1824, the local chief offered to transport him to the village on the opposite bank and ordered him to lie down in the bottom of the dugout. McCoy wrote later, "When I was thus adjusted he said he believed he could get me across as I did not appear to be so heavy as a deer he had once taken over in the same canoe."[10]

*The steamer **Grand** at the Grand Rapids steamboat landing behind Island 3 about 1908.*

River Deemed "Navigable for Steamboats" in 1836

When settlement was just beginning along the river, an 1836 gazetteer of the almost-state of Michigan noted that 240 miles of the 270-mile length of the river were navigable for "bateaux." Further, "It is navigable for steamboats 40 miles to the Grand Rapids, below which it has not less than four feet of water." [11]

Early white settlers bought, or traded for, Indian canoes which they used for personal transportation. But as agricultural products and lumber began to be produced in saleable quantities businessmen built pole boats for transporting goods to neighboring communities and to the mouth of the river, where they connected with steamboats going around the Great Lakes. These river vessels, more like rafts, were powered by the current and the "white ash breeze" – that is, men with poles who pushed against the bottom of the river urging the vessel onward. Some of the bigger pole boats required a crew of six, eight, or more.

Many of the rude rafts were sold for the lumber in them when they reached Grand Haven, and the raftmen returned home on foot. According to early accounts, some of the first rafts were simply let go at the end of the river and allowed to float out into Lake Michigan.

The First Steamboat: the Gov. Mason

In 1835 several Grand Rapids businessmen contracted for the construction of a steam-powered vessel with a shallow enough draft to run between the rapids and the mouth of the river. In 1837, when the vessel was actually launched, she was named **Gov. Mason**, and it was said her namesake, Governor Stevens T. Mason, presented a set of colors in honor of the occasion.

In December of 1837, with high water providing safe passage over the usually shallow places and smoothing the rapids, the Gov. Mason went upriver as far as Lyons. With wonder, Edward Lyon described the scene to his stepbrother, Lucius Lyon, one of the investors:

> Yesterday was a great day for the people of this part of Grand River – the Steamer Gov. Mason arrived at Lyons at 1 o'clock with a large company of Gentlemen and Ladies on board. It being the first time that a Steamboat descended the beautiful River to this part it was one of the most pleasing moments we have witnessed in a long time.[12]

Shortly afterwards the vessel ended up on dry land in the flood of 1838, and it took time and financial outlay to return her to the river. In May of 1840 the Gov. Mason had completed a run from Grand Rapids to Grand Haven, and several passengers were eager to pay their passage onward to Muskegon. A storm arose on Lake Michigan and the shallow draft of the vessel designed to ply the river made navigation difficult. The boat was washed onto a sandbar and dashed to pieces by the strong wind and waves. The passengers and crew escaped uninjured.

The next vessel with an eye on the upriver run had an even less successful life. The little steamer **John Almy**, named for a Grand Rapids representative in the legislature, sank on its maiden voyage near the mouth of the Flat River.

Navigation to Jackson Explored

In the earliest days of settlement, when the first river improvements at Grand Rapids were under way, some of the material needed in construction was brought down the river on flat-bottomed scows from Jackson. The success of these trips brought up the question of permanent slack water navigation from Lyons to Jackson. In 1842 the Grand River Navigation Company was organized, but the plan did not succeed even though the Michigan State Geologist expressed the opinion that the scheme of such improvements was wholly practicable at a small expense..

Boats Built on the Grand River

Boatbuilding was a common activity along the Grand for the next 70 years. A list compiled for the *Historical and Business Compendium of Ottawa County* in 1892 of vessels constructed between 1860 and 1890 in Ottawa County listed:

    89 at Grand Haven
    13 at Ferrysburg
    9 at Spring Lake
    1 in Crockery Township
    4 at Blendon Landing

Vessels constructed in Ottawa County included: **Owashtanong**, a 140-foot sternwheeler, launched 1837 in Grand Haven; the **Humming Bird**, launched at Lamont by Henry Steele in 1847, a center-wheel vessel with twin hulls,

STEAMBOAT LINE.

Grand Rapids, Grand Haven and Chicago Direct.

STEAMBOATS
L. G. MASON & DAN'L BALL
On Grand River.
PROPELLORS
Truesdell and Ottawa
On Lake Michigan.

The Steamer L. G. MASON, Capt. J. GANOE, will leave Grand Rapids every morning, (Sunday's excepted,) at 8 o'clock. Returning, leave Grand Haven at 2 o'cl'k, P. M.
The Steamer DANIEL BALL, Capt. J. M. KELLY, will leave Grand Rapids every Monday, Wednesday and Friday at 9 o'clock, A. M. Returning, will leave Grand Haven every Tuesday, Thursday and Saturday, at 8 P. M.

GOOD ACCOMMODATIONS FOR PASSENGERS,
FREIGHT
Forwarded with despatch at lowest rates.
GANOE & PARKS, Proprietors.

Grand Rapids Steamboat advertisement from 1895.

because of a blocked safety valve – it was said that the engineer often hung his hat on the valve – the vessel blew up just as it reached the city in 1854; **Olive Branch**, built at Ottawa Point in 1856, was fitted out like a Mississippi River sternwheeler with staterooms and a large banquet hall, she was 146 feet long and had a draft of 3 feet, 10 inches. Earlier a lakes-going schooner had been built in the small shipyard at Ottawa Point. (See page 30 for an account of a trip on the Olive Branch in 1857.)

After the **Gov. Mason**, an active boatbuilding industry continued at Grand Rapids. Some of the best-remembered

The Grand steaming out in 1907.

vessels built there included: **Patronage**, 85 feet in length, built in Grand Rapids in 1838, with an engine constructed in Grandville; **Paragon**, 97 feet long, built at Grand Rapids; **Michigan**, launched in 1853 at Grand Rapids, 100 feet long, she burned at her Grand Rapids dock in 1860. She is most famous for winning a race from Grand Rapids to Grand Haven against the **Algomah.**

A number of boats had connections to businesses run by John Ball of Grand Rapids including: **Enterprise**, built to carry freight for the Granger and Ball Plaster Mill, which was located on Plaster Creek, two miles south of Grand Rapids. Granger and Ball also had two stores in Grand Rapids and one in Ionia; **Empire**, the flagship of the John Ball fleet, built in 1846, 130 feet, with a four foot draft; **Great Western**, built in 1845; and **Odd Fellow**, launched in 1846, at Grand Rapids. She was a propeller vessel, and made only a few trips on the Grand before going into service on Lake St. Clair.

Other boats included: **Kansas**, built in 1854 at Grand Rapids, 104 feet long with a 3 feet 3 inch draft, built by W. C. Heyden for J. B. Parks. Also in 1854 Robert S. Parks built five boats for use on the Illinois Canal. **Pontiac**, 124 feet long, was built at Grand Rapids in 1855 and was used both up and downstream. The same year the **Nawbeck**, only 96 feet long, but with a draft of 3 feet, 3 inches, was built by C. P. Parks and put on an upriver run, until the railroad came in 1858, then the Nawbeck was taken over the dam and used below the rapids.

One of the best known, and most often pictured, boats on the Grand River, the **Wm. H. Barrett,** was built at Grand Rapids in 1874, and operated for 20 years until destroyed by fire at the Wealthy Street dock on November 6, 1894.

A Day on the Olive Branch by Charles E. Belknap

One spring morning in 1857, drifting away from the pier at the yellow warehouse, the steamer Olive Branch set forth for the Haven with a cargo of package freight, a top deck loaded with passengers, and Capt. Robert Collings, Pilot Tom Robbins and Cook Jim Dailey, with a full crew of husky Irishmen. We were soon winding between banks heavily wooded and bordered with wild fruit trees in full bloom – plum, cherry, crab and thornapple – all festooned with wild grape vines.

At the dock of Hovey's plaster mills a hundred barrels of land plaster were taken aboard. Then angling across the river we were against the bank at Grandville, the place nature intended should be a town site. The settlement got an early start with some of the best men who came out of the east in those pioneer days. Here we left package freight and took aboard passengers.

At Haire's landing we gathered up a lot of maple sugar in tubs and a pile of slabwood for the boilers.

At the mouth of Sand Creek, where there had once been an Indian village, we added a couple going to the Haven to be married. Coming down from the upper road they crossed the creek on a tree footbridge and the young lady had taken a tumble and had to swim out. They built a fire to dry out as well as to signal the boat. Once aboard the women passengers fitted the young woman out in dry clothing and the couple were seated at the captain's table for the noon meal. The bride-to-be had come west to teach the Sand Creek school, but the first month she found a better job and the log shack's pupils had a vacation.

At the Blendon hills two families of Hollanders all wearing wooden shoes, were met by a man with a yoke of cattle. Their goods were piled high on his cart and the boat tooted a goodby as they trailed away into the forest.
It was a short run to Lamont, a beautiful place so spread along the bluffs – for every man wanted a home on the river front – that it looked four miles long and four rods wide.

All the morning a couple had occupied a bench on the top deck in front of the pilot house. The man smoked a fancy shaped pipe and they talked only in German. Lamont evidently touched his heart and with arm outstretched he recited "Bingen on the Rhine." I did not understand then as I did in the Civil war days, when I served with men who often on battle days sang of "Bingen on the Rhine."

At Eastmanville Mr. Eastman came aboard with a party of ladies and gentlemen. The ladies were carrying many things made by the Indian women of the vicinity, beaded belts and loaded money bags; some had traveling bags of smoke-tanned buckskin ornamented with native dyes and woven designs of porcupine quills. The freight taken here consisted of many packs of ax hafts shaved out of white hickory.

The dining table was crowded at the evening meal. Capt. Collins toasted the bride-to-be who was garbed in the best that several "carpet sacks" afforded.

At the landing at Bass river Mr. Eastman took charge of the dining cabin and with song and story the Olive Branch rounded Battle point, paddling past great river bottom meadows of cattail and wild rice, from which flocks of wild duck came swirling overhead.

There were many inviting channels and waterways and the pilot needed to be well informed. As we neared the Haven the sun in the golden west disclosed smoking mill stacks, forests of ship masts and drifting sand dunes. Beyond was a great sea of white caps. this was the end of a perfect day.[13]

*The **George P. Savidge** coming in for a landing at Spring Lake about 1880.*

Railroads Take Over

When the Detroit, Grand Haven & Milwaukee Railroad came to Grand Rapids in 1858, it had an immediate effect on river traffic. The boats, except those owned by manufacturers, lost most of their freight business.

By 1900, when most had given up on river traffic, the Grand River Transportation Company brought in a boat from Oshkosh, Wisconsin, renamed it the **City of Grand Rapids**, and put it on a route between Grand Rapids and Grand Haven. With a capacity for 400 passengers, the vessel could run to the mouth in four hours and forty minutes. The upriver trip took just over six hours. In 1901 a second boat, the **Heath**, was added. However, the railroad, which ran in conjunction with vessels from Grand Haven to Chicago, made it so difficult to make onward connections at the mouth that by the end of the 1901 season the Grand River Transportation Company was defunct.

One more attempt to restore river traffic was made. In 1905 the Grand Rapids and Lake Michigan Transportation Company built the **Grand** and the **Rapids**, each 134.8 feet long. The vessels began regular service in 1906, but by 1907 the venture ended and the boats were sold.

The End of the River Traffic

In 1915 a feasibility study by the U. S. Army Corps of Engineers recommended abandoning navigation above Lamont, but approved continued dredging of a channel from Lamont to Grand Haven. An extensive study from 1928 to 1930 recommended limiting the federal dredging operation to the river below the Bass River where considerable gravel mining operations continued until the 1970s.

In 1912 the **May Graham**, a small sidewheeler, was moved from the St. Joseph River to the Grand and began making daily trips Grand Haven to Grand Rapids and back, delivering goods that arrived by boat at Grand Haven and gathering passengers and farm produce for the Crosby Transportation Company's Chicago-bound boats. To add interest to a trip on the May Graham, numbers had been painted around the rim of the paddle wheel. Passengers would choose a number and ante up a nickel. When the boat stopped, whoever had the number at the top of the wheel received the entire pot.

The last steamer to pass through the old swing bridge at Eastmanville was the May Graham. She made her last trip in 1917, and then the hinges on the old bridge rusted shut.

Lakes Boats Call at Grand Haven

In addition to river boats there were many lake boats constructed at Grand Haven. An 1893 compilation lists 59 vessels launched at that port: 28 steamers and propellers, four lake barges, 18 tugs, and nine schooners, but many others went unrecorded.[14]

Even after boat traffic to Grand Rapids was nearly non-existent, lake-going vessels continued to call at Grand Haven. In 1926 a federal study noted four lines of steamboats which entered the mouth of the Grand River on a regular schedule, all carrying both freight and passengers. They were the Grand Trunk Railway car ferries to Milwaukee, Goodrich Transit Line which went south to Chicago and north to Muskegon, the Peninsula and Northern Navigation Company, and the Wisconsin and Michigan Transportation Company which provided service to Milwaukee and Muskegon.

In addition there were a number of freight vessels carrying gravel from the mining operations about 17 miles upriver to the Construction Aggregate docks in Ferrysburg.

Excursions Between Islands, Communities

Pleasure craft were on the Grand River well before 1900.

At Lansing the Loomis Steam Ferries Company, run by Captain A. P. Loomis, ran three steam ferries, the **Minnie Case**, **Searbird** and **Pickwick**, from the North Lansing dam about two miles south to the Mineral Wells Hotel, which was built in 1867 to take commercial advantage of a mineral-rich spring which flowed near the confluence of the Grand and Red Cedar rivers. The healing waters attracted a broad clientele until

The Lanota was one of several small steamboats which served visitors to the Seven Islands Resort on seven islands in the river just west of the downtown bridge in Grand Ledge, 1880s to about 1910. At right, the high bridge which carried the railroad over the river.

February of 1876 when the hotel burned, just as the spring was going dry.

At Grand Ledge, beginning in 1877, a series of small steamers served visitors to the Seven Islands Resort, including the **Lanota**, the largest and most famous which could carry as many as 30 visitors at a time.

Other small boats, at various towns along the river including Grand Rapids, specialized in picnic outings and Sunday School excursions. The small excursion steamers were a regular and important means of communication up and down Spring Lake and the other bayous near Grand Haven, and between the tri-cities of Grand Haven, Spring Lake and Ferrysburg.

At Lyons about the turn of the century a small sidewheeler called the **Island Queen** took passengers on Sunday afternoon jaunts to scenic Green View Point for picnics on the riverbank east of town. A little later the **Creeping Bear** served excursionists from Muir on the Maple River just north of the Grand River junction and also ferried passengers between the two villages.

Modern Excursion Vessels

A 64-foot steel-hulled sidewheel vessel was built by Clyde Curtis in 1967 to be used for pleasure excursions from a dock near Ann Street in Grand Rapids. She was named the **City of Grand Rapids** and had two decks. Power was supplied by a 1938 John Deere diesel tractor engine. The boat ran from the north end of Grand Rapids, 11 miles upstream to Ada and back, at a speed of 7 miles per hour until about 1973. On May 31, 1975, the boat was renamed the **Grand River Queen**, under the ownership of Gerald

*The **City of Grand Rapids** was launched in 1968.*

Elmer who added a Dixieland band for a few seasons.

Harbor Steamer was built in 1983 in Saugatuck and taken to the Grand River where she was put in service making 90-minute excursions from the Grand Haven Municipal Pier both up and down the river and into Spring Lake. She was 57 feet in length, had a draft of three feet, and was modeled after some of the boats that had plied the Kalamazoo River at Saugatuck since 1956. A few years after launch she moved upriver slightly to a new anchorage at the rear of Chinook Pier, a charter boat dock and shopping center on the river in downtown Grand Haven. After her retirement Grand Haven began offering sailing excursions on the river.

In 2006 the only sternwheeler left running below Grand Rapids was the **Grand Lady**, a 105 foot boat with twin stern wheels and a 22 inch draft. The Grand Lady docks in Grandville, just south of 28th Street (Wilson Avenue) near the Norton Indian Mounds. The vessel can carry up to 150 passengers and can make the trip to Spring Lake in five hours when the water level is high enough.

Michigan Princess at Lansing

The largest and most elegant of the 21st Century boats is the **Michigan Princess**, a 110-foot, three story vessel which can accommodate up to 500 guests. The boat has two dance floors and frequently hosts parties which include theatrical events, musical groups and weddings. The Michigan Princess operates year-round with both regularly scheduled cruises and private parties. In 2007 a smaller, open vessel, the **Princess Laura**, was also in operation for J & K Steamboat Line operating only in the summer with short scenic cruises on the river near Grand Ledge, or occasionally at other festival sites.

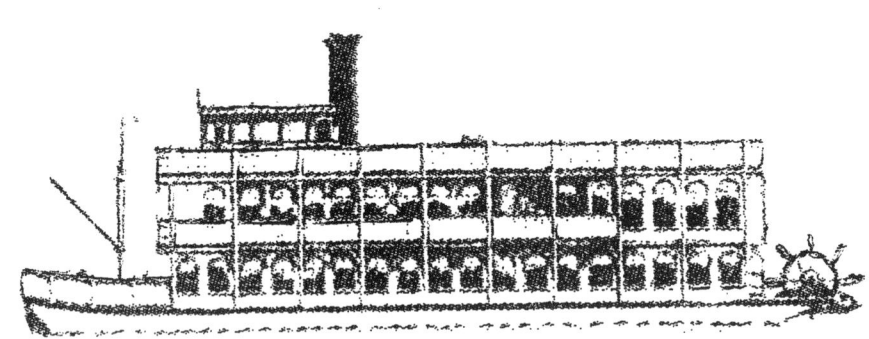

*The **Michigan Princess***

Turning on the Lights

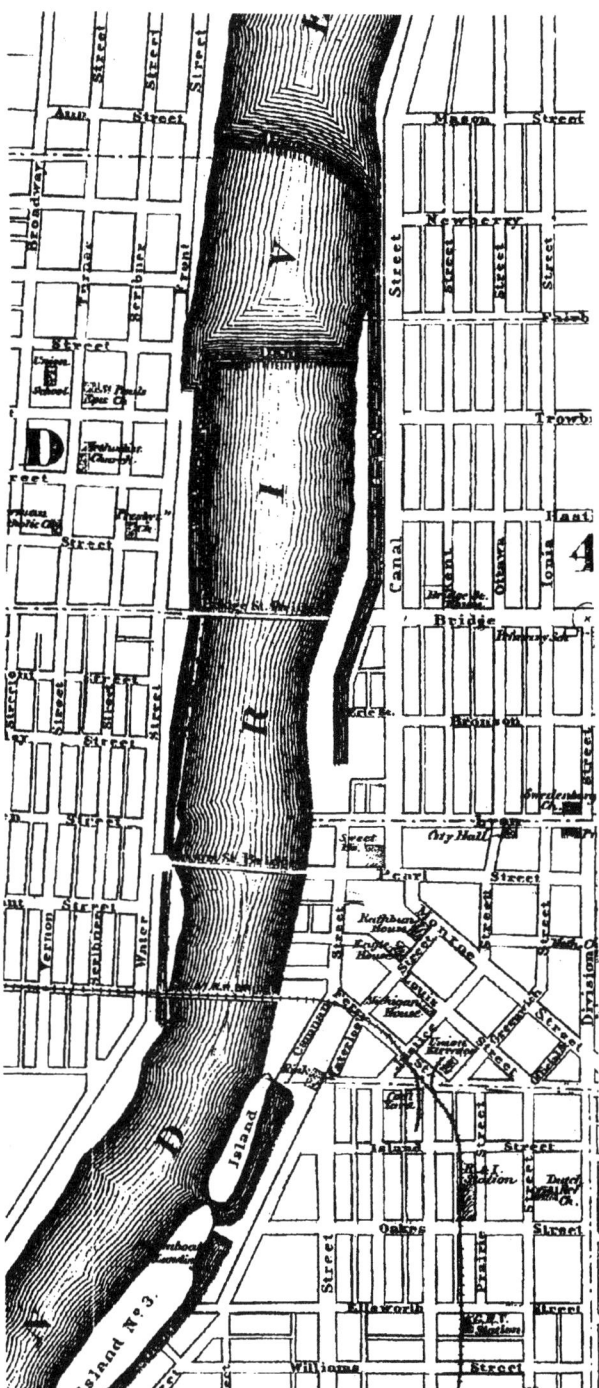

The Grand River at Grand Rapids showing the old wing dam (top) which channelled water through the power canal, right, and the 6th Street Dam which fed the westside canal. Note also the steamboat landing behind Island 3.

Because the rapids on the Grand River are concentrated in a small area, there was never the extended hydropower development which marked the history of the Kalamazoo River to the south, and the Muskegon River to the north. Today only the Webber dam near Lyons, a municipal plant at Lansing, and two small dams near Eaton Rapids still produce electric power. The Grand River, however, was important to the beginnings of hydroelectric history.

First Industrial Use of Electricity from Hydropower

The nation's (some sources say the world's) first industrial use of hydropower to generate electricity occurred in 1880 when 16 brush arc lamps were powered using a water turbine at the Wolverine Chair Factory on the Grand River in Grand Rapids.[15]

The Grand Rapids Electric Light and Power Company was organized March 22, 1880, with a capital stock of $100,000. The company purchased a 16-light Brush dynamo and the lamps and wire needed for the installation. The dynamo was set up at the Wolverine Chair Factory at the corner of Pearl and Front streets and the power company rented water power on the canal to propel it.

The lights were first turned on July 24, 1880, in Sweet's Hotel, the E. S. Pierce clothing store, Spring & Company's Dry Goods Store, A. Preusser's Jewelry Store, Mills & Lacey's Drug store, Star Clothing House and the Powers' Opera

House. Business increased rapidly and in September the equipment was moved to a sawmill building at the lower end of the westside canal and a larger dynamo added.

For many years the commonly accepted birthdate of commercial electricity was 1881, the year a small hydroelectric central station was begun in Appleton, Wisconsin, and Thomas Alva Edison's central steam station went into operation in New York City. The Grand Rapids installation predates both of these by several months. Author George Bush writes in his 1973 history of Consumers Power Company, "The fact that the birth of electric utilities has been pegged somewhat erroneously on these two installations is probably due to Edison's great fame and influence." The Grand Rapids claim has since been recognized by most encyclopedias and reference works.[16]

Webber dam under construction in 1906 for Commonwealth Power Company near Portland. The postcard notes: "at a cost of $1,000,000."

The Webber dam in operation..

The Beginnings of Consumers Power

The Grand Rapids Light and Power Company continued to operate until 1902, when it joined with the Edison Light and Fuel Company, the Lowell Water and Light Company and the Peninsula Light Power and Heat Company to form the Grand Rapids Edison Company. The holdings of this firm were purchased in 1906 by the Grand Rapids-Muskegon Power Company, which would also eventually supply power to Grand Rapids, Muskegon, Big Rapids, Coopersville, Grandville, Ada and Lowell. Grand Rapids-Muskegon Power Company was one of the companies which formed Consumers Power in 1910.

In 1917, under Consumers Power, a new semi-automatic hydroelectric plant was built adjoining the old one and gradually took over the generation of power. At least as late as 1940 the water turbine and crown head, part of the shaft and one pulley from the historic original equipment were still standing in part of the old plant by the river, then used as a warehouse.[17]

But by 1925 Consumers was getting the major portion of its power from dams on the Muskegon River, having determined that the development of hydroelectric power on the Grand River at Grand Rapids was "impracticable and non-economical."[18] That year the company offered to give up their share of the East Side Water Power Company canal, so the city could save money by using the trench to install a new sewer downtown. But Consumers agreed to maintain the dam to provide water for its steam plant on Wealthy Street, and recommended the erection of "small dams below the present dam to maintain the level of the river without unnecessary loss of water." These dams were built in 1927, and remain in place, providing some control over water levels, and some excellent fishing spots.

Power Production Leoni to Grand Rapids in 1893

An 1893 tabulation of power-producing dams on the Grand River noted water powers, varying from 75 to 2,000 horsepower, at: Michigan Center, Liberty and Jackson, in Jackson County; Dimondale and Grand Ledge in Eaton County; North and South Lansing, and Onondaga in Ingham County; Portland and Lyons in Ionia County; and "the greatest of all" at Grand Rapids in Kent County.[19]

In addition power dams were located on tributaries of the main river, at Dixon's Creek, Prairie Creek which entered the river near Ionia, Child's Mill on the Rogue River, Hubbardston on the Maple River, and at Lowell on the Flat River. Also, "the Thornapple, a few miles nearer the city offers like opportunities."[20]

Webber Dam Near Lyons

In April of 1906 H. R. Wager of Ionia sold to Commonwealth Power Company (later Consumers Power, still later Consumers Energy) the rights and contracts for a 28-foot dam across the Grand River in Lyons Township, Ionia County. Work was started at once, building an earth embankment with a concrete core wall. The generator was connected to the transmission line by three transformers of 1,000 kilowatts each. The lines were carried to Lansing

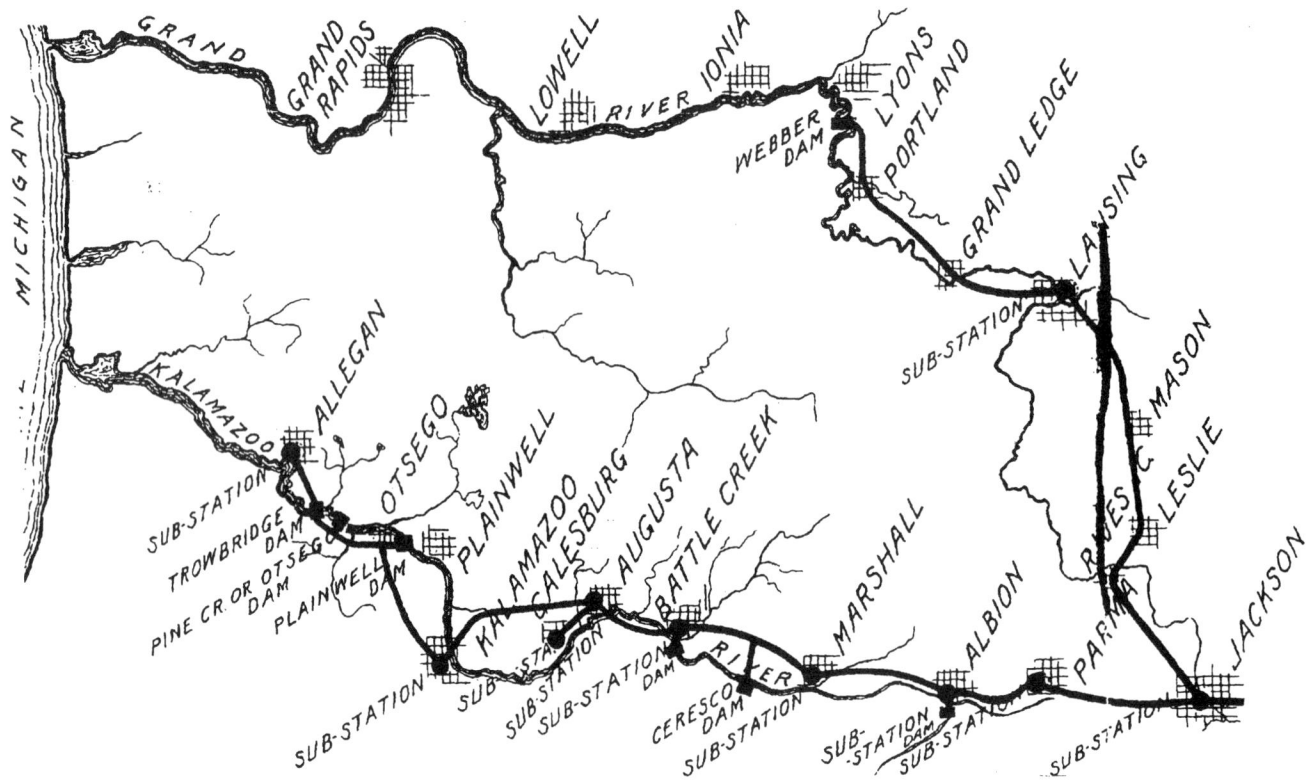

The Commonwealth system in 1908.

by rows of three-legged towers, using pin-type insulators. The dam was named for the Portland banker who handled some of the land purchases.

In 2007 the Webber Dam continues to provide 3,225 kilowatts of power for Consumers Energy Company.

Lansing Board of Water and Light

In 1885 the City of Lansing decided that safe drinking water and fire protection should be the responsibility of the municipality. In 1892 this was extended to providing electrical service, beginning with 110 arc street lamps and 136 customers. Today the Lansing Board of Water & Light is the third largest electric utility in Michigan.

Despite having two dams very little hydroelectric power is produced in Lansing today. The Moores Park Dam, built in the 1920s to create a pond for the Otto E. Eckert coal-fired generating plant, has two 540 kilowatt horizontal Francis turbines which produce some hydropower; however it is limited to one to two percent of the city's total power production.

The North Lansing Dam was constructed in 1936 near the site of the first dam built in the city in 1838. The purpose of the dam was to provide a pond for a proposed Ottawa Street Power Station and secondarily to provide hydropower. The hydro generator unit was officially decommissioned on December 27, 1990, and the entire plant officially shut down in 1992. The hydro unit is still in place, but has been rendered inoperable in accordance with Federal Energy Resource Commission procedures.

21st Century Hydroelectric Installations

In the 1970s the Federal government offered incentives to companies which would develop power sources not dependent on fossil fuels. Several small companies bought or leased no-longer-used river dams to produce hydro-electric power, selling the power to area distributors.

Two dams near Eaton Rapids were put back into service. The Mix Dam, in the downtown area, was built in 1933. It uses the waters of Spring Brook at its junction with the Grand River, just off the main shopping street. The Smithville dam is on the Grand River three miles upstream from Eaton Rapids.

The two installations were purchased by Cameron Gas and Electric and put back on line. In 2007 the Cameron Gas and Electric Company has become the Grand River Power Company, a subsidiary of the American Energy Company, a holding company under California ownership, and power production continues.

American Energy owns other small power companies including Seneca Falls Power Corporation, Tomahawk Power and Pulp, and Commonwealth Power Company, in the East.

A 2007 Census of Grand River Dams

In 2007 there were 15 existing dams on the Grand River. Only four were actually producing power: Webber Dam near Portland, Moores Park at Lansing, Smithville near Eaton Rapids, and the Mix Dam at the mouth of Spring Brook at Eaton Rapids.

Others which were still operating, mostly for scenic purposes included North Lansing, Lyons, the State Street (or upper mill race) dam at Eaton Rapids, a small dam on the river near Knight Street at Eaton Rapids, Grand Rapids' 6th Street Dam, Fitzgerald Dam at Grand Ledge, Liberty Mills, Michigan Center at the east end of Center Lake, two dams on Lake LeAnn, and one on Mirror Lake near the headwaters..

The Smithville Dam in 2007.

High Water on the Grand

An 1836 gazetteer, while extolling the virtues of the Grand River, admitted:

> The river is subject to freshets, and at intervals, in some places, to inundations, though the high banks generally afford them sufficient protection. At the mouth it is never known to rise more than a foot, but at the rapids it sometimes rises to the height of 15 feet.[21]

Flooding Every Spring

The banks of the Grand River, for most of its course, are meandering and surrounded by low-lying terrain. It was not until dams were constructed across its flow, and the industrial structures of the cities began to impinge on its banks, that extra water was a serious problem.

However, even before much work was done a terrible flood swept over Grandville and Jenisonville in 1838. When the settlement at what would become Lansing was just beginning, in 1843, high water washed out the dam requiring the settlers to start over before lumber could be obtained for building. In 1852 the whole river valley was covered with water.

Lansing Bridges Take a Ride in 1875

By 1875 the three communities that made up early Lansing had agreed to build five new bridges across the dam. These spans were constructed of iron, rather than wood, so that they might withstand spring flooding.

However, builders had not reckoned with the "hard winter" of 1874-75. By April 1 a mass of ice was banging against the Mineral Wells bridge near the confluence of the Red Cedar and the Grand. It stood for hours. Finally the center span caved in and sank into the water, then seemed to float up again and began to move to the north – downstream toward the bridge at Michigan Avenue. This was the earliest of the iron bridges built in 1871, a single-arch "bowstring" bridge. Because there was no center pier, the debris from the Mineral Wells bridge passed beneath the Michigan Avenue bridge and moved northward.

Without pause the ice and the remains of the Mineral Wells bridge took out the bridge at Shiawassee Street. Next the remains of two bridges smashed into, and demolished, the Saginaw Street bridge. Then the debris from three bridges attacked and the Franklin Street bridge surrendered. Finally the ice and tattered residue from four bridges made short work of the span at Seymour Street. As the water moved on to Delta Mills bits of bridge were left on the banks, and the force of the mass dissipated.

Although the citizens of Lansing turned down the first proposal offered in July, a second ballot in August passed and a bond issue of $14,000 was issued to replace the bridges.

Logjam of 1883

There was a lot of rain in the summer of 1883, and the rising river, coupled with

The logjam of 1883, once loosed, is just a blur as it passes under the Pearl Street bridge in Grand Rapids.

(Grand Rapids Public Library)

the enormous number of logs on their way to mills downstream, caused a log jam at several locations – trouble spots included the Ottawa County Boom Company's big boom, located just upstream from the entrance to Stearns Bayou; the Grand Rapids Boom Company sorting boom, on the Big Bend, upriver from the city; and ten million feet of logs on the Flat River at Lowell threatening to break into the main stream, which already had more water and logs than it could handle.

With quick pile driving and lots of rope the workers at the booms were able to hold the logs back, but water backing up in the fields was ruining crops. The situation, which had reached a crisis as early as June 25, worsened a month later when the Flat River jam broke loose and smashed into the rear of the jam at Grand Rapids. With the added pressure the Detroit, Grand Haven & Milwaukee Railroad bridge gave way. This brought the rushing water, hundreds of tumbling logs, and a large section of railroad bridge which was floating on top of the logs into the Chicago & Milwaukee Railroad bridge, which, too, succumbed. Downstream part of an iron bridge lodged in the channel creating a new jam. For two days workmen labored frantically to dismantle the bridge and drive new pilings to contain the logs.

By the time the channel was open much of the pressure had been relieved by water and logs shunted into nearby fields. The rest of the summer was spent retrieving logs which had floated more than a mile from the river bed. These logs were returned to the city by railroad.

Lyons Besieged by Ice in 1887

In February of 1887 ice formed at the island about one mile west of the junction of the Grand and Maple rivers. The ice increased and eventually reached the north limit of the village of Lyons, cutting off the natural flow and the water began to rise. Efforts to dynamite the blockage were unsuccessful and more ice formed at the bridge to the height of the bridge railing.

The ice jam forced the river out of its banks and sent it down Bridge Street in downtown Lyons, flooding buildings as far east as King Street. The river continued on this course for two weeks, inundating 83 businesses and residences. Kelley's store became the post office, private offices, and a temporary residence for the homeless. As the water rose, even that refuge succumbed, and the post office and bank set up in the Methodist church.

It was later estimated by the *Lyons Herald* that more than 5,000 people visited the town in those two weeks to see the river running down main street. A slightly exaggerated sketch of the devastation appeared in *Harper's Magazine* spreading the fame of the small village worldwide.

Flood of 1904 Becomes the Measure

The most serious flooding in the written history of the river occurred in March of 1904. The problem was not unique to the Grand River. A generous winter's snowfall, compounded by frozen soils that could not absorb the runoff, had streams far over their banks all over the Midwest by the beginning of March.

Ice was also a major problem. The March 17, 1904, *Grand Rapids Herald* reported:

MICHIGAN.— THE VILLAGE OF LYONS, PARTIALLY DESTROYED BY AN ICE-GORGE AND INUNDATION IN GRAND RIVER.

The Maple River in Muir in 1904.

That the ice breakers of the city bridges were seriously menaced by the heavy ice this spring was shown when the large ice field above Fulton street bridge moved out at 5 o'clock yesterday.

Massive pieces which were thrown up against the second pier from the west side of the river tore up portion of the pier as if the heavy timbers had been matches. Assistant Engineer Carpenter and his force had to blast a series of holes just above the bridge to loosen the ice from the piers. When the last shot was fired the whole field extending to the Pere Marquette railroad bridge was set in motion by the current. To the crowd of spectators on the bridge the sensation was similar to that of being on board a steamer which was ploughing her way through a sea of ice.

On March 16 the water stood at 12.15 feet, and there was much hope that when

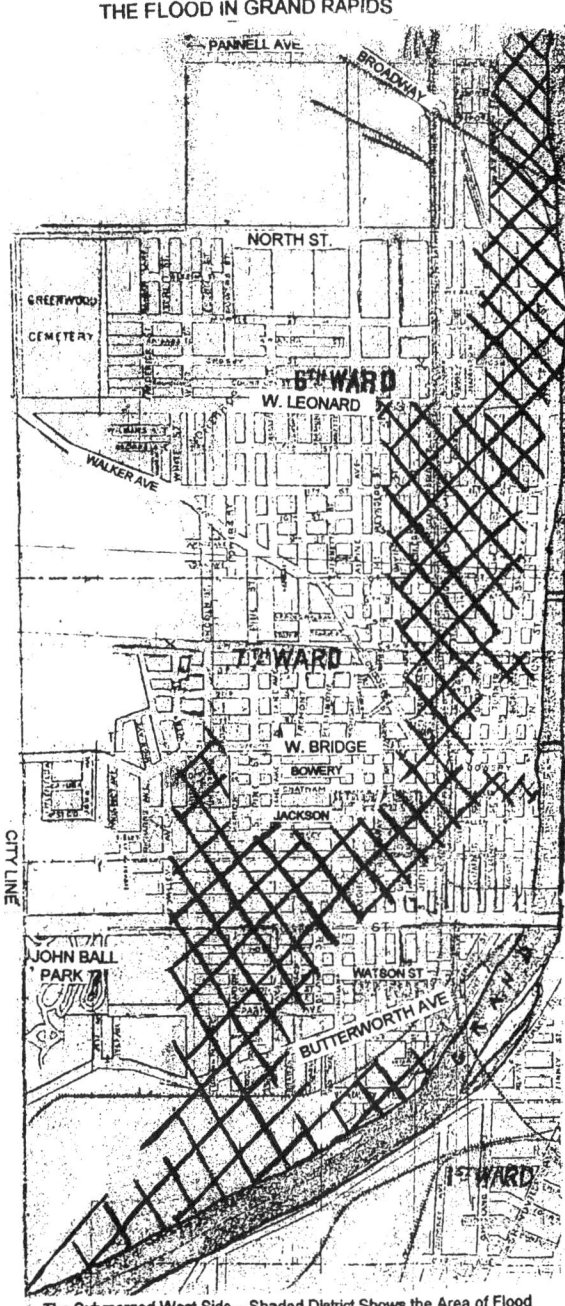

The Submerged West Side – Shaded District Shows the Area of Flood

the ice had passed the bridges the water level would begin to drop rapidly. The water level did begin to fall, but then it started to rain.

Rains Add to Overflowing River

The water level rose steadily. March 26 the paper reported 19.30 feet, a rise of

Jackson's Main Street on July 15, 1909, with 3 ½ feet of water.

2.30 feet in the previous 24 hours. The headline read:

IT'S A WILD DAY IN CITY

Downtown stores closed early. Workers wading in water to their necks removed "hundreds of dollars of stock" from the stores on Monroe Street. "A crowd of spectators gathered in front of Johnson's cigar store on Canal street watching a man clad in a rubber suit throw boxes of water-soaked cigars and valuable tobaccos out of the basement window."

The electric lighting plant was flooded and shut down, leaving the city in darkness. There was also some disruption of telephone service, an important link with those suffering in their flooded homes. Bridges were strained, and two of the railroad spans were ballasted with coal cars, but the only serious flood damage in Grand Rapids was a washout on the Grand Trunk Railroad near the east abutment.

The flood was widespread. In Lowell the Pere Marquette Railroad tracks bridge washed out and the newspaper reported that the road bridge was "leaking." In Ionia more than $10,000 worth of lumber from the wagon company simply floated off and was carried downstream, and more than 100 homes were destroyed.

Bridge Destroys Powerhouse in Lansing

In downtown Lansing spring floods sent the Kalamazoo Street bridge floating downstream where it jammed against the Michigan Avenue bridge, causing the already-swollen stream to backup behind the obstruction. Later in the same day the Logan Street bridge broke loose and demolished the Piatt powerhouse at the Moores Park Dam.

Jenison was deluged, the highway to Grand Rapids was covered and train service suspended. A boat at the Jeness Hotel brought people to their businesses. The station agent in Grandville reported that the bridge at that point "had been raised from its piers and was floating." In Lansing the bridge which led to Mt. Hope Cemetery was washed out, so burials could not be completed. In Grand Rapids pallbearers carried a casket through 18 inches of flood waters.

As April began, residents along the river began to feel that the worst was past until the whistle at Horner's Woolen Mill in Eaton Rapids began shrieking at midnight. An aroused populace was told that the Spicerville Dam on Spring Brook east of the town had gone out and they had less than a half hour to prepare. The deluge of water was followed by an ice jam and men worked around the clock to save the bridges.

Stemming the Tide in 1905

In 1905 waters were only a foot lower than they had measured in 1904, but experienced residents knew better how to cope with the problems. A dike which had been built since the flood of 1904 at Grand Rapids held back the swollen river. Tended constantly by men with fresh sandbags, the effort managed to stem the tide. The river crested at 21.6 feet on June 9. The *Grand Rapids Herald* had a banner headline:

WORST IS OVER, RIVER IS RECEDING

But other articles in the same paper warned residents of the 8th Ward that their cellars were in danger of flooding as the result of water backing up in the sewers. With no advance warning many goods in cellars, including hundreds of jars of canned food, had to be abandoned, especially in the low ground between Shawmut Avenue and West Bridge Street.

Ice at Grand Rapids January 24, 1907.

City Works to Wall Out Flood

Following the 1904 flooding at Grand Rapids a wall was begun in 1905 to help contain the river and beautify the downtown riverbanks. It was not finished in time to alleviate the 1905 difficulties, but the work, continued in 1906, until a high wall was finished on the west side of the river between the Grand Trunk Railroad tracks and Crosby Street. In 1907 a contract was let to continue the wall through the city.

By 1911 flood walls were under construction between Fulton and Wealthy streets on the west side, and from Wealthy south on both sides of the river. Most of these walls still stand.

Fishing in the Backyard in 1912

The water officially crested at 19.20 feet at Grand Rapids on April 7, 1912. Spring rains caused problems all along the valley. The waters at Lansing crested the same day, but did not immediately recede. Eaton Rapids, Grand Ledge, Portland and Lowell all showed a drop of less than a foot. The April 8, 1912 *Grand Rapids Herald* reported:

> Almost every basement on Canal street was flooded yesterday. Syphons and pumps of all descriptions were being used to keep the water down as low as possible. The current still continued to eat into the unprotected embankment of the Grand Trunk railroad near Leonard Street. A large number of sand bags had been laid above 6th street bridge and these prevented a further washing out at this point.
>
> Yesterday afternoon, men were fishing in their backyards along Market street. One had his nets sunk near his wood-shed, while another was fishing from a raft not far from his house.

Water and Ice Combine in Portland

Flooding, as the winter ice was melting and the springtime rains began, was a continuing problem in the springtime. In March of 1920 heavy ice on the river itself thawed rapidly in warm rains. The river rose and with the raging water large "bergs" of ice were sent downriver. This loose ice would cause ice walls as it tried to get under the bridges, imperiling the structure of the span, but also redirecting the river down the easiest path, usually a nearby city street.

A photograph taken in Portland March 15, 1920, shows citizens posing on top of some of the foot-thick ice chunks left along a city street when the water receded. Many of these bergs were packed in sawdust and taken to area ice houses for use the next summer.

Floods in 1948 Bring Back Memories

Memories of the devastating floods of 1904 and 1905 had faded in 1947 and 1948 when melting snow and spring rains brought the water levels to within two feet of the 1904 record for two years in succession. Waters crested at 19.42 feet on April 9, 1947, and reached 20.02 feet on March 23, 1948.

Some of the most serious devastation in 1948 occurred at Lowell where the Flat River, on its way to the junction with the Grand River less than a mile south of town, overflowed its banks and gushed

The caption on this postcard reads: "The Big Flood and Ice Scene at Portland Mich. Mar 15, 1920."

onto Main Street, cutting the village in half. Power was threatened as water rose in the municipal power plant.

At Grand Rapids catch basins were sealed off to prevent water from backing up and flooding the streets. Consumers Power workers in sheriff's department boats toured the flooded sections of the city turning off electric power. Untreated sewage poured into the river. In Wyoming Township officials voted to buy boots for members of the police department "for emergency use."

Gerald R. Ford, Jr., who was president of the United States 1974-1977, was a resident of Grand Rapids in 1948 and was chairman of the Kent County Red Cross Disaster and Preparedness Relief Committee. He announced reassuringly that the Red Cross "stands ready to help flood victims, on a basis of need, beyond their own resources, in replacement of shelter, clothing, food and basic necessities."[22]

Later High Water Records at Grand Rapids

According to a 1960 publication of the Grand Rapids Watershed Council the highest floodwaters in the decade of the 1960s occurred April 3, 1960, when flood water crested as 19.25 feet. Many spectators were out to see the high water on a sunny day with a high of 69 degrees. In Lowell, caught between the swollen Flat and Grand rivers the fairground was under water, which threatened the downtown area.

In 1973 below freezing temperatures compounded the problems with water-soaked streets. One man reported that his car, left out near the mailbox, was frozen in 20 inches of water and ice. Marooned residents had been traveling by boat, but the half inch of ice that formed on the top of the waters made boat travel difficult. The river crested at Grand Rapids nearly four feet above flood stage.

Another Set of Back-to-Back Floods

High water in the Grand River valley has a tendency to occur two years in a row. The four highest water levels ever recorded at the rapids occurred in 1904, 1905, 1947 and 1948. Another set of twin high water years was recorded in 1975 and 1976.

In 1975 continued rains kept water levels high for several days in late April. One of the hardest hit areas was Lansing, where both the Grand and the Red Cedar were far out of their banks and many of the stores in the business district were closed because of high water.

In 1976 the river crested at the Pearl Street gauge in Grand Rapids at 19.2 feet on April 8; it was the highest reading since 1960. In Grand Rapids the swollen river was undermining weak spots in the pavement at Welsh Civic Auditorium and at least one car was damaged when it began to sink in a caved-in section of pavement. At the city's waste treatment facility a hastily completed earthen levee prevented flooding and a discharge of sewage into the river, a problem the plant had experienced in 1948.

At Ionia the water was two feet over flood stage and most of the downtown business district was shut down.

Three ladies (left) wait for a boat to take them across the road in Jackson during a spell of high water

Ecological Future

Early settlers at Grand Rapids saw the Grand River as both the source of their water, and the destination of the municipal sewage. Households nearby simply ran their lines directly into the river. Others paid $1.50 for the privilege of draining their cellars into public sewers which reached the river near a railroad bridge a block west of Louis Street downtown, producing, according to one historian. much "public nosepinching."[23]

"A Glimpse of the Future"

As early as 1905 the pollution problems were recognized. The New Year's edition of the *Evening Press* ran two pages labeled, " A Glimpse of the Future," which were datelined "January 1, 2005" and gave the news the writer expected to appear in the newspaper of that date, one hundred years after the actual date of publication. The articles included news of a cow that was bred to give condensed milk, a sports report on a game of base ball (the sport was two words until about 1920) between London and Chicago played entirely with robots, the development of a new fruit called the "peachorine" which would give five crops a year, and the recent annexation of Holland giving Grand Rapids a port on Lake Michigan. The page also included a little history:

> Out at 45,573 Plainfield Avenue there lives a man who says he is 110 years of age. This old man makes one statement that seeming almost unbelievable in many ways, is undoubtedly true. He says that the present trunk sewer which enters the city at Plainfield Station and empties into Lake Michigan at the suburb of Grand Haven was once called the Grand River and that the village secured its water supply there. The river, a century ago, was noted for its beauty. Billjones remembers well when, in 1945, it was decided to build a cement covering over the river and use it for a sewer. The exact line of the old river would be hard to find now, as great manufacturing and office buildings have been erected on it. In the early days there were factories scattered along the river bank, and bridges connected what were known than as the East and West Sides.

For years state agencies, pressured the city to improve its handing of sewage. In 1913 the City of Grand Rapids was cited by the Michigan State Supreme Court for polluting the Grand River. The State Health Department took up the case and, in 1922, issued a firm order directing the city to construct a sewage disposal plant. Troubles with the financing forced the city to build a less comprehensive plant than it had envisioned. Despite an addition and extensive work in 1953, combination lines, which serve both storm and sanitary sewers in the greater Grand Rapids area, are frequently overloaded during high water and dump untreated sewage into the river into the 21st Century.

Waste from factories sliding into the river in Grand Rapids in 1908.

And Grand Rapids was not the only municipality where completely raw sewage occasionally reached the river. In a Michigan Department of Environmental Quality report for 2004, the 196 million gallons of untreated effluent contributed by the city of Grand Rapids paled beside the 420 million gallons which was reported from the city of Lansing. In 1991 Lansing began a plan to completely separate the storm and sanitary sewers before the year 2021.

Industrial Pollution Causes Red Feet

Industrial pollution, once a major source of impurities, has lessened since the Toxic Substances Control Act of 1976 which banned the discharge of harmful chemicals. This act was followed by an even more stringent federal law which became effective in 1977. Some of the worst polluters were required to build their own waste treatment plants or hook up to municipal wastewater treatment facilities.

As recently as the 1950s industrial pollution was often clearly visible. A former resident of Grand Haven said that when she was growing up near the river in the late 1940s and early 1950s she and her sister liked to sneak out on a dock near the Eagle Leather Company factory and fish, or just paddle their feet in the water. Some days the river would be blue, or red, or yellow depending on what color dye the leather factory was using. "The red days were the worst," she said later. "When we would dangle our feet in the water while we fished, the dye would turn them red. Mother would take one look at two little girls with red feet and know where we had been."[24]

Fishing in the River Called "Different"

An 1893 publication, *Michigan and Its Resources*, put out by the state and designed to lure new residents and visitors, curiously described fishing in the Grand River:

> The Grand River . . . pursues its winding way from Jackson to Lake Michigan, creeping through valleys, rolling over rapids, tumbling over falls, meandering majestically through romantic scenery, occasionally dividing itself, forming beautiful little islands, frequently deepening to make homes for the finny tribe, with which it is abundantly stocked. Fishing in Michigan streams is and always will be pre-eminently great sport, unlike fishing in canals and navigable streams where it is about as good one place as another. To catch fish you must go where they are. An Irishman speaking of the fishing in Michigan said it was just as good in one place as another, and a great deal better.[25]

As pollution increased the fishing declined. Waste used up the oxygen in the water, and the heavy nutrient level made weed growth a nuisance. Another difficulty some fishermen of the era remember was toilet paper in the water which snagged on flies and line. Even when the fishing was good there wasn't much to catch. Fishing in the Grand was, in general, bypassed by Michigan fishing guides. A tourist guide published in 1927 does not list as "the best fishing" any west Michigan river south of the Muskegon.[26]

Clamming for Buttons

In addition to fish and turtles the Grand River was one of many in southern Michigan with a marketable clam crop. The clams were usually sold to factories to make buttons, and the meat inside to farmers as hog fodder. Rarely the shell would contain a pearl, crude and small by ocean standards but saleable – the best would bring over $100 to a collector. Fairly large button manufacturing facilities were located at Lamont and at Ada, near Grand Rapids.

The simplest sort of clamming occurred when young boys seeking extra pocket money would just walk around on the sandy river bottom feeling with their feet, then cook the resulting clams in a big bucket over a campfire, removing (and sometimes eating) the clam inside prior to scrubbing the shell. Larger operations included a flat-bottomed boat with one or more iron bars aboard with dangling lines attached to four-pronged iron hooks tied on at intervals. The bar would be dragged along the bottom and, as the hooks touched the open clams on the bottom, the shells would close, holding tight until they were brought to the surface.

On the Grand River, because of the swift current, clammers often used a "mule" for propulsion. This was simply a piece of canvas, usually about four by 10 feet, but the size varied with the size of the boat. This was sunk in front of the boat and bowed out in the water, and used the current to provide the forward impetus – usually about the right speed for clam-

"Could this be possible?" September, 1967 cartoon in Grand Rapids Press.

ming. Later some boats used small motors. Pollution, overfishing and buttons made from other material caused the clam industry to decline; it was virtually over by 1930.

River Looks Better – Still Smells

A Department of Natural Resources guide from the early 1960s notes, "Although not known for its fishing, the Grand is a beautiful river with some outstanding scenic attractions. . ." The guide goes on to recommend, instead, a canoe trip covering 185 miles in 10 days, beginning two miles north of Jackson at Parnell Road and ending at Grand Haven including several portages.

However, a report of a canoe trip on the Grand in the August 8, 1968, *Grand Rapids Press* noted, "The scenery along the way is often not bad, but in a canoe your nose is too close to the water to enjoy it." The paddler went on to describe the water as "brownish-green, frequently scummy, and it bears an occasional dead carp or sucker. . . Here and there a pipe or a stream outlet adds a discolored flow to the river, the new water usually even more unsavory-looking than the river."

Foam, caused by detergents in the waste water, still appeared occasionally, but as one canoeist pointed out, "Things have improved since the early days of detergents in the sewage outflow. I remember when foam was all across the river, a couple of feet thick."[27]

"Salmon in Grand? Could Be"

In terms of recreational fishing, the efforts made by state and federal programs to clean up the river began to make a real difference by the beginning of the 1960s. Local fishermen who had continued to wet their lines expecting a channel catfish, suckers, or, if they were very lucky, a pike, walleye or smallmouth bass began to notice that the weeds (and toilet paper) were less troublesome, and some days the water was almost transparent.

In 1968 the Grand River was suggested as one venue for a new State of Michigan stocking program. This announcement prompted the headline in the September 19, 1967, *Grand Rapids Press*, "Salmon in Grand? Could Be."

The stocking program had been test marketed on the Manistee and Platte Rivers and Bear Creek up north, and fishermen up there were literally elbow to elbow when the fall runs began. Besides giving a needed boost to the sport fishing, bringing salmon and other game fish to Michigan had a secondary purpose. A small herring called the alewife had invaded the Great Lakes following the construction of the Welland Canal and reached Lake Michigan in the early 1960s. The alewife had about a four-year lifespan, and every spring thousands of the silvery fish would die off and litter water and beaches with rotting fish. The salmon were expected to grow fat on vast quantities of alewives.

Chinook, Steelhead and Coho – Oh, My!

Starting modestly in 1969 the number of fingerlings planted in the river grew, along with the number of locations. A portion of the chinook salmon each year is placed in net pens near the mouth of the river and fed while they acclimate to their surroundings before release. Others are taken to Riverside Park, upstream

---

FISH CONSUMPTION ADVISORY

Certain kinds and sizes of fish contain levels of toxic chemicals that may be harmful if those fish are eaten too often.

The amounts of chemicals found in Michigan fish are not known to cause immediate sickness. But chemicals can collect in the body over time. It may take months or years of regularly eating contaminated fish to build up amounts that are a health concern. Chemicals may eventually affect your health or that of your children.

GRAND RIVER

Above Webber Dam:

General Population, unlimited consumption of Carp, Channel Catfish, Northern Pike, Suckers and Walleye.

Women & Children: Carp, Suckers, Channel Catfish under 18" one meal per month; Northern Pike, Walleye, and Channel Catfish over 18": one meal per week.

Below Webber Dam:

General Population, unlimited consumption of Carp, Channel Catfish, Northern Pike, Suckers and Walleye.

Women & children, Carp, Suckers, Walleye over 18" and Channel Catfish over 18": one meal per month. Northern Pike, Channel Catfish under 18" and Walleye under 18" one meal per week.

A summary of the State of Michigan Fish Consumption Advisory issued in 2007

from the 6th Street Dam in downtown Grand Rapids. Coho salmon have been released as far inland as Lansing, and another load was released near Lyons. Steelhead (a kind of rainbow trout) smolts are placed in waters of the Grand at Lansing, and in Crockery, Prairie and Fish Creeks, and the Flat and Rogue Rivers. Brown trout released in Lake Michigan have been migrating up the river where some of them have spawned.

All of this river cleaning and fish stocking has made the Grand River a destination for fishermen. Ironically no place on the river is as popular as downtown Grand Rapids near the 6th Street Dam, where the fishing seems to go on year around. There is still pollution in the river; analysis has shown the presence of polycholorinate biphenyls (PCB), a byproduct of paper manufacturing, in the fatty tissue of fish in the Grand. The State of Michigan has issued a series of advisories stating that there is some health risk in consuming too many fish from polluted streams. (See box on page 53 for a summary of the 2004 advisory concerning the Grand River.)

Downriver a 1994 study "The Identification of Heavy Metals, Their Movement and Their Impact on Life in the Lower Grand River," identified traces of lead, cadmium, and also manganese in soil and fish samples from Bruce and Pottawatomie Bayous in Ottawa County. The study concluded that most of the harmful substances had settled to the bottom of the silt layer and, "The most important management strategy would be to see that the sediments remain undisturbed."[28]

Park Land Along the River

In the earliest days the scenic value of the river took third place to the practical need to generate energy for sawmills, wheat grinding and other tasks, and provide water for steam boilers. But as the industries turned to other forms of energy, and moved farther from the riverbank, the scenic value of having a body of water winding through your municipality was recognized.

In 1922 the City of Lansing hired Harland Bartholomew, then city engineer for St. Louis, Missouri, to write a comprehensive city plan for Lansing. He began his report which was presented to the Lansing City Council on April 4, 1922, by noting:

> . . . the Capitol City can not afford to sacrifice the distinctive charms of the two rivers on which the city is founded.[29]

Then Bartholomew goes on to recommend the development of linear parks along the riverbank, a process Lansing has diligently pursued. Most of the other communities with riverfront acreage have similarly responded, and townships, counties and the State of Michigan have added many more miles and parks, recreation lands, and designated game areas to the scenic banks.

Partnering with Industry

The Ottawa County Parks Department is working on a plan to partner with the gravel mining industry along the river to add a multi-recreational park to their

Grand River Greenway project. The operation may have been partially inspired by Millennium Park, built by Kent County on a large property of former gravel and sand mining near the western Kent County boundary.

Ottawa County parks officials have tentative agreement from gravel miners for the Bend Area Mine Reclamation project which would create a master plan for a 500 acre area along the south bank of the river about half a mile west of the eastern boundary of Ottawa County. The miners would do their work following the plan, creating lakes and other topographical features, and the parks department would contract to purchase the land for a park when the industrial operations are completed.

The Role of Rivers

In his 1977 volume *Michigan: Heart of the Great Lakes,* Richard A. Santer, then associate professor of geography at Ferris State College, wrote:

It is difficult to overstate the important role that the 36,360 miles of classified rivers has played in the history and present-day economy of the state. . . Frequently in a modern urbanized society, people fail to interact daily with the flowing streams of their community, especially those that may have been channeled with concrete banks and lined with buildings, or put underground by hundreds of meters of sewer conduits. Yet, the influence of rivers on the daily lives of citizens has undoubtedly increased in importance as population and technology have grown. While a skyscraper water tower may proclaim engineering achievement of a proud community, what needs to be appreciated is that the lifegiving waters which it holds still come from an out-of-sight pipe in a flowing river or well whose purity must be continually protected.[30]

Sourcenotes

[1] Blois, John *Gazetteer of the State of Michigan*, (Sydney L. Rood & Co.: Detroit) 1838, p 294.

[2] Baxter, Albert "Some Fragments of Beginnings in the Grand River valley," *MPHC* Vol. 17, p. 325.

[3] Hamilton, Claude T. *Western Michigan History: Colonial Period* (Merchants Life Insurance Company: Des Moines, Iowa) 1927 [?] p. 23.

[4] Campbell, J. V. "Account of a Plot for Obtaining the Lower Peninsula of Michigan from the United States in 1795," *MPHC*, Vol. 8, p.410.

[5] Journal entry from *John Askin Papesr*, (Burton Historical Records) p.350. Speculation on the places visited, extrapolated from maps and the journal data by Jim Woodruff in *Across Lower Michigan by Canoe 1790* (Published by author: 2004).

[6] Baxter, Albert *History of the City of Grand Rapids, Michigan* (Munsell & Company: New York and Grand Rapids) 1891, p.53

[7] Miller, Judge Albert "Incidents in the early history of the Saginaw Valley," *MPHC*, Vol. 13, p. 351.

[8] *Michigan and Its Resources* (Robert Smith & Co., State Printers: Lansing) 1893., p. 246.

[9] *Grand Rapids Morning Press*, March 11, 1891.

[10] *History of Baptist Indian Missions, Memoirs of Isaac McCoy*, introduction by Robert F. Berkhofer Jr. and George A. Schultz (New York) 1970. Originally published, 1840.

[11] Blois, p. 294.

[12] Edward Lyon to Lucius Lyon, December 8, 1837, Lyon Papers, Clements Historical Library, University of Michigan, Ann Arbor, Michigan.

[13] Belknap, Charles E. *The Yesterdays of Grand Rapids* (The Dean-Hicks Company: Grand Rapids) 1922. p. 56-58.

[14] *Michigan and Its Resources*, p.189.

[15] Baxter, *History of the City of Grand Rapids*, . p. 215.

[16] Bush, George *Future Builders: The Story of Consumers Power Company* (McGraw-Hill Book Company: New York) 1973, p. 58.

[17] Anderson, Seth "First Hydro-Electric Plant was Built Here," *Grand Rapids Herald*, October 20, 1940.

[18] Grand Rapids City Commission, regular session minutes, April 27, 1925.

[19] *Michigan and Its Resources*, p. 96.

[20] *Michigan and Its Resources*, , p. 246.

[21] Blois, p. 294-295.

[22] *Grand Rapids Herald*, March 22, 1948.

[23] Lydens, Z. Z. *The Story of Grand Rapids* (Kregel Publications: Grand Rapids) 1966. p. 36.

[24] Interview with Sharon Noell, former Grand Haven resident, 2006.

[25] *Michigan and Its Resources*, p.96

[26] Newnom, Clyde L. *Michigan's Thirty-Seven Million Acres of Diamonds* (the Book of Michigan Company: Detroit) 1927, p 149.

[27] LaBelle, Tom "Grand River Looks Better – But Phew!" *Grand Rapids Press*, August 8, 1968

[28] Thorpe, Patrick A. *The Identification of Heavy Metals, their Movement and Their Impact on Life in the Lower Grand River, Michigan* (Grand Valley State University Water Resources Institution) 1994.

[29] Bartholomew, Harland *The Lansing Plan: A Comprehensive City Plan Report for Lansing, Michigan, submitted to the City Council, April 4, 1922.*

[30] Santer, Richard A. *Michigan: Heart of the Great Lakes* (Kendall/Hunt Publishing Company: Dubuque, Iowa) 1977, p. 102.

From Beginning to End

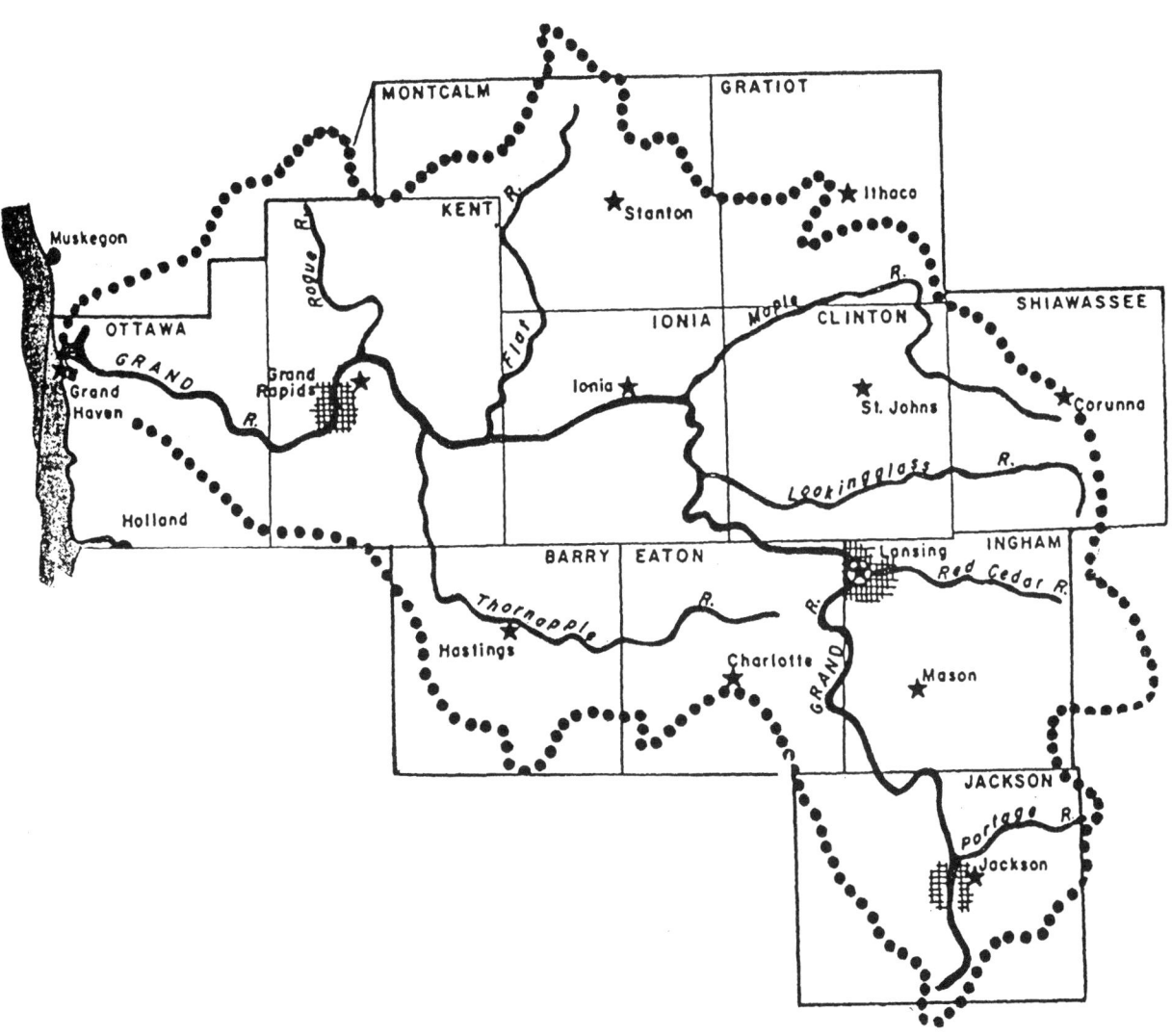

This tour of the Grand River is based on U.S. Corps of Engineers surveys published in 1919 and 1929. It is a mile by mile account of what you would see if you were paddling a canoe down the river, despite the fact that such a trip would be impossible over some of the river's length because of shallow water, weed-choked channels, culverts, bridges, dams and other manmade improvements. Maps, both old and new, and many historic photographs show the changing face of the river.

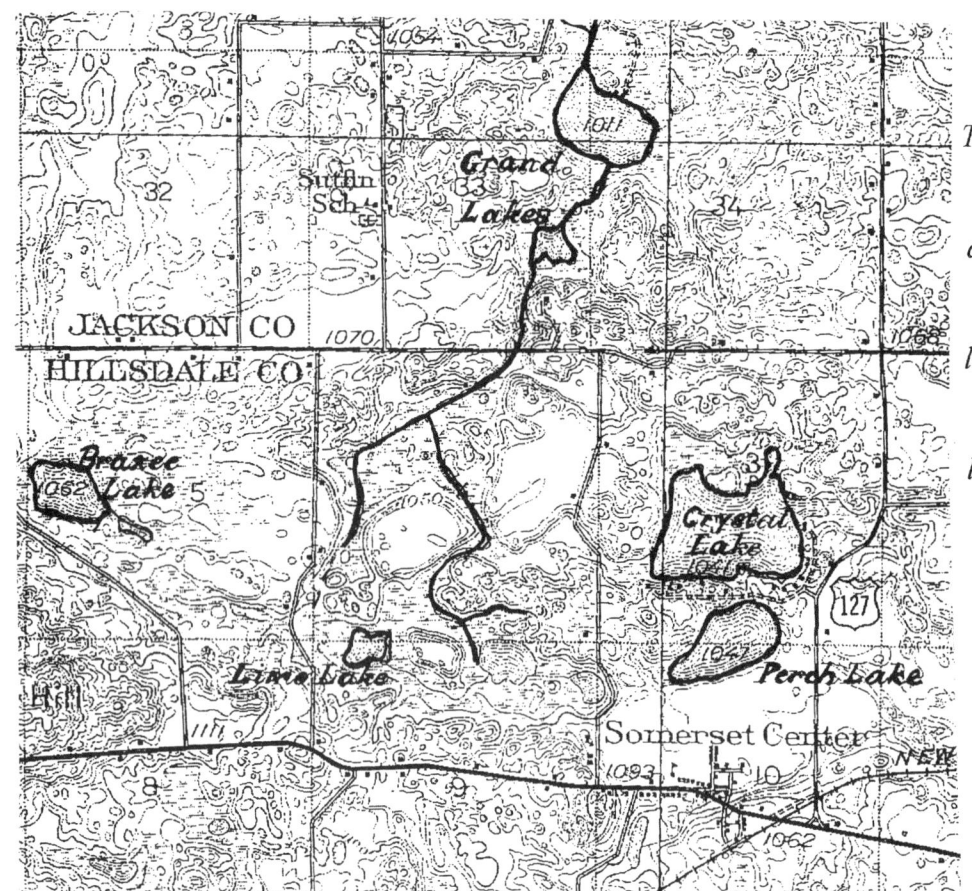

This 1927 survey map shows only a swampy area and tiny, shallow Lime Lake south of the county line. Note Braxee Lake on the left, and a big and a little Grand Lake to the north.

By this 1971 map the dams which formed Lake Le Ann had been built, and the smaller of the Grand Lakes had been enlarged and renamed Mirror Lake. Somerset Center is on the lower right of both maps.

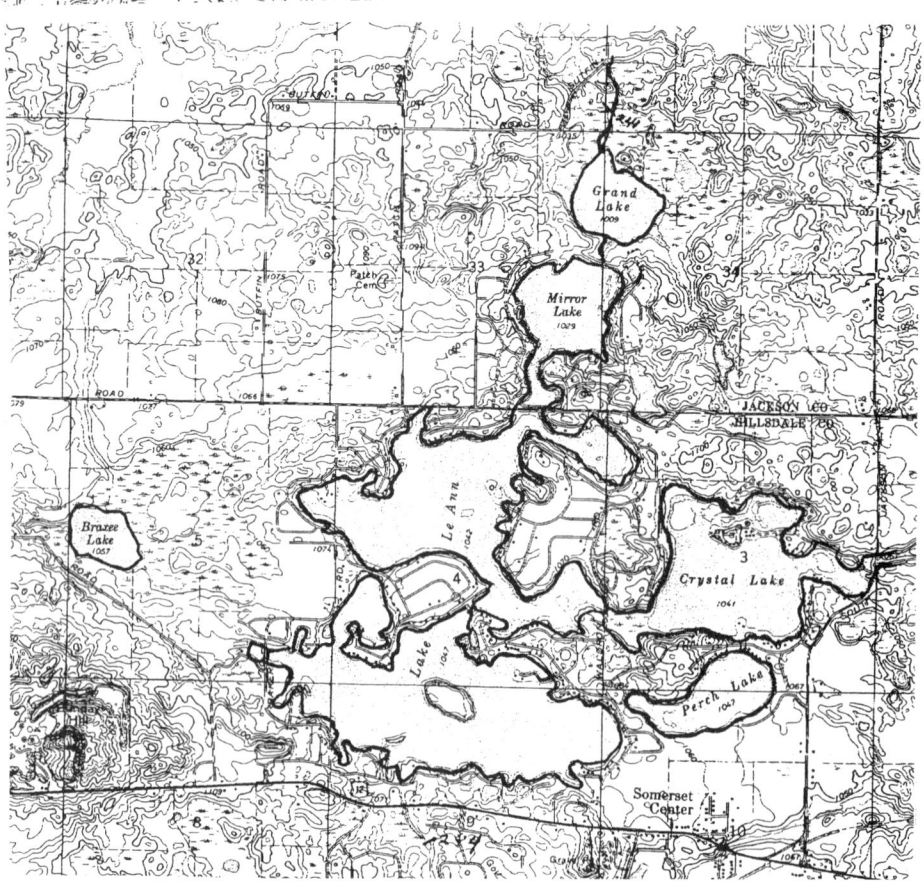

The Sources

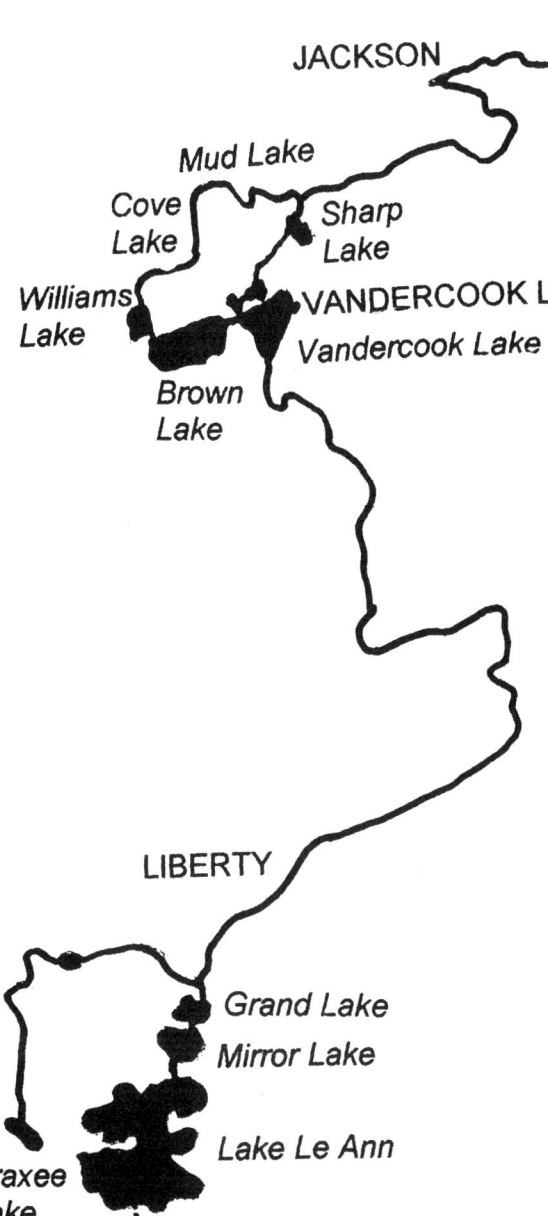

The Grand River from its mouth at Grand Haven to its source south of Jackson is approximately 250 miles in length. These measurements take into account most of the meander of the river, but cannot be exact since change in the river, especially in the lower swampy area, is common as water levels vary depending on the amount of precipitation and other factors.

The mileage figures which measure the distance from the mouth to the site being described are based on a 1929 Corps of Engineers study supplemented with updated information from USGS maps of the 1970s and 1980s. Mileage markers should be considered only approximate, and useful as a general estimate of the distance between points.

An 1881 history of Jackson County describes the beginnings:

> The Grand River may be said to have its source in the extreme southern portion of Liberty Township in a marsh and pond southwest of Grand Lake. Its course is north east toward Clarke lake in Columbia; thence north by west through a series of windings, until it enters Jackson City at the southeast angle. . .[1]

On a 1927 survey map there is a continuous stream into the Grand Lakes from the south. Just south of Hillsdale County's north boundary the stream ends in a swampy area east of Braxee Lake and Bunday Hill. One portion of the swamp, deeper than the rest is labeled Lime Lake. The elevation at its shoreline is 1050 feet.

In 1960 developers built two dams in the swamp which have created Lake Le Ann, a large irregularly-shaped lake in Somerset Township, Hillsdale County. Vestiges of the former swamp extend even farther to the south and in some seasons and at some water levels water from this swamp remnant flows under U.S. 12 and into the new lake.

246.9 Culvert. Chicago Road (U.S. 12) crosses east-west over a small culvert, less than three feet in diameter which sometimes flows into Lake Le Ann from the south. The community of **Somerset Center** is located on the Chicago Road about a mile east. The farming town became Somerset Center because it was in the center of Somerset Township which had been named for Somerset, Niagara County, New York.

246.9-245.4 Lake Le Ann, a large manmade lake, covers parts of sections 4,5,8,9, and 10. Its elevation is 1047 feet. The lake is really two lakes linked by a small passage. The southern dam is located between two subdivisions called Royal Shores and Grand Point and forms the southern half of Lake Le Ann. There are residential areas on several large peninsulas, also two small islands within the lake. The northernmost dam was built near Vicary Road and forms the north half of the oddly shaped lake.

245.4 Enter Liberty Township, Jackson County.

245.4 Bridge. On the county line Vicary Road crosses the channel between Lake Le Ann and Mirror Lake on the north in an east-west direction.

245.4–244.8 Mirror Lake. Water flows through a small channel to Mirror Lake (1029 feet elevation). On old maps Mirror Lake and the lake to the north are referred to as Little Grand and Big Grand, but they are approximately the same size now as the result of a dam on the smaller and southernmost of the two.

244.4–244.8 Grand Lake (1009 feet elevation) is fed by a narrow channel from the spillway at Mirror Lake. Many most intimately connected with the Grand River consider Grand Lake as its primary source. A map of Michigan printed in the late 1830s shows the Grand River beginning at "Great Spring" south of Jackson. Grand Lake is spring-fed and, it is claimed, that even when the water level is low and dams at Lake Le Ann and Mirror Lake are not permitting water to flow out, the Grand River continues to flow because of the continuous influx of water from Grand Lake. To settle the matter a 1990 expedition which canoed the entire Grand River, led by well-known canoeist Verlen Kruger with James Woodruff as historian, began in Grand Lake with a solemn ceremony declaring it to be the source of the river. Grand Lake is privately owned, the only access is to put in down river and paddle upstream.

This late 1830s map shows the Grand River beginning south of Jackson at "Great Sp." (bottom left)

The dam at Liberty Mills with a pedestrian bridge across the top.

244.3 A small stream from Braxee Lake, located just west of Lake Le Ann in Hillsdale County, curves northward through the Putney Millpond and enters the main river from the west. This small stream rises less than a half a mile from Farewell Lake, a primary source of the Kalamazoo River. Braxee Lake is located in section 5, Somerset Township, just north of Bunday Hill, which is the highest point in elevation in the southern lower peninsula at 1282 feet, The elevation at Braxee Lake is 1057.

242.9 Bridge. South Jackson Road crosses the river north-south. The river is a tenth of a mile wide at this point and narrows to go under the road.

242.8 **Liberty** (or **Liberty Mills**) This tiny settlement on the east bank in section 23 of Liberty Township was founded in 1835 by Moses Tuthill. Jesse Bivins proposed the name, believed to have been suggested by the speech given by Patrick Henry prior to the Revolutionary War which stated, "Give me liberty or give me death!" However, the first post office, which opened April 13, 1837, with Franklin Pierce as postmaster, was named **Montgomery**. The office was renamed Liberty, after the township on January 19, 1839, and operated until March 31, 1903.

By the highway near the general store, there is an engraved boulder, moved from near Bunday Hill, engraved:

> Here at Liberty Mills is the first dam on the Grand River originating in nearby hills, the river flows nearly 300 miles north and west to where it joins Lake Michigan at Grand Haven. The Grand is Michigan's longest river.

242.75 **Liberty Dam**. There is a narrow dam at Liberty which produces a 10 foot waterfall. It is located behind the general store and has a footbridge over the dam.

242.7 Bridge. Liberty Road crosses the river east-west just east of Gillette Road which runs along the west bank of the river for about a half a mile.

242 Culvert with guard rail. Culver Road crosses the river north-south.

241.8 Outlet from Skiff Lake enters the river from the northwest.

240.9 Bridge with guard rail, built in 2004, carries Gates Road over the river north-south.

240.5 Enter Columbia Township, Jackson County, crossing the prime meridian of Michigan.

At the township line the river crosses diagonally under the intersection of Meridian Road and Jefferson Road.

239.5 Outlet from the swampy area north of Clark Lake enters the river from the north. The west end of Clark Lake itself, a body of water approximately a mile and a half long and a half mile wide, comes within half a mile of the Grand River, but under normal drainage conditions water from the lake, when it drains at all, exits to the southeast into Lake Columbia, eventually flowing into the Raisin River and entering Lake Erie at Monroe. A small community called **Clark Lake**, or Clarklake, (named for Robert Clark of Monroe, a government surveyor in the area), grew up near the west shore of the lake. It was a station on the Cincinnati, Jackson and Mackinaw Railway. A post office opened there April 25, 1896.

238.5 Culvert with guard rail. Reed Road crosses the river east-west utilizing a double culvert..

237.5 Re-enter Liberty Township, Jackson County.

237.5 Bridge. Meridian Road (U.S.127) again crosses the river in a north-south direction at the township line. At this point the river is about 12 feet wide.

237.1 The meandering river passes to the south of the Blue Ridge, a glacial esker which stretches approximately two miles southwest to northeast at an elevation of about 1000 feet.

236.2 Bridge. Loomis Road crosses the river east-west.

235.5 Enter Summit Township, Jackson County.

235.2 The outlet from Hammer and Peter White lakes flows into the river from the northeast.

234.8 Bridge. Draper Road crosses the river north-south, near the intersection of Ayers Road. A new crossing was under construction in the spring of 2007.

234 Bridge. Hague Avenue crosses the river north-south before entering Vandercook Lake village on the north. It is a crumbling concrete bridge with a central pillar.

232.8 Sharp Creek, from Mercedes Lake, enters the river from the southwest.

At this point the river flows through several small to medium-sized interconnected lakes.

232.1-232.7 Vandercook Lake, with the settlement of **Vandercook Lake,** named for pioneer settler Henry H. Vandercook, on the northeast bank. On the southeast shore is **Vandercook Lake Park**, which can be reached by car off 4th Street on Avenue A. Facilities include basketball and baseballs areas, a swimming beach, public toilets, playground and a boat ramp.

232 Bridge. Browns Lake Road crosses the short channel between Vandercook and Brown Lake in a north-south direction.

232-231.2 Brown Lake, a large lake with residences around much of its perimeter. Elevation is 947 feet.

231.1-230.8 Williams Lake a small undeveloped lake connected by a .3 mile channel from the northwest end of Brown Lake. River flows northwesterly into Williams Lake and then out at the northwest corner, once again forming a stream.

230.2. Bridge. The road which goes to the WKHM radio tower crosses, east-west. The riverbed turns east and flows just north of, but apparently does not connect to, Wyckoff Lake before it turns again north.

228.8 Bridge. Badgley Boulevard (called Hinkley Road to the east) crosses east-west on a concrete bridge with massive end abutments.

228.7 Bridge. Stonewall Road crosses the river north- south.

228 Bridge. Probert Road crosses northwest-southeast on a span built in 2003 with a separate bicycle and hiking path..

228.2-227.8 The Grand River, including a long bayou which reaches to the north, flows through **Ella Sharp Park**. Formerly a large farm the land and family home, which is now a museum, was willed to the City of Jackson in 1912, by Ella (Merriman) Sharp. The 563-acre park includes a golf course and learning center, swimming pool, sports fields, playground areas, rose garden, picnic shelters and the Peter F. Hurst

Before 1930 the lakes around Jackson were well-known entertainment venues. This postcard is the slide at Vandercook Lake in 1912.

Planetarium. Sharp Park is accessible by vehicle from 4th Street.

226.9 Bridge. Francis Road crosses the river north-south on a short concrete bridge built in 1993.

(Most maps show the official channel of the Grand River the route that flows from Vandercook Lake east to Brown Lake and north to Williams Lake. However, at the same time there is water flowing from Vandercook Lake north to Cove and Mud Lakes, and then through a channel .8 miles long into Sharp Lake. North of Sharp Lake, Park Drive crosses the flow, east-west.)

226.7 East of Francis Street the loop through the lakes is completed and the Grand River becomes a single stream.

225.8 Booth Drain enters the river from the south.

225.4 Bridge. Brooklyn Road (or Airline Drive, also designated M-50 and business U.S.127) crosses the river northwest-southeast.

224.8 Railroad bridge. The old Cincinnati Northern tracks cross the river parallel to the highway bridge.

224.6 Bridge. Meridian Road crosses north-south. The road retains the name (although it was earlier called Oak Lane), but curves off of the actual prime meridian at this point.

224.55 Enter Leoni Township, Jackson County.

224.5 Bridge. River flows east under U.S. 127 which crosses north-south on twin bridges.

224.2 Outlet from Ackerson Lake enters the river from the south.

223.6 Bridge. South Street crosses northwest-southeast and the river turns northwest.

222.6 Bridge. The Grand River passes under U.S. 127 flowing west. Just east of the bridge the flow is increased with water from a series of lakes to the east of Jackson. Some sources indicate that this is an "eastern" or "northern" branch of the Grand River. Its beginnings are worth noting:

"North Branch"

The waters of the "North Branch" begin just off Cady Road, east of Wolf Lake Road northeast of the small settlement of **Napoleon**

Bridge. Wolf Lake Road crosses north-south.

The flow is northward into Little Wolf Lake where **Little Wolf Lake County Park**, off Wolf Lake Road in Napoleon Township, provides the public access to a swimming area, picnic facilities and restrooms.

Water flows through a short channel into Wolf Lake with the settlement of **Oak Point** on the southwest bank

Willow Creek enters Wolf Lake from the northeast.

Enter Olcott Lake

Bridge. Napoleon Road crosses north-south over the small reed-choked channel between Olcott Lake and Little Olcott Lake.

The casino at Wolf Lake in 1906.

Enter Little Olcott Lake, on some maps the eastern portion of Little Olcott Lake is called Dollar Lake.

Bridge. Moon Lake Road crosses east-west

Outlet from Price Lake enters the river from the north.

To the south, what is probably an old river bed forms Moon Lake.

Enter Center Lake. A stream enters Center Lake from the northeast bringing the Grass Lake Drain and passing through an old millpond near the community of **Leoni**. The outlet from Round Lake enters Center Lake from the northwest. There is a public access about midway on the north bank.

Michigan Center. A settlement was begun just north of the outlet on the extreme northwest shore of Center Lake in 1834 by Martin Schumacker, Abel F. Fitch and John Allendorf. The first post office was established February 1, 1838. It was named because of its location, at the approximate east-west center of the lower peninsula.

Center Lake Dam. At the Center Lake spillway, built in 1918, the elevation is 939 feet. The spillway's primary purpose is flood control. There is a boat ramp at **Leoni Township Park,** on 5th Street between Broad and South Lakeside streets. The park also features playground facilities, restrooms and picnic tables. Near the outlet, on a long narrow section of water which flows to the northwest, there is a canoe livery and launch.

Bridge. 5th Street crosses the flow of the North Branch at the spillway north-south.

Bridge. Falahes Road crosses north-south.

The North Branch flows into the main river just east of the U.S.127 bridge, mile 222.6.

Jackson to Eaton Rapids

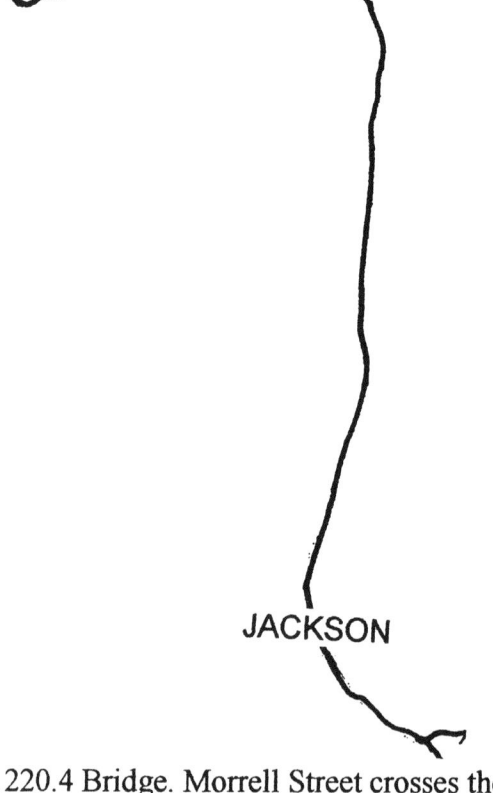

221.4 Bridge. Losey Street crosses the river north-south on a bridge built in 2004.

221 Bridge. High Street again crosses the river, this time east-west.

220.7 Bridge. Lewis Street crosses the river east-west

220.6 Railroad Bridge. An old New York Central Railroad bridge crosses the river east-west.

222.6 The flow from the south meets up with the flow from the lakes to the east, in section 7, Leoni Township, Jackson County, just outside the city limits of Jackson.

In earlier days the river became navigable for small boats from this point, and it was near here that settlers from Detroit would put rafts in the river with household goods bound for Ionia, Grand Rapids, Lansing and other points west.

Jackson. Horace Blackman built a log cabin at the site of Jackson in 1827. The settlement was named **Jacksonburgh** for President Andrew Jackson, and first platted in 1830. A post office named Jacksonburgh opened in 1830, the same year the first dam was built. The name of the settlement was changed to **Jackson-opolis** in 1835 and to Jackson in 1838. It is the county seat of Jackson County. Jackson was incorporated as a village in 1842 and as a city in 1857. The population of the city was 36,316 in 2000. It had an area of 11.1 square miles.

222.5 Bridge. Just west of the U S. 127 bridge High Street crosses the river north-south.

220.4 Bridge. Morrell Street crosses the river east-west The Jackson Water Department and the Department of Public Works are nearby.

220 **Holton Dam** stood at this point until 2001. In the 1920s the river, from the

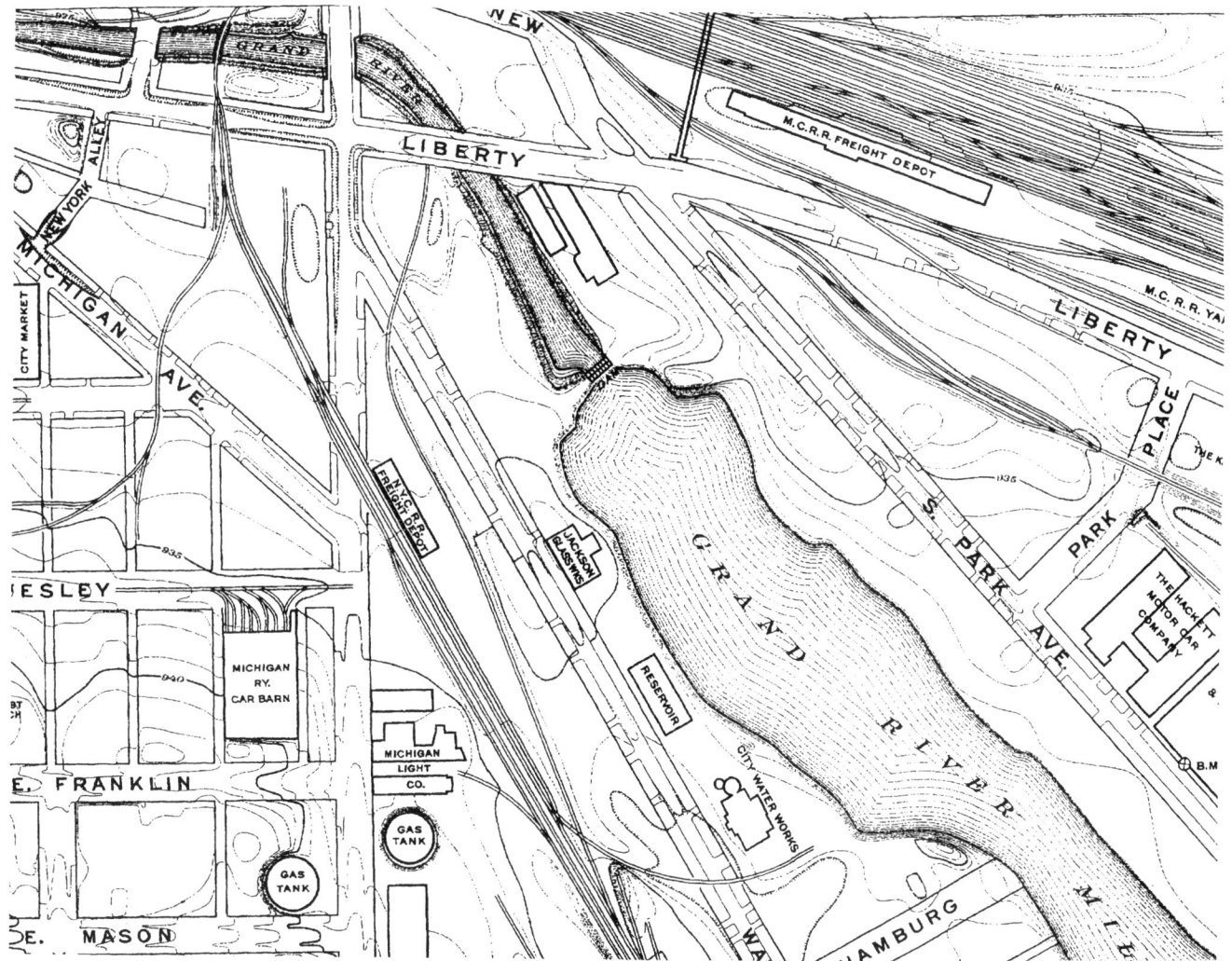

Holton Dam in downtown Jackson from a 1917 city map. Note the Hackett Motor Car Company at lower right.

dam to Michigan Avenue, a distance of about 2,280 feet of river, was forced into a cement channel. Later that channel received a cement cap to decrease the amount of trash which was dumped into the stream and also to mitigate the smell. After several children were trapped under the cap and drowned, the cap and the dam were removed in 2001 and the mill pond was drained. The banks of the river within the city are now full of plants and small trees.

219.8 Bridge. East Washington Street crosses the river east-west.

219.7 Bridge. Cooper Street, a major north-south street in downtown Jackson crosses the river north-south.

219.5 Bridge. Francis Street crosses north-south. Nearby the sculpture "Summer Night Tree" by sculptor Lourse Nevelson stands by a state office building..

219.45 Bridge. Mechanic Street crosses the river north-south.

219.4 Bridge. East Michigan Avenue (Louis Glick Highway) crosses the stream east-west near the municipally-run Grand River Market.

219.35 Railroad bridge. This track crosses the river north of Michigan Avenue. It marks the end of the part of the river which was capped and the stream widens slightly here.

219.2 Bridge. The William D. Monroe Bridge carries Trail Street across the river east-west. It was named for a former city engineer. Early writers record a ford at this point in the river.

219.1 Bridge. Ganson Street crosses the stream east-west

219.1-218.8 Jackson County Fairgrounds and Jackson Harness Raceway are on the west bank.

218.9 Michigan's first state prison was authorized by the legislature in 1837 and built on the east bank of the river at the north end of Mechanic Street. It was a temporary structure, built of tamarack poles. A more permanent building was erected three years later. In 1934 a new, modern prison was constructed north of Jackson. Some of the exterior walls of the old prison on Mechanic Street remain.

218.75 Bridge. North Street crosses the river east-west.

218.5 – 218.35 **Lions Park**, a seven-acre city park on the west bank, provides sports fields, a playground, picnic shelter and a view of the river. It is at the corner of Adams and Blackstone streets.

218.25 Bridge. Monroe Street crosses the river east-west

217.95 Leave the City of Jackson, enter Blackman Township, Jackson County.

217.8 Bridge. I-94 crosses the river east-west on twin bridges.

The Michigan State Penitentiary with the Grand River and the North Street bridge in the foreground, from a 1914 postcard. The railroad crossing at this point was the main track of the Grand Trunk.

217.4 Railroad Bridge for Penn Central tracks north of interstate.

217 Hurd Marvin Drain, on at least one old map called Tobin-Wheeler-Snyder Drain enters from the west.

216.4 Bridge. Parnall Road crosses the river east-west.

216 Southern Michigan State Prison is high up on the east bank. This is the prison complex built in 1934 to replace the first prison in Michigan which had been constructed in 1839 in downtown Jackson. It was closed in 2001, but was expected to be reopened when the space is needed.

214.6 Portage River enters the river from the east, with the settlement of **Puddleford Bridge** a half mile upstream on the Portage River at Cooper Road (M-106). The Portage River has, at that point, already joined with water from Pickett Drain, Thornapple Creek, Cahogan Creek, Orchid Creek, Wildcat Creek, the outlet from Brill Lake, and drains from other small lakes in the area.

Just past the Portage River junction the grounds of the old State Prison Farm stretch for two miles along the east bank.

212.5 Bridge. Maple Grove Road crosses east-west on a bridge constructed in 1977. Off the northwest corner of the bridge there a DNR access site with a boat ramp and public fishing pier.

2115.7 Twin Lakes Creek (or Drain) enters from the east.

209.9 Bridge. Berry Road crosses the river east-west on a crumbling cement bridge. Survey maps show **Berry Bridge** at this crossing.

209.8 Outlet from Allen Lake enters the river from the east, earlier maps show

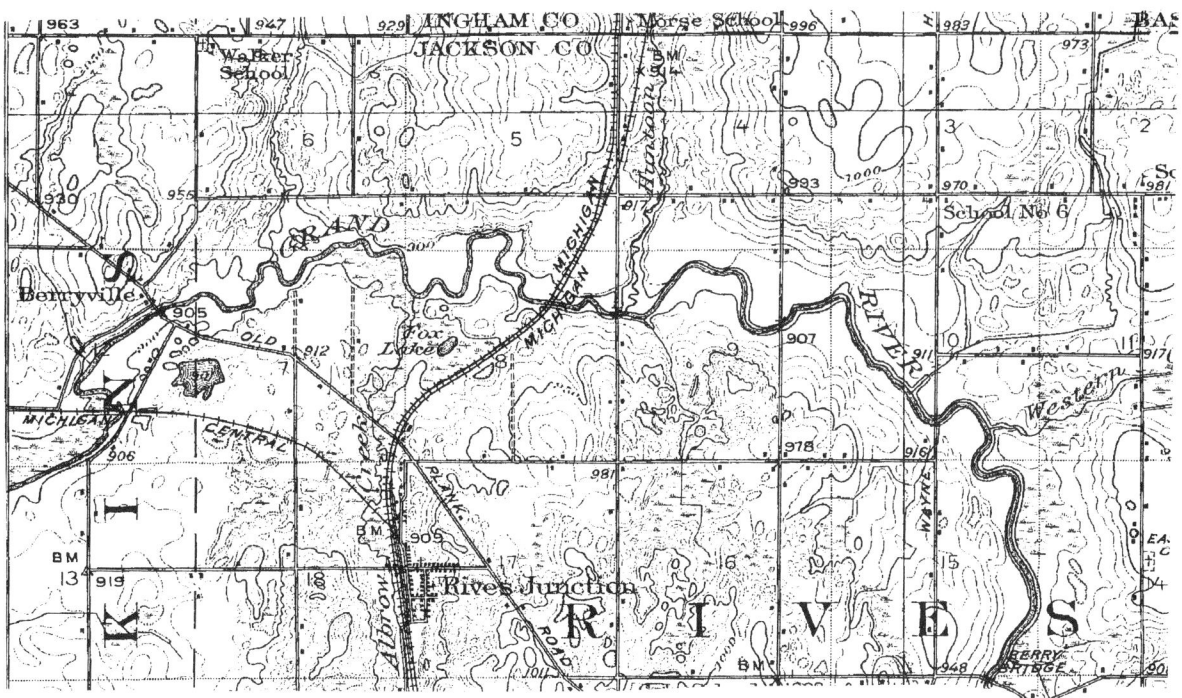

Berryville and Rives Junction, left. *Berry Bridge (lower right) in 1921.*

the same stream flowing from Perry (or Berry) Lake.

208.5 Western Creek enters from the east having already picked up Shaw Branch. At this point the river bed begins a leisurely turn to the west.

206.8 Bridges. U.S.127 crosses the river north-south. The bridge has been removed from State Street, (old 127) which runs parallel to the new road on the east.

205.7 Huntoon Creek, from the village of Leslie, enters the river from the north having already picked up Royston Drain.

205.54 Bridge. Churchill Road crosses the river north-south on an old concrete bridge.

205.3 Railroad Bridge. The old Michigan Central (later Penn Central) line to Lansing crosses north-south.

203.9 Albrow (or Albrau on some old maps) Creek enters from the south through a swampy area from the settlement of Rives Junction. Nearby is **Youth Haven Recreation Area** which provides access to the river.

About two miles south of the river is the community of **Rives Junction**, established where the main Michigan Central track split, one going north to Lansing, the other west to Chicago.

203.2 Perry Creek enters from the north.

202.1 Enter Tompkins Township, Jackson County.

201.9.6 Bridge. Rives-Eaton Road crosses the river northwest-southeast.

Berryville About 20 buildings is all that is left of the settlement of Berryville at this point, where the river meets the Rives-Eaton Road.

201 **Trestle Bridge Park**, at the site of an old Penn Central Railroad bridge which crossed the river supported by five wooden trestles. There is a carry-down boat ramp and small parking area east of the river reached from Dixon Road.

196.9 Sandstone Creek enters from the south having already picked up McKay Brook.

About a mile up the creek is **Tompkins Center** which was first settled by Richard Townley in 1836, and named for the New York State township where he had formerly lived, which had been named for Daniel D. Tompkins, a former New York governor. A post office called Tomkins operated from January 22, 1839 to 1904. The settlement was located on the Old Clinton Road.

196.3 Bridge. Tompkins Road crosses north-south on a concrete bridge with metal rails. Nearby is a hard-surfaced boat ramp with a 20 vehicle parking lot.

An 1873 map shows a community, post office and railroad station called **Arland**. a mile and a half east of the river on the Arland Road. Robert T. Todd became the first postmaster May 1856. The post office officially closed October 31, 1904.

192.5 Enter Onondaga Township, Ingham County

190.8 Outlet from Lanes Lake enter the river from the northeast.

190.4 **Baldwin Park** near the west bank is a 16-acre facility on the site of a former Indian campground. It has a picnic shelter, restrooms, playground, softball diamond, fishing and a canoe launch.

190.2 Railroad Bridge. Conrail tracks, formerly Michigan Central, cross the flow southeast-northwest.

190.1 Bridge. Old Plank Road crosses northwest- southeast. In 2007 this bridge was being totally rebuilt.

190.1-189.4 **Onondaga** The first settlement at this site was by Oliver Booth in 1834, Warren B. Buckland became the first postmaster on October 16, 1838. The village was platted in 1870 and named after the township which had been named by Orange Phelps after his old home, Onondaga County, New York. It was later a station on the Michigan Central Railroad. Onondaga is an unincorporated part of Onondaga Township which, in 2000 had a population of 2,958.

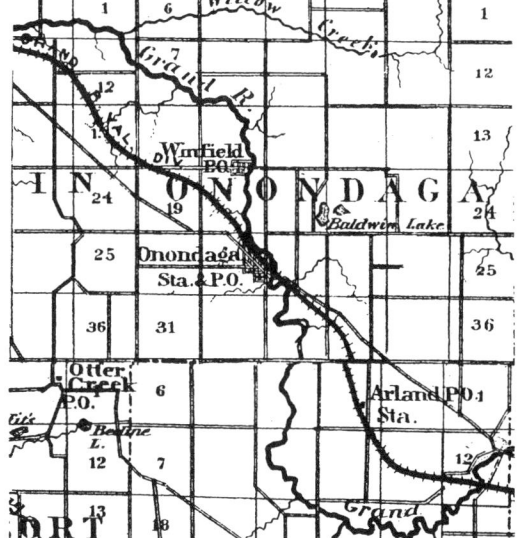

This 1873 map shows Winfield (also called Kinneville), Onondaga station and post office, and Arland.

189.8 Bridge. Onondaga Road crosses the river north-south. Railroad tracks run parallel to the highway on the south bank of the river.

187.8 Bridge. Kinneville Road crosses the river east-west.

187.8-187.6 **Kinneville** The name of this small settlement near the west bank of the river is spelled several different ways, including Kinneyville and Kinnieville. In 1849 Stephen Van Kinney recorded a village plat which he called **Nova Scotia**. It received a post office called **Winfield** on April 29, 1862, with William Earll as its first postmaster, the office operating until March 14, 1903.

186 Bridge. Gale Road crosses north-south on a one-span truss bridge. The river is very wide.

185.4 Kettler and Norris Drain enters from the southwest.

184.8 Enter Hamlin Township, Eaton County.

Bridge. On the county line Waverly Road crosses the river north-south. It is a long concrete bridge with grill fencing. Two miles south along Waverly Road in Ingham County is the VFW National Home opened in 1925 to care for the widows and orphans of deceased veterans.

184.2 Willow Creek enters from the northeast, having already picked up North Onondaga Drain.

183 **Smithville Dam** About 1886 a man named Smith built a dam at Smithville. In 1890 his mill burned. Today there is a

The Smithville dam and power station.

larger dam with a power station on one bank. The installation is owned by Grand River Power Company, a subsidiary of the American Energy Company. The power produced by this dam is sold to area power distributors. In January of 2006 the American Energy Company, was cited for safety violations at this dam, and also at the nearby Mix Dam, and three others on the Thornapple River, and ordered to pay $300,000 to resolve the issue. As compensation for resource damage, the Michigan Department of Natural Resources was slated to receive $50,000 to be spent specifically on fish passage and habitat improvement projects around the hydroelectric facilities.

182.9 Bridge. Smithville Road crosses north-south just below the dam. The four-acre **Hamlin Township Park** near the bridge, sponsored by the Hamlin Township firefighters, provides fishing access and a picnic area. There is also an artesian well near the river bank, with iron-rich water which was an important part of the area's early mineral baths. Additional park land is in the process of development.

182.1 South and slightly east of Eaton Rapids is the Michigan State Holiness Camp Meeting Ground, on a 1912 survey map it is labeled "campground" and many postcards mention that campground and show canoeing and camping in a woods. The campground was begun by the Methodists in 1885 on a 32-acre wooded lot. The central building in the facility is the Memorial Auditorium, a 1000-seat many-sided wooden tabernacle with sides that can be lifted to allow the summer breezes in, but keep the rain out. Over 70 little cottages provide accommodations, and there is a two store-frame hotel. The roads are carefully laid out to spell the word "Holiness."

Eaton Rapids to Lansing

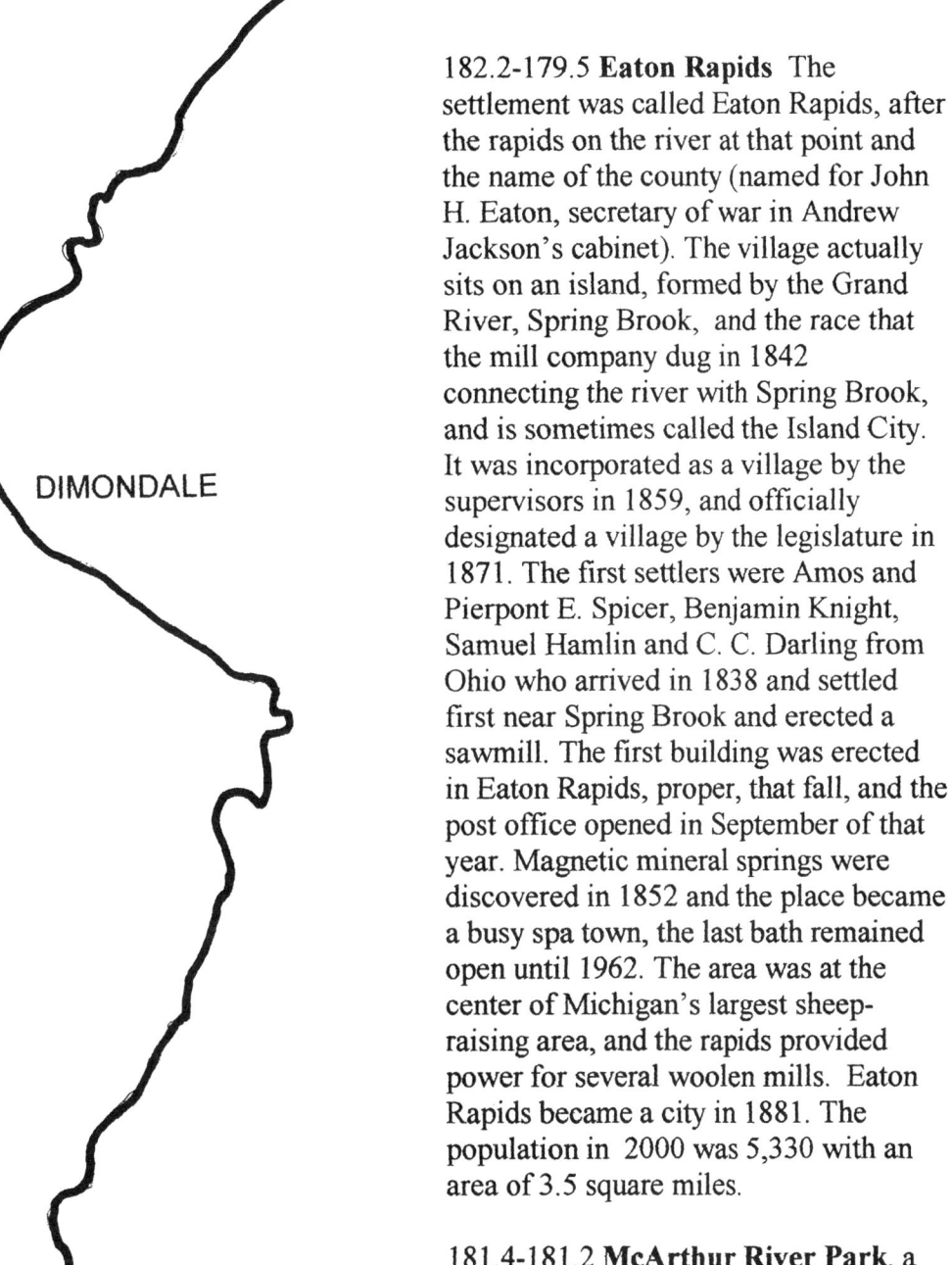

182.2-179.5 **Eaton Rapids** The settlement was called Eaton Rapids, after the rapids on the river at that point and the name of the county (named for John H. Eaton, secretary of war in Andrew Jackson's cabinet). The village actually sits on an island, formed by the Grand River, Spring Brook, and the race that the mill company dug in 1842 connecting the river with Spring Brook, and is sometimes called the Island City. It was incorporated as a village by the supervisors in 1859, and officially designated a village by the legislature in 1871. The first settlers were Amos and Pierpont E. Spicer, Benjamin Knight, Samuel Hamlin and C. C. Darling from Ohio who arrived in 1838 and settled first near Spring Brook and erected a sawmill. The first building was erected in Eaton Rapids, proper, that fall, and the post office opened in September of that year. Magnetic mineral springs were discovered in 1852 and the place became a busy spa town, the last bath remained open until 1962. The area was at the center of Michigan's largest sheep-raising area, and the rapids provided power for several woolen mills. Eaton Rapids became a city in 1881. The population in 2000 was 5,330 with an area of 3.5 square miles.

181.4-181.2 **McArthur River Park**, a linear city park along the riverbank on the northeast side of the river is reach on land off River Street. It has a boat ramp, playgrounds and picnicking facilities.

180.9 South Mill Race and Dam. The

channel of water which connects Spring Brook to the Grand River and is sometimes calls the south mill race. The original plan was to augment the water of Spring Brook as it flowed past the mill dam. Today at most water levels the flow of the main river is discouraged from entering the brook by baffles in the big river. There is about a eight foot waterfalls just beyond the race.

180.8 Bridge. State Street (called Plains Highway in the township) crosses, the river east-west carrying M-50 and M-188 over the river. The bridge was built by the city in 1948.

180.7 A foot bridge which connects with Hamlin Street crosses from the downtown Eaton Rapids area to Island Park (sometimes called G.A.R. Park). In 1892 the small island was privately owned and described as "a shady retreat for pleasure seekers with a fine collection of animals and a museum of rare specimens." In 1897 it was purchased by the city for use as a park. Following the Civil War the Eaton County Battalion held annual encampments from 1908 until 1929 and it was officially renamed G.A.R. Park. Two Civil War cannons were erected on the island and the G.A.R. monument to "Our Fallen Heroes 1861-64" was moved there in 1915. When the old fire alarm bell was no longer needed it was taken to the island to serve as a tribute to 80 years of Eaton Rapids firemen in 1954. Another foot bridge, connects the island to the east bank.

180.6 Bridge. Knight Street crosses the Grand River east-west, and continues westward, through the business district, to cross Spring Brook.

180.55 A small dam, about two feet in height, connects an island in the river with the mainland creating a small waterfall.

Island Park at Eaton Rapids

(Top) The Horner Brothers Woolen Mill on the Grand River at its junction, with Spring Brook. (Bottom) An old paper mill (at left in top picture) has been recycled into apartments, said to have more rooms than the Grand Hotel at Mackinac Island.

180.4 **Mix Dam**. The main body of Spring Brook enters the Grand River through the turbines at Mix Dam. The creek was dammed at its juncture with the Grand in 1933 to provide power for the woolen mills and the city. The dam has been used in recent years by the Grand River Power Company to produce hydroelectric power. The same company runs Smithville Dam a little over two miles upstream. The Mix dam powerhouse is located about a quarter of a mile downstream from the dam on M-50. Before Spring Brook enters the Grand River it has already picked up the waters of Hobart and Booth Drains.

Water from Spring Brook enters the Grand through Mix Dam.

Just up Spring Brook from the dam on the north bank, a large paper-making factory buildin, constructed about 1900, is being converted into apartments.

179.5 Enter Eaton Rapids Township, Eaton County.

179.4 Spicer Creek enters from the northwest.

178.4 Harris Drain enters from the south.

177.9 Bridge. Petrieville Highway crosses east-west. The river is very shallow here.

Petrieville or Petreville is on both sides of the river on the Petrieville Highway, First settled in 1880 the community had a post office from 1898 to 1901. Alice E. Jenks was the first postmaster.

177.5 Odell, Benton and Bentley Drains enter from the west.

176.2 Bunker Highway crosses the river east-west. **Bunker Road Landing,** at the southeast corner of the bridge, west of M-99, is a five-acre park with a carry-down boat ramp, suitable for small boats and canoes, with a 13-car parking area..

175.7 County Line Drain enters from the southeast.

173.7 Columbia Creek enters from the east

173 Enter Aurelius Township, Ingham County.

172.8 Enter Delhi Township, Ingham County

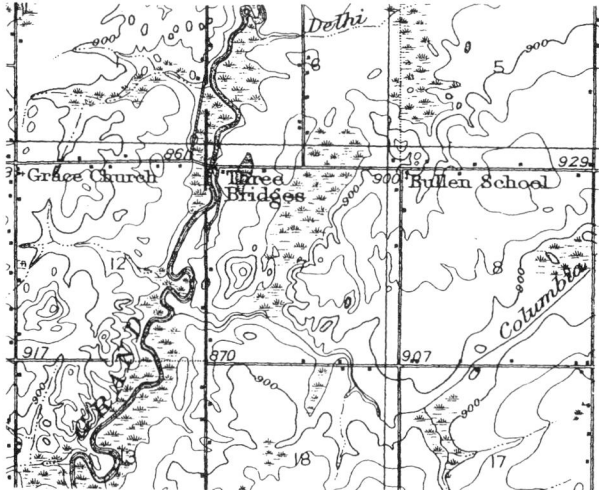

Three Bridges on a 1912 survey map. Here, or on Columbia Creek to the south, stood the settlement of Columbia.

172.8 Bridge. Columbia Highway crosses east-west. Nearby, a 1912 survey map shows the community of **Three Bridges**. In this vicinity a settlement called **Columbia** was begun in 1837 and grew to include 18 families and a sawmill. Columbia had hopes that it would be designated the county seat, but lost the bid to Mason and vanished from the maps.

172.8-169.7 **McNamara Landing,** on the west side of the river near the Columbia Highway bridge, marks the beginning of three miles of parkland along the east bank of the river. There is a boat ramp at McNamara Landing with a small parking area. This area also serves as a trailhead for hiking and biking trails that meander along the riverbank. To the north, **Riverbend Natural Area** has a small pond, a landing on the Grand River and hiking and mountain bike trails open in the summer. By land it is reached from Nichols Road. The northernmost of the three parks, **William M. Burchfield Park**, is sometimes used as a label for them all. It officially begins at the big bend, near the foot of Burke Highway, and includes both the east and the west banks of the river. The total area is 540 acres. The park is reached by vehicle from Grovenburg Road. There is a per vehicle fee. In the summer facilities include a picnic area, a stocked fishing pond, playground, an inland swimming area, hiking trails, a regularly scheduled nature day camp, and canoe and kayak rentals and trips. The park is run by the Ingham County Parks Department. In the winter cross-country skiing trails, and two 700-foot toboggan runs are an attraction.

172 Aurelius and Delhi Drain enters from the east.

168.8 Grovenburg Drain enters from the northeast having picked up Blakeslee and Abbot drains.

168.3 Bridge. Waverly Road crosses north south on a three-pier concrete bridge with metal tube railings.

168.3 Enter Windsor Township, Eaton County.

168.1 Skinner Extension Drain enters from the southwest, on old maps it is called Howard Drain.

Millett Station, Dimondale and Windsor from an 1873 railroad map.

167.4 Gilbert Drain enters the river from the northeast having already picked up West Town Drain.

167.2 Bailey Road formerly crossed the river southwest-northeast at this point, but the bridge has since been removed. A community called **Windsor** is a half mile northeast on Bailey Road on an 1873 map. It was settled by Orange Towslee in 1837 and received a post office in 1894. The town and township was named by citizens from Windsor, Vermont.

166.9.2 Michigan Road (M-99), a divided highway, crosses the river north-south. The road becomes Martin Luther King Highway in Lansing.

The old bridge at Dimondale from a 1903 postcard.

165.4-164.3 **Dimondale** in Eaton County. Isaac M. Dimond began to build a dam and a sawmill on the river in 1856 and he had the village platted by Hosey Harvey in 1856 naming it Dimondale for himself and family. A post office was opened in July 3, 1872 with Bradley Sloan as postmaster. It was a station on the Lake Shore and Michigan Southern Railway Company line although the station was called **Diamondale**. The settlement incorporated as a village in 1906. The population in 2000 was 1,342, with a land area of one square mile.

165 Bridge. Bridge Highway crosses the river southwest-northeast and goes into Dimondale. The bridge was built in 1932 and refurbished in 1986. There is an small park near the northwest corner of the bridge.

164.8 **Dimondale Weir**. The first dam at about this site was constructed about 1840, an earthen dam on a three-foot fall, which turned mills and powered other industry in early Dimondale. The dam and 15 acres surrounding it were purchased by the Lansing Board of Water and Light as a potential source for hydroelectric power, but never operated by them. About 2001 it was acquired by the village of Dimondale and a decision made to remove the remnants of the old dam to restore the flow of the river. Because of the fall in the river at that point a W-shaped weir, made from large rocks, was constructed to stabilize the stream bottom, while allowing the water to pass through the rocks without accumulating sediment. Weirs of this type have been used in other states, but the Dimondale site was a first for the State of Michigan. It was expected to improve water quality and fishing, and reduce the potential for flooding without hindering shallow draft navigation.

164.8 Silver Creek enters from the southwest, after picking up Whaley Drain.

164.3 A five-acre island just downstream from the weir near the west bank has been earmarked for development as a village park with a bridge connecting it to the riverbank

The old mill race and gristmill at Dimondale photographed about 1910.

163.1-163 Bridges. Twin bridges carry the Interstate highway, I-96, across the river southeast-northwest.

162.8 Bridge. Crietz Road crosses north-south on a concrete, two-pillared bridge.

160.5 **Woldumar Nature Center** on the northwest bank has five miles of nature trails some along the river. In the summer Camp Discovery offers events for families, children and teens. Displays at the nature center include live animals and geology. On land it is reach from the Old Lansing Road.

160.2. **Millett** A settlement located about a half mile west of the river on the Lansing road began around coal and clay beds owned by S. E. Millett. It was given a station named **Milletts** on the Chicago and Lake Huron Railroad Company, later the Grand Trunk Western Railroad, in 1877. The same year a post office named Millett was opened with Franklin P. Wells as its first postmaster. The post office closed in 1910.

158.3 Bridge. Waverly Road crosses north-south. marking the Ingham County line and the city limits of Lansing.

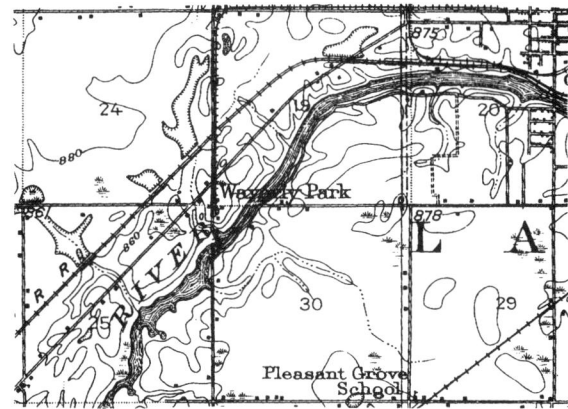

Waverly Park on a 1912 survey map, the City of Lansing is at upper right.

Waverly Park. A 1912 survey map shows Waverly Park off the northeast corner of the bridge. Opened in 1892, it was first called **Leadley Park**, after its proprietor, Gottleib Leadley, who died in

Waverly Park entrance in 1909.

1897. It was sold to the Lansing City Electric Railroad Company and became a popular picnic area and amusement park. In the early days boats also would take passengers to Waverly Park from the Logan Street dock in Lansing. The park once included refreshment stands, a boat livery for outings on the river, games, rides and a hotel. Today the City of Lansing has reached the old park site which is partly occupied by the Deepdale Memorial Gardens.

The boat landing at Waverly Park about 1910.

Lansing to Ionia

159.2-150.2 Lansing The first settlement at Lansing was centered around a saw mill located near the present North Lansing dam. It was known as "Lower Town" or "North Town" after the North family which settled there. The second settlement was "Upper Town" which began with the construction of a bridge across the Grand River near its junction with the Red Cedar River. When Michigan had became a state in 1837 the legislature, having enough on its mind, decided to continue to have the state capitol at Detroit and voted to not consider the question for ten years. In 1847 there was considerable wrangling in both houses of the state legislature and finally it was agreed to build a new capital in a new settlement to be created at the approximate east-west center of the lower peninsula in Lansing Township, Ingham County. This created a "Middle Town" which, with the construction of the first capitol, became the dominant area. Michigan was the name given to this new capital city, but citizens and newspapers did not like the idea of Michigan, Michigan. The *Detroit Free Press* wrote that it was "more like a hiccup than a name," so, on April 27, 1847, the name of the settlement and post office was changed to Lansing, after the name given the township. The township had been named by settler Joseph H. North Jr. after his hometown Lansing, in Tompkins County, New York, which had been named for John Lansing, a New York Revolutionary War hero and jurist. Lansing, including all three of the original settlements, was incorporated as a city in 1859. In 1898 native-son Ransom E. Olds, who was experimenting with an early automobile became the first person in the world to actually sell one of the contraptions. His vehicles were also the first to use liquid gasoline to provide internal combustion, and Olds developed an improved spark plug. In 1901 city fathers purchased the old fair grounds on the river downtown, and offered it to Olds as a manufacturing facility for his Oldsmobile car line. Lansing's population in 2000 was 119,128 making it the state's sixth largest city, with an area of about 35 square miles.

Michigan Avenue bridge and the capitol about 1912.

157.6-156.9 Frances Park is on the south bank, nearly directly opposite Grand River Park. Frances Park includes a linear park along Moores River Drive on the south shore, two scenic outlooks on the Grand River, a hiking trail and a formal rose garden with more than 150 varieties of roses. It is a popular place for weddings.

157.4-156.9 Grand River Park on the north bank. In 2007 the J & K Steamboat Line docked at this park. The Michigan Princess is a 110-foot, three story vessel which can accommodate up to 500 guests at theatrical events, concerts and receptions. Two of the decks are enclosed and the boat operates year-round with both regularly scheduled cruises and private parties. There is also a public boat launch at Grand River Park.

156.4 **Riverside Park** on south bank is a small park along the river with playgrounds, picnic facilities. It is reached off River Drive.

156.2 Bridge. Logan Street crosses the river north-south. It was on the west edge of the site of the old Oldsmobile plant.

155.8 A pedestrian-bicycle bridge at the west end of Moores Park.

155.8-155.5 **Moores Park,** named for lumberman and wagon maker John Henry Moores who donated the land, is on the south bank in downtown Lansing There is a boat ramp, several playgrounds and picnicking sites, a handicapped access fishing area, a large shuffleboard layout where the annual Senior Citizen Shuffleboard Tournament is held, and an unusual round swimming pool, which was designed by Wesley Bintz and opened in 1928. It is also the place to view the Moores Park Dam. The park is reached from Moores River Drive, east of M-99. Lansing's nearly seven mile **River Trail** begins at Moores Park and travels, mostly on the east bank of the river, until just south of the Seymour Street bridge, north of the downtown area..

155.7 **Moores Park Dam**. A dam was constructed at approximately this site in 1898, by the Piatt brothers, who also built a steam generating electric plant nearby. The installation was bought by the Michigan Power Company, which tried to lure electric business from the municipal operation, but eventually sold to the Lansing Board of Water and Light in 1919. The Moores Park Dam was rebuilt in the 1920s to create a pond for the Otto E. Eckert coal-fired generating plant. There are three smokestacks on top of the powerhouse, all 624 feet in height, the tallest self-supporting structures in south central Michigan. They are known locally as Wynken, Blynken and Nod, after the fishermen in a Eugene Field poem. The dam has two 540 kilowatt horizontal Francis turbines which produce some hydropower, however it is limited to one to two percent of the city's total production. The elevation at that point is 833 feet.

155.4 Bridge. Island Avenue, a short street, only a quarter of a mile long, crosses the river on a slant and provides authorized vehicles access to the power plant from the south bank. It is a picturesque bridge with lamps on each end.

Washington Avenue bridge about 1912.

155.35 The river, which had been flowing east and slightly south, takes an abrupt turn to the north.

155.35 Railroad bridge for the Grand Trunk Western railroad.

155.2 Bridge. A graceful bridge with decorative lamps carries Elm Street over the river east-west.

154.9 **Scott Park** on the north bank.

154.8 Bridge. The Washington Avenue bridge crosses the river north-south. A modern span has replaced the earlier bridge which had two elliptical arched spans and was often photographed.

154.75 **Biddle City**. Before there was a Lansing there was the proposed village of Biddle City platted in 1836 just south of the junction of the Cedar River and the Grand River by Jerry and William Ford of Jackson and named for Major John Biddle of Detroit. The city was never realized.

154.6 Junction with the Red Cedar River which enters from the south in downtown Lansing. The Red Cedar River rises from Cedar Lake, south of Fowlerville in Livingston County. It flows north and picks up Middle Branch at Fowlerville, South Branch, and then Kalamink Creek and Wiley Creek just west of Webberville, Deer Creek at Williamston, Coon Creek, the outlet from Lake Lansing, Pine Mud Lake Drain, Sloan Creek, and Button Drain. The Red Cedar merges with Sycamore Creek near Lansing's Potter Park. Before this junction Sycamore Creek has already merged with Talmadge Drain, Willow Creek, Mud Creek, Banta Drain and Mud Lake Drain.

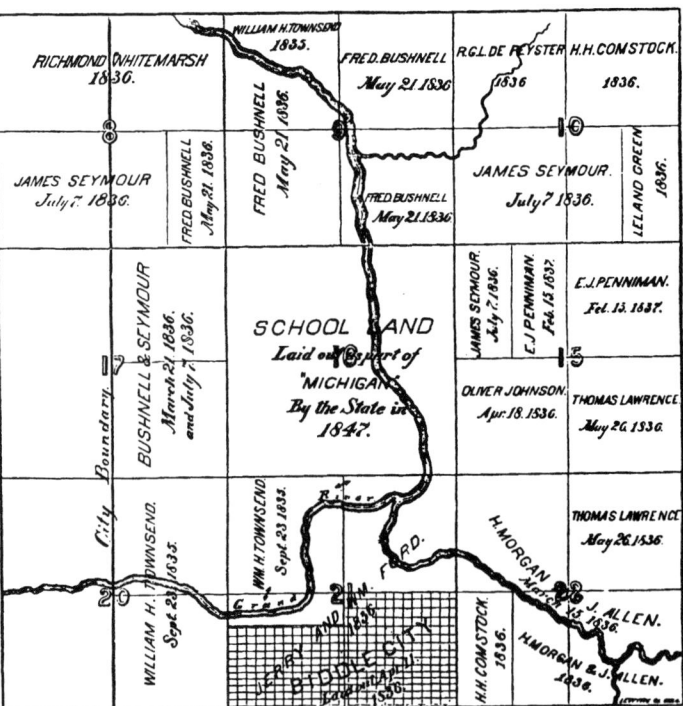

A map of the junction of the Red Cedar River (right) and the Grand (left) showing early land owners and the site of Biddle City.

About 1847 there was a bridge built across the Grand River near the confluence with the Red Cedar, but it was hard to maintain and was not replaced when it washed out during the flood of 1860.

154.45 Bridge. River Road crosses the river north-south, practically under the interstate bridge.

154.4 Bridge. Twin bridges carry I-496 over river east-west.

154.35 **Sweeney's Landing**, on the west side of the river just north of I-495. North of the Red Cedar River junction is a small park with a hard-surfaced boat ramp, reached from River Street, nearby is **River Street Park.**

154.2 Bridge. Kalamazoo Street crosses the river east-west.

The River Trail between Kalamazoo Street and Michigan Avenue has several museums including the R. E. Olds Transportation Museum. the Museum of Surveying, Impression 5 Science Center (a hands-on science museum for children), and Riverwalk Theatre. There is also an outdoor Planet Walk, with the entire solar system laid out along the riverbank. On land the area is accessed from Museum Drive off Michigan Avenue.

153.8 Bridge. Michigan Avenue which leads directly to the capitol crosses the river east-west. The first bridge at this point was of timber construction, built in 1848. It was replaced in 1856 with a timber lattice bridge, resting on a central pier. In 1871 a bowspring single span truss bridge was erected, which was one of two bridges in the city to survive the flood of 1875. In 1894 a steel arch bridge 234 feet long and 155 feet wide (at the time of its construction said to be the widest bridge in the country) was erected. It was replaced by a concrete structure dedicated, in 1975-76 as Michigan Veterans Memorial Bridge.

153.7 Pedestrian bridge. Near the end of Ottawa Street, just north of Michigan there is an enclosed, all-weather pedestrian bridge between the Radisson Hotel and the Lansing Center at Riverfront Plaza.

153.65 Just north of the Michigan Avenue bridge stands the Ottawa Street Power Station for the Lansing Board of Water and Light. The 16-story structure is built in Art Déco style, with a color scheme that ranges from polished black granite (symbolizing coal) at the base, to purple-gray and progressively lighter shades of red, orange, yellow and ending at the top with a yellow-gray. It sits on the northeast corner of Grand Avenue and Ottawa Street, on the west bank of the river. The plant is located on the site of an earlier power plant built in 1908 by Michigan Power Company. The hydro-generator unit was decommissioned on December 27, 1990, and the entire plant officially shut down in 1992. The hydro unit is still in place, but has been rendered inoperable in accordance with FERC procedures.

The Michigan Avenue bridge, Lansing, with an electric trolley and large horse-drawn carriage, about 1912.

153.6 Bridge. Shiawassee Street crosses the river east-west.

153.8-153.2 **River Front Park** occupies both banks of the Grand River from Michigan Avenue to Oakland Avenue. On land it can be reached from Grand Avenue. The first phase was opened for the Bicentennial in 1976. It is built mostly on reclaimed land with former industrial buildings removed, but an old salt storage shed was remodeled into an amphitheater for performing arts events, and an old railroad bridge is now a pedestrian walkway that allows visitors to either side to cross the river. Facilities include a biking, jogging and walking trail and a small boat ramp. The eight-mile River Trail Walk runs along the east bank of the river from Michigan north of town nearly to Martin Luther King Jr. Boulevard.

On the east bank of the river between Michigan and Shiawassee streets, Oldsmobile Park plays host to the Lansing Lugnuts, a minor league professional baseball team.

153.4 Railroad bridge. An old Michigan Central spur track crosses the river southwest to northeast.

153.5 Bridge. Saginaw Street crosses east-west.

153.2 Bridge. Oakland Avenue crosses east-west. Looking north from the bridge there is a view of the North Lansing Dam.

153 **North Lansing Dam.** The first dam was constructed just north of the present structure in 1838, by Lansing's first settler John W. Burchard. According to family history the dam was damaged in 1843, and Burchard and three other men were inspecting the damage the following spring when their small boat was swamped and he was drowned. The old mill race is still visible nearby, but is plugged. The present North Lansing Dam was constructed in 1936 by the Lansing Board of Water and Light to provide a pond for the Ottawa Street Power Station, and, secondarily, to provide hydropower. The powerhouse is on the east bank with the Lansing Board of Water and Light nearby.

In 1981 the Brenke Fish Passage was completed allowing fish to move upstream. The ladder was designed by artist Joseph E. Kinnebrew, who had created a similar installation in 1975 at Grand Rapids, and by landscape architect Robert O'Boyle. It was named for William Brenke, to honor his contribution in bringing salmon fishing to Lansing. In 2004 there was a preliminary study concerning removing the North Lansing Dam and restoring the river to its more normal course, which would allow small pleasure boating craft in the urban Lansing area.

152.9 Bridge. Grand River Avenue West, an old road to Detroit, which was named after the river, crosses it east-west. This is the old M-16 and which ran more or less continuously from Detroit to Grand Rapids.

152.7 Bridge. Grand River Avenue North crosses the river north-south.

151.9 Bridge. North Logan Street (De Witt Road in the township) crosses the river north-south.

Just east of the bridge the Turner-Dodge House stands high up on the north bank.

Oak Grove just north of the Lansing city limits, from a 1927 survey map.

The Classical Revival style home was designed by Darius Moon and built in 1858 by Lansing merchant James Turner. It was enlarged by his son-in-law, Frank Dodge (a state legislator in the late 1880s) and is now owned by the city of Lansing. The house is open for tours May to October, with a special tour at Christmastime.

151.7 Railroad bridge. Site of the bridge which carried the old track of the Manufacturer's Beltline Railroad, which served the city power station and the Oldsmobile plant across the river.

151.5 **Oak Grove** A 1927 survey map shows the community of Oak Grove on the north side of the river between Grand River Avenue and the railroad tracks to the north. The old community is now within the city limits of Lansing.

151.2. Reynolds Drain enters the river from the north. Nearby Horsebrook School may show an older name for the stream.

151 **Tecumseh Park**, run by the City of Lansing, on the north bank, off Tecumseh River Drive. The park has a playground and picnicking facilities.

149.8 Bridge. Waverly Road crosses north-south. This is the fourth time that Waverly Road has crossed the Grand River.

149.8 Leave the City of Lansing and enter Delta Charter Township, Eaton County.

148.2 Edwards Drain enters the river from the north.

147.6-146.9 **Delta Mills** (or **Delta**) The settlement was named for the township, which had been named for the bend in the river that formed a Greek letter Delta (with Carrie Creek forming the third side). The first settler was Erastus Ingersoll who purchased land between the Grand River and a turnpike that had been surveyed from Detroit to Grand Haven. Since the place is approximately half way across the state, he was also speculating that the new capital would be built nearby. When the village was first platted it was called **Grand River City**, but was given a post office named Delta on September 6, 1842, with Whitney Jones as the first postmaster. The post office closed on November 15, 1910. The settlement was also a station on the Detroit, Lansing & Lake Michigan Railroad The community was never incorporated.[2]

147.2 Bridge. Webster Road crosses the river north-south and enters Delta Mills.

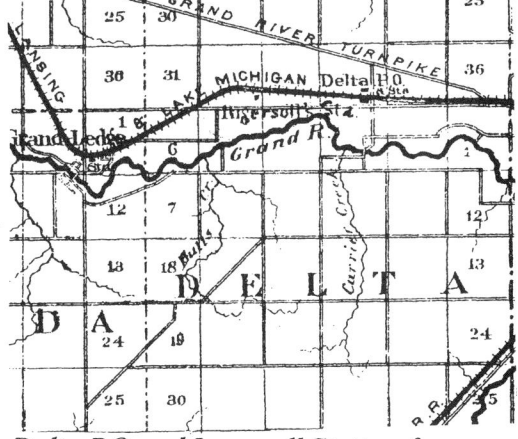

Delta PO and Ingersoll Station from an 1873 railroad map.

The Palisades at Grand Ledge, still a busy rock-climbing venue.

The old dam across the river at Grand Ledge originally built to power a gristmill near the downtown area. This picture was probably taken from the bridge.

147.2-146.9 **Delta Mills Park** begins at the southwest corner of the bridge and runs along the south bank. The park includes fishing, a canoe landing, a playground and picnic areas, and is part of a larger park across the road to the south.

146.9 Carrier Creek enters from the south having already joined with Holly Drain near Delta Center.

146.9 **Ingersoll's Station** is labeled, just west of Delta, on the 1873 Tackabury map where the Delta River Road runs near the north bank.

146.7-146.8 **Hunters Orchard Park**, run by Delta Township, on the south bank has fishing access, picnic facilities and a canoe landing.

145.8 Bridge. Twin bridges carry I-96 over the river north-south.

143.9 Miller Creek enters the river from the south, having already received Bulls Creek.

142- **Grand Ledge** is on both sides of the river. The first permanent settlement here was made in 1848 by Edmund L. Lamson, although there had been abortive settlement efforts prior to that time. It was named for the high ledge of rocks on the north side of the river.

The post office opened in 1850. Grand Ledge was incorporated as a village in 1871 and a city in 1893. In 2000 its population was 7,813 with a land area of 3.6 square miles.

140.8 **Jaycees Park** is located east of the Bridge Street bridge, on the south side of the river off River Street. There is a hard-surfaced boat ramp, play-ground, and a small parking area. The log cabin serves as a senior center and Scout building.

140.7 Old photographs show a dam just east of the bridge. The first dam at this site was built in 1849 by John W. Russell, David Taylor and Abraham Smith, who went before the state Legislature to secure a grant for its construction. The dam was 230 feet in length and provided power for a sawmill on the south bank of the river. The power was later used by a planing mill as well. Nothing is left of the old dam.

140.6 Bridge. Bridge Street crosses southwest to northeast in downtown Grand Ledge. The first bridge built at this approximate point was a wooden structure in 1853, replaced in 1870 by an iron span, and in 1910 by a graceful, three span concrete bridge. A 1989 inspection showed cracks and crumbling cement and a completely new bridge was constructed in 1991.

Second Island and Hotel.   *First Island and tame deer.*

New bridge at Grand Ledge in 1912.

140.6-140.1 Seven islands in the river in this mile, were once part of the Seven Islands Resort. Begun about 1870 it was said to have been second only to Petoskey as a resort with 12 trainloads a day in the summertime flocking to its scenic facilities. The small first island, which featured an animal park, was linked by bridge to Second Island, which held the Island House Summer Resort, built in 1894. It grounds were showcased with ornate porches and garden houses. Also on Second Island was a cylindrical structure later dubbed "Mudge's Folly." It was constructed by J. S. Mudge and was intended to be a mechanical tower with verandahs revolving at different speeds, topped off with a giant centrifugal swing. It was damaged by high water and never worked as intended, although it stood for many years. On Third Island there was a large pavilion which sold refreshments and was sometimes used as a ballroom and by visiting theatrical troupes. For a short period of time in the early 1890s there was a roller coaster which linked islands Two and Three, but it was destroyed in the flood of 1893. Islands Four, Five, and Six were left wild and Seven was a favorite picnic spot for boaters. In the summertime, in addition to canoes and rowboats for hire, small pleasure steamers provided visitors with an outing on the water and a view of the famous rocks to the musical accompaniment of an on-board stringed duo. With the advent of the motor car, the resort lost business and closed although some of the old buildings stood for many years. In 2003 the city under-took restoration of Second Island as a park. been. Today a bridge connects it to the mainland and there is a paved walkway the entire length of the island and a bandstand for entertainment.

The boat landing on Second Island with one of the excursion boats at the dock. Mudge's Folly is behind it.

139.9 Railroad Bridge. Probably it was the Detroit, Grand Rapids & Western Railroad which first bridged the river at this point about 1888. Because this bridge is high off the water it is often referred to as the "High Bridge." It is just beyond Island Seven.

139.85 **Oak Park** is located on the northeast side of the river, practically under the old railroad bridge. This is the most popular place to actually climb the ledges. It is the largest outcropping of rocks in central Michigan and the seventh largest in the state. Rock climbing lessons and assistance is available locally. Facilities at the park include a picnic area, stairs to the river and a cantilevered overlook. After crossing the bridge from the main downtown area, turn west on Front Street to the park entrance.

139.7 Sandstone Creek enters from the south.

139.6-139.2 **Fitzgerald Park**, a 78-acre city park on the west bank, includes some of the famous rock ledges for which Grand Ledge is named. Early Indian tribes visited the area in the spring to tap the abundant maple trees. In 1894 the Grand Ledge Spiritualist Camp Association built a summer meeting area, including a large partially stone pavilion which still stands. The area was purchased by the city of Grand Ledge in 1919. Facilities include three miles of nature trails, picnicking, baseball, volleyball and basketball areas, an 18-hole disc golf course and a skateboard park. In the winter there is a sledding hill and cross-country skiing trails. Canoes can be rented for river excursions. The park is named for Michigan Governor Frank D. Fitzgerald, who was a native of Grand Ledge. There is a vehicle entrance fee April through October. On land it is reached off Jefferson Street just west of downtown Grand Ledge.

139.4 **Fitzgerald Dam** The first dam was built in this area in the 1870s to provide a water depth suitable for boating between the islands. It was improved by J. S. Mudge and was sometimes called the "stone dam." In April of 1922 voters approved $10,000 to build a new permanent concrete dam with "ample waste gate capacity to flush the pond as often as necessary to keep it in a good sanitary condition."[3] On the western side of the present installation a section of the 1922 construction still stands. A fish ladder was built on the park side in the 1970s.

139.4 Lincoln Brick Park Across from Fitzgerald Park, on the east bank of the river, Eaton County operates Lincoln Brick Park, a 90-acre facility located on the site of a former brick factory. The park includes two picnic pavilions, playground, nature trails, fishing, and, in the winter cross country skiing. There is also an interpretative center recounting a decade of brick production. Vehicle entry fees are in effect may through September. On land the park is near the intersection of Main Street and Tallman Road.

139 Stone Coal Creek enters from the southwest.

Clay pit just northwest of Grand Ledge.

138.8 Enter Eagle Township, Clinton County.

137.5. River Bend About three-quarters of a mile south east is the community of River Bend which shows on an 1873 map. The community had a post office from 1871 to 1891, named for the large bends of the river in the vicinity.

136 Bridge. State Road crosses east-west.

Mining gravel is a major industry in the area.

133.6 Bridge. Jones Road (an extension of Benton Road) crosses north-south

133.0-118.2 Portland State Game Area begins in Clinton County and continues in Ionia County with patches of land on both sides of the riverbank until about mile 115. The area is contains a total of 1,991 acres and is a controlled hunting area run by the Michigan Department of Natural Resources. There are no bridges for more than 10 miles. The terrain is characterized by large sweeping meanders of the river bed with high banks on one side..

132.1 Enter Danby Township, Ionia County.

130.85 Frayer Creek enters from the south having already picked up Guinan Drain..

129.5 Bridge. Formerly there was a vehicle bridge on Turner Road (called Boyer in Eaton County) which crossed the river north-south. The bridge approach road has been closed for more than a decade, but the framework of the old Parker through truss bridge, in 2004 said to be one of only three in the state, remains.

River Bend PO from an 1873 map.

129 Cryderman Lake Drain enters from the south.

127.1 Bridge. Charlotte Highway crosses north-south. The bridge was built in 2001. There is a public access off the southwest corner of the bridge. Southeast of the bridge a large rock sits in the water that has been used by generations of river goers (probably even the Native Americans) to measure the water level.

126.1 **Chief Okemos Grave.** High up on the north bank, in section 21, Danby Township, there is a large stone which reads:

> Grave of Okemos
> Noted Chippewa Chief
> 1858
> Placed by S. T. Mason D.A.R.
> Chapter in 1921.

It marks the grave of Ogimaans (it means "Little Chief" and is usually anglicized as Okemos). In 1896 he was enlisted by the British to act as a scout and was severely wounded by the Americans in battle. Afterwards he signed a treaty of peace with Lewis Cass. In later years he retired to Shimnecon, an Indian mission village near this site, where he died in 1858 and was buried near his cabin. Indians, and others, often leave small offerings in his honor at the gravesite which is deep in the woods in a section of the Portland State Game Area.

125.4 Gardner and Hiar Drain enters from the south.

124.4-119 At this point the Portland State Game Area extends solidly for more than five miles on the north (or east) bank of the river.

121.5 Sebawa Creek enters from the southwest having picked up Winchell and Union Drain and Ramsey Drain.

119.9 **Towner Road Park** provides a boat ramp and a 20 car parking lot. Take Towner Road to Pohl Road. The park is on the south bank of the river behind a large island.

117,3 A small community called **Frost Corners** is located a mile and a half east of the river at the corner of Peake and Frost roads.

116 Enter Portland Township, Ionia County.

115.2 Bridge. Kent Street crosses north-south as the river begins a hairpin turn.

114.5. Stiffler Drain enters from the south.

114.25 Bridge. Twin bridges carry I-96 over the river east-

114.2 Pedestrian Bridge. In the shadow of the Interstate bridge, an interesting "erector set" style bridge carries the bicycles and pedestrians using the Portland River Trail across the river east-west. The bridge is manufactured of metal, to compliment other historic bridges used on the trail including the old Burroughs bridge from the Flat River near Lowell, which has been recycled and moved to the area to carry the trail over the Looking Glass River.

114.2-111.8 **Portland** The settlement is located where the Looking Glass River joins the Grand and was so named because it was considered a good port and many goods were shipped from this point, both on the Grand River and up its nearby tributaries, the Flat and the Maple. The first government land purchased in what was later Portland was by Elisha Newman in 1833, although there is some evidence that he did not actually move to the area until 1836. The post office was opened March 11, 1837 with Joshua Boyer as postmaster. Portland incorporated as a village March 30, 1869 and as a home rule city December 9, 1968, It was a station on the Chicago & West Michigan Railway, later the Pere Marquette. Portland now bills itself as "City of Two Rivers." In 2000 the population of Portland was 3,789 with an area of 2.4 square miles.

113.3 Bridge. A two-span metal through truss bridge carries Bridge Street over the river. It was built in 1890 and has unusual decorative detailing. The bridge was rehabilitated to celebrate the city's centennial.

113.2 Bridge. Grand River Avenue crosses northwest to southeast on a concrete structure built in 1936. **William Toan Park** is located next to the bridge.

113.1 Looking Glass River enters from the east. This twisting body of water begins in the northwest corner of Livingston County and flows north into Shiawassee County where it turns west. On its way to the Grand at Portland it picks up Howard Drain, Kellogg Drain, Perry Drain, Osborn Creek, Mud Drain, Clise Drain, Mud Creek, Turkey Creek Drain, Rouge Drain, Remey Chandler Drain, Prairie Creek, Faiver Drain, Summers Drain, Smith Drain, Cutter Drain, Pierce Drain, Openlander Drain,

The south Portland River Trail bridge.

The Bogue Flats just around the bend from downtown Portland from a 1910 postcard.

The Portland municipal dam, photo taken in the 1920s.

Shaddock Drain, Husted and Landenburg Drain, the McCausey Branch and several other small streams. Vermilion Creek south of Laingsburg In Clinton County it passes through the communities of Dewitt and Wacousta. The Looking Glass River is approximately 70 miles in length.

112.9 Pedestrian bridge. The old C & O tracks crossed the river northwest to southeast. The railroad bridge is now a crossing for the Portland River Trail. The steel truss bridge was constructed in 1881, and in times of high water and ice jams would be weighted with loaded railroad cars. The last train passed over it in 1984. There is an island in the river just north of the bridge.

112.5-112 **The Bogue Flats Recreation Area** has ballfields, biking and hiking trails, a playground, restrooms and is the beginning of Portland's 8.2 mile riverwalk. It was named for the Bogue family which once owned the property.

111.25 Balderson Drain enters from the northeast.

109.9 Dam. **Portland Municipal Dam.** The dam was built in 1898. The old brick powerhouse with arched windows still stands on the south bank. There is a DNR fish ladder south of the channel and a gravel boat launching ramp. At the base of the dam Friend Brook enters the river from the west. There is a small rocky island just below the dam.

108.8 An 1873 map shows a post office name **Kossuth** on the west bank between the river and the railroad. The office opened December 6, 1855, with George W. Dickinson the first postmaster, and operated until 1868. It was named for Lajos Kossuth, a Hungarian patriot, who visited the United States in 1851.

107.9 Bridge. The bridge on Goodwin Road, which crossed the river east-west, is no longer open to traffic although the framework remains in place. It is a double truss bridge with an unusual level (not arched) top.

105.6 Bridge. David Highway crosses east west. **Collins** is about three miles west of the bridge. On an 1873 map **Stebbinsville Station** is just south.

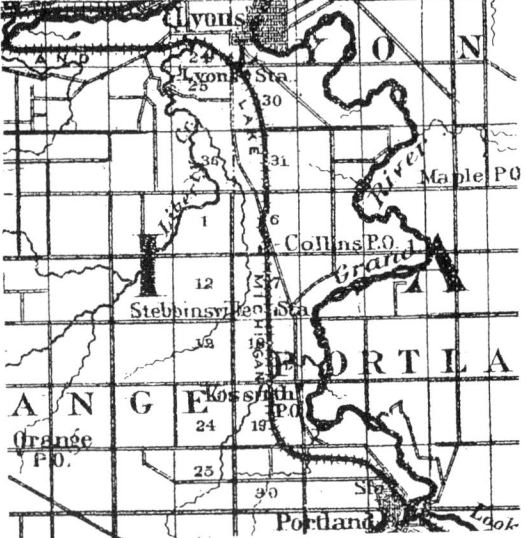

Kossuth, Stebbinsville, Collins and Maple on an 1873 map.

103.8 Enter Lyons Township, Ionia County.

On an 1873 map there is a bridge which crosses the river, east-west, on Maple Road, which marks the township line. Old postcards refer to this bridge as Centerline bridge, using the name for the road still used in Clinton County. On the same map there is also a small community called **Maple** just east of the river. The post office located there had opened in 1838 in Lyons Township with

Webber dam in 1907.

Zena Lloyd as the postmaster. When he moved he carried the post office with him. The post office closed in 1901. Today there is a residential development on the east bank of the river, but no bridge, although there is a fish access point at the end of Maple Road.

102.7 Webber Dam Boat Access. There is a hard-surfaced boat ramp, small parking area, and public toilet on the north side of the impoundment, take Peckins Road to Webber Road. Behind the dam the impounded river is more than a half mile wide for two miles.

102.3 Webber Dam. Consumers Power Company (earlier Commonwealth Power, later Consumers Energy) acquired the rights and contracts for a dam across the Grand River in Lyons Township, Ionia County, in 1906. Work was started at once, building an earth embankment with a concrete core wall and a 28-foot head. The installation went on line March 12, 1907. Most of the electricity created was sent by high power transmission lines to the Lansing area. The dam was named for the Portland banker who handled some of the land purchases. In 2007 it remains an active part of the Consumers Energy system with a capacity of 3,250 kilowatts. The DNR operates ladder to give river-spawning fish access to the upper river.

Sandpits just downriver from the dam on the west bank may have been a source of materials for dam construction.

102 Goose Creek enters from the east, having already picked up Cook Drain and Clinton and Ionia Drain.

101.7-101.3 Moore Island, so named on an 1875 map. Elevation is 658 feet.

100.5 Wagar Dam was built at a community on the river known as **Willing** in 1898. It was constructed by the Ionia Water Power Electric Company, H. R. Wagar, president, to provide power for the growing city of Ionia, nine miles downriver. The dam which had a nine-foot head, was seriously damaged by the 1904 flood and rebuilt, then refurbished again after

Wagar Dam and powerhouse between Portland and Lyons about 1909.

World War II. The facility was purchased, in 1925, by Consumers Power Company. Wagar Dam was removed from production in 1956, and most of the dam was demolished by dynamite, although there is still a small dam in the water.

98.4 Green View Point A scenic overlook on north bank, reached from Kimball Road. It overlooks the site of a large Indian battle fought about 1785. According to legend, a tribe of Potawatomi Indians built earthworks just west of Muir for defense. Chippewa Indians, 30 miles up Maple River planned to attack them in conjunction with the Menominee Indians on the Grand River. They want to take both the stronghold and the fields of cleared land in the valley. However, the fast-flowing current in the Grand River brought the Menominees onto the field the day before their allies arrived. The Potawatomi warriors met them at the bend of the river east of Lyons and defeated the Menominees, and the following day finished off the Chippewas. Early settlers found many skulls and skeletons on the old battlefield.. The roadside park was opened in 1927 and dedicated to Fred W. Green "Ionia County's Leading Citizen" and governor of Michigan 1927 to 1931.

97.4-95.8 Lyons The first settlers were H. V. Libhart and his family from Naples, New York in 1833, and the community was called **Arthursberg**, but the place did not begin to boom until Lucius Lyon (who would become the state's first senator after statehood was granted in 1837) bought the entire town site in 1836 and sent at least a dozen members of his large family to settle there. The name was changed to Lyons because it was full of people named Lyon. Truman H. Lyon became its first postmaster in 1836. In 1847, ten years after statehood when the legislature was looking for a more centrally-located capital than Detroit, Lyons was a hot contender. One legislator howled, "What! Shall we take the capital from a large and beautiful city and stick it down in the woods and mud on the banks of the Grand river, amid choking miasma, where the howl of wolves and the hissing of massasaugas and groans of bullfrogs resound to the hammer of the woodpecker and the solitary note of the nightingale?"[4] Instead, they chose Lansing, at that time an even more remote place on the banks of the same river. Lyons was incorporated as a village on January 6, 1869. Its population in 2000 was 726, with a land area of 3.6 square miles.

97.1 There is a hard-surfaced boat ramp and a small parking and picnic area at the south end of Tabor Street in Lyons.

96.2 **Lyons Dam**. After three abortive attempts a dam was finally built across the Grand River at Lyons about 1860. It was completed by local men who formed the Lyons Water Power Company and had the power to turn 34 runs of stone. On an 1874 plat map a 279 foot mill raced flowed off the east side of the dam and along Mill Street, rejoining the river just east of a big triangular island. In 1898 an electric power plant was added. The predecessors of Consumers Powers bought a partial interest in the dam in 1914, and the entire operation before its rebuilding in 1929. The facility was retired in 1957 and sold to the Village of Lyons for a dollar in 1960. Remnants of the old mill race are still visible.

96.15 Bridge. South Bridge Street crosses the river east-west in Lyons, just north of the dam. The present bridge is built approximately where the 1837 bridge was constructed by Henry A. Leonard and Andrew Hanse. It was washed out in the ice jam of 1857, but replaced. In 1881 the old wooden bridge was replaced with a Whipple truss wrought iron span. It fell into disrepair

and a modern structure was built at the crossing in 1975.

Just northeast of the bridge is a stone memorial to founder Lucius Lyon and a restored comfort station and water pump which were part of what was believed to be the state's first tourist camp, established in 1923.

96.1 **Hazel Devote Park** furnishes picnicking facilities, rest rooms and sports fields. It is reached off Prairie Street in town.

94.5 Maple River enters from the northeast. The Maple River rises near Vernon, southwest of Corunna in Shiawassee County It receives the

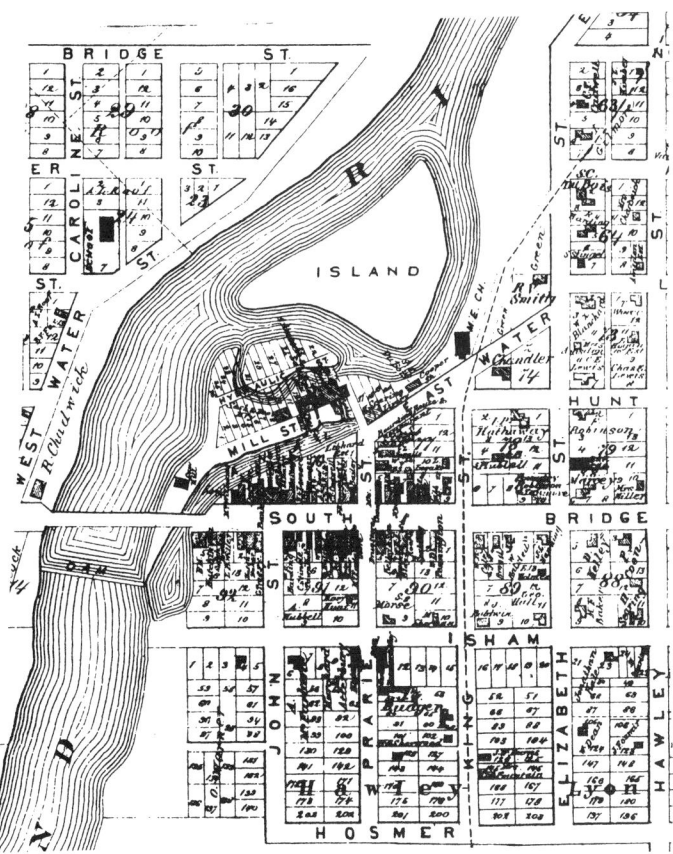

Lyons from an 1874 atlas, showing mill race and dam.

Lyons under water during the flood of 1887. Ice blocked the river and sent it flowing through the downtown.

waters of Duplain and Ovid Drain, Sturgis Drain, Baker Creek near Elsie (Baker Creek having already joined with Wise Creek and Wait Drain), Newsome Creek, Halterman Creek, Boyce Creek, Ferdon Creek, Collier Creek, Bradley Drain, Pine Creek (having already joined with North Shade Drain, the River Styx, Cox Drain, Hayworth Creek, Peel Creek and several small drains in the vicinity), Waters Drain, and Bower Drain before joining the Grand near Muir. The Maple River is approximately 75 miles long and passes through the communities of Ovid, Elsie, Bannister and Maple Rapids. About six miles northeast of Muir the Maple River receives the waters of Fish Creek, itself more than 40 miles in length, which comes down from Montcalm County passing through Carson City and Hubbardston.

Muir located a half mile up the Maple River was the site of a lumbermill in 1854 built by Soule, Robinson & Company. In 1857 the first post office was opened called **Montrose Station**, because many of the early settlers had come from Montrose, New York. Andrew Robinson was the first postmaster. The Detroit, Grand Rapids & Western Railroad came through the settlement largely because of the efforts of H. K. Muir, and in 1860, the name was changed to honor him. Muir was incorporated as a village on March 25, 1871. The population of the village was 634 in 2000, with an area of .8 square miles.

94.5 Enter Ionia Township, Ionia County.

93.65 **Generauxville** (sometimes spelled Generauville) About 1830 Louis Genereauville helped his son, Louis Jr. establish a trading post at a place described as "west of Lyons," probably where at old dirt track leads down to the water from a road still known as the Generaux Road. The young man caused the death of an Indian and was sent to prison and the post was later taken over by Louis Campau. Some old histories say that the first bridge built across the Grand River was constructed at this point shortly after 1830. It was a connecting link between Detroit and Ionia, via Lansing.

92.7-90.4 Grand River Mini-Game Area is located on the south bank between the Grand River and the old C & O railroad bed. It is a small state game area run by the Michigan DNR.

90.5 Prairie Creek enters from the north. A 1916 survey maps shows a dam at Prairie Creek just north of the railroad, and a small settlement called **Prairie** west of the creek, it was replatted in 1872 as **Prairie Creek** but was never incorporated.

90.4 Railroad Bridge. The **Ionia Rivertrail,** 3.2 miles long, which starts on the south bank at Cleveland Street, follows an old railroad bed into town. The bridge formerly served as part of the C & O tracks.

89.3 Bridge. Cleveland Street, which marks the east city limit of Ionia, crosses north-south. The present bridge was constructed in 1931.

Grand Trunk Railroad at left.

The Maple (at right center) meets the Grand between Lyons and Muir.

Ionia to Grand Rapids

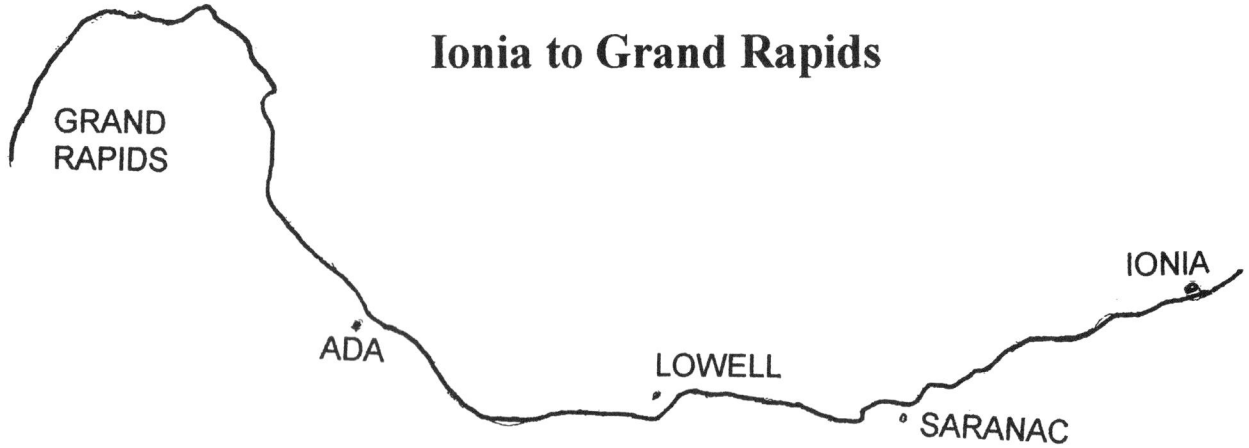

89.3-87 **Ionia** A party of 63, led by Samuel Dexter of Herkimer, New York, arrived here in late summer of 1833. Since it was too late to plant crops they purchased for $25 sufficient food from the local Odawa Indians to survive the winter. The payment also included use of five Indian bark huts in the vicinity for the party's women and children. Erastus Yeomans was the first postmaster when the office opened August 29, 1835. Ionia incorporated as a village in 1865, and as a city in 1873. The settlement and post office were named for the county, which took the name of an ancient Greek province. In 1836 a land office, where early settlers would have had to go to register their land, opened in the town. In addition to the usual sawmills and gristmills, industries included the quarrying and exporting of a reddish sandstone and the state's second prison. The population of Ionia in 2000 was 10,569 (about 3,000 of this number were prisoners incarcerated in local state-run facilities), with an area of 5.2 square miles

87.9 Bridge. Dexter Street, crosses the river north-south and enters Ionia. South of city limits it is known as State Road. The fairground northwest of the bridge is the site the Ionia Free Fair. It is one of the largest fairs in Michigan. Facilities include 48 acres of landscaped grounds, a grandstand, race track, children's playground, hiking and bike paths, and a campground. Just west of the bridge on the north bank of the river there is a boat ramp and parking.

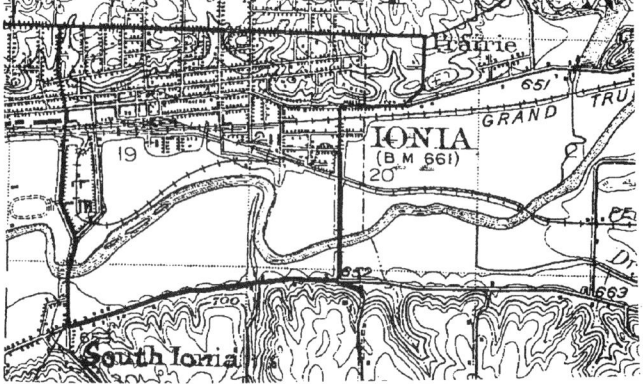

This 1916 survey map shows Prairie, on Prairie Creek, at upper right. Ionia, center, and South Ionia at lower left

86.5 **South Ionia**. Oliver Arnold who came to the area with the Dexter colony moved across the river and set up a blacksmith shop. In 1876 his son, G. W. Arnold, platted a village called South Ionia. It was never incorporated but still shows on some maps at the south end of the bridge and Riverside Drive, where there is some commercial development.

The Dexter Street (or State Road) bridge into Ionia about 1915.

The central tower of the Michigan Reformatory at Ionia about 1908.

86.3 The old Michigan State Reformatory and Prison complex is located on a hill overlooking the river. It was the second prison built in the State of Michigan. Construction was approved by the legislature in 1875 and completed in 1880, although there have been many additions over the years. It was operated continuously until 2001, but there are plans to reopen it, when needed, after remodeling. In addition there are five other state prisons, with varying levels of security, in the Ionia area, two near Riverside Drive, and three other institutions on the Blue Water Highway on the north edge of town.

85.8 Railroad Bridge. The old Grand Trunk Western track crossed the river north-south on this bridge.

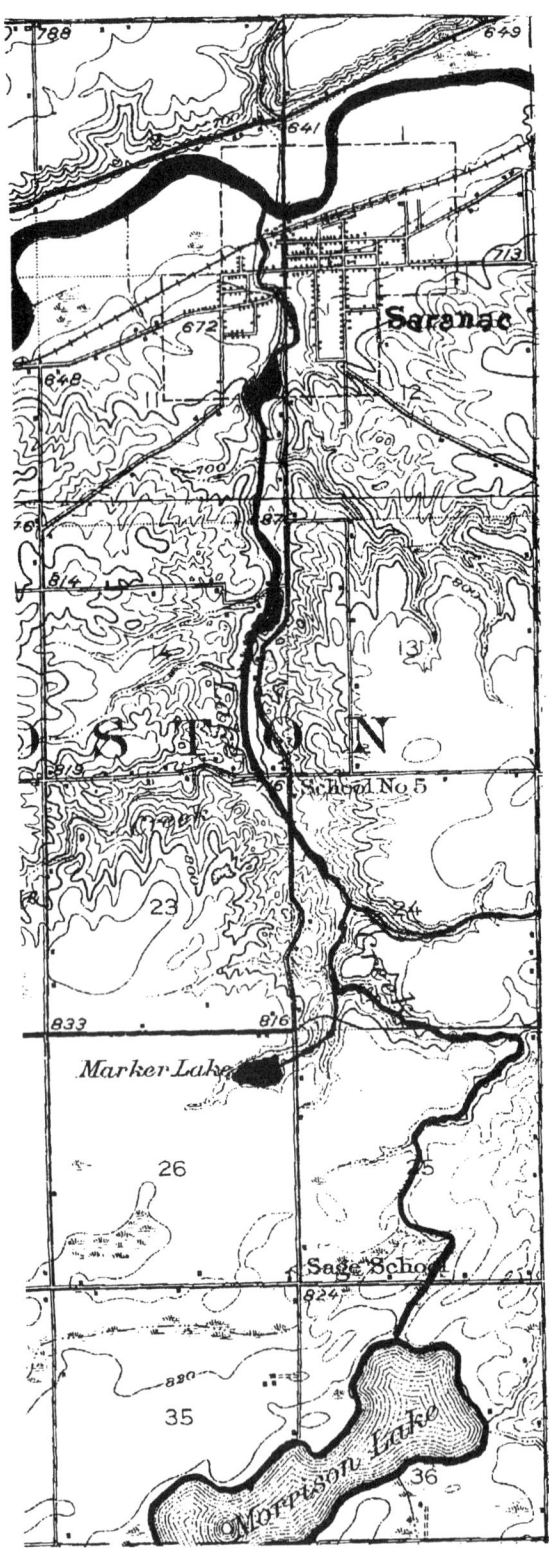

(Left) There is little fall on the Grand River near Saranac to furnish hydropower so settlers instead built two dams on Lake Creek as it dropped into the valley. The southernmost, in section 14 ran Waterville Mill. The larger dam, in section 11, provided power for the Huhn Mill. This map is from a 1912 survey.

84.9-80 **Ionia State Recreation Area** has four miles of frontage on the Grand River, which forms the northern boundary of the 4,500 square acre park. Facilities include horseback riding trails, a dog trial area, swimming at an inland lake and hunting and trapping in season.

84.1 Bellamy Creek enters from the north after passing through **Brock County Park**. Almost directly opposite, Sessions Creek enters from the south, having received the waters of Peacock Ditch. On the south bank there is a picnic area which is part of the Ionia State Recreation Area with a boat launch.

82.8 Timberland Creek enters the Grand River from the north.

79.8 Red Creek enters from the north.

79.6 Crooked Creek enters from the south.

79.5 Enter Boston Township, Ionia County

78.5-77.8 **Saranac** Judge Jefferson Morrison bought government land south of the Grand River in 1836, and sold it to Detroit businessmen who platted a village. The first post office was called **Boston**, after the township, but on February 12, 1859, it was renamed Saranac. The village was named for a

The lower dam on Lake Creek at Saranac about 1920, probably when it was owned by Consumers Power.

The lower mill pond remained in place until the 1970s when a developer removed the boards for repair and did not replace them. Today the dam is a picturesque ruin in the woods just off Morrison Lake Road on the north edge of Saranac.

New York State resort town to attract settlers from that state. The Waterville Mill on Lake Creek dates to 1838. The dam has been partially removed, but the mill building is still standing on McArthur Road. Just inside the south limits of Saranac a dam on Lake Creek provided power for the Huhn mill. In 1903 mill owner Daniel G. Huhn obtained a franchise for an electric light plant. Before World War II the dam was purchased by Consumers Power, but may never have been operated by them. Saranac incorporated as a village in 1869. Population in 2000 was 1,326 with a land area of 1.2 square miles.

78.15 Bridge. Hawley Road, north of town, turns into Bridge Street in Saranac and crosses the river north-south. South of Saranac it is known as Morrison Lake Road. There is a park on the southeast corner of the bridge with a restored Grand Trunk Western depot which houses the Boston-Saranac Historical Society museum. Southwest of the bridge is a hard-surfaced boat launch with a small parking area. Nature trails in front of the museum run along the river to the Nature Center.

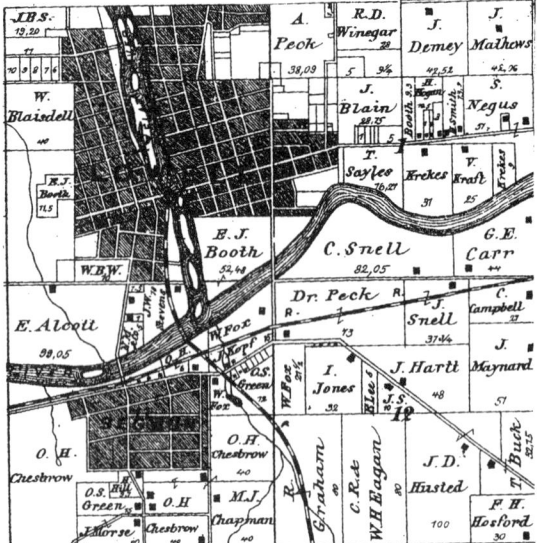

Lowell and Segwun from an 1876 map.

78 Lake Creek enters from the south. having already joined with Little Creek, and the drains from Peck Lake, Morrison Lake and Marker Lake.

74.6 Toles Creek enters from the north.

74-71.3 Lowell State Game Area is north of the river.

71.85 Enter Lowell Township, Kent County

70.5 Bridge. South Division Street crosses north-south and enters Lowell.

70.3 Railroad Bridge A heavy double truss bridge carried the old C & O railroad over the river north-south.

70.1 Flat River enters the river from the north just south of downtown Lowell. The Flat River begins in Montcalm County north of Greenville near Six Lakes. It collects the waters of Brimmer Creek, Wolf Creek, the drain from Hemmingway Lake, Paulson Creek, Clear Creek (from Lincoln Lake), Black Creek, Butternut Creek, Coopers Creek, Dickerson Creek, Wabasis Creek, Lake Creek, Seely Creek, the outlet for Murray Lake and Page Creek before entering the Grand River at Lowell.

Lowell Downtown Lowell is about a half mile up the Flat River. The first settlement at the confluence of the Grand and Flat rivers was by Daniel Marsac of Detroit, a fur trader who built a trading post on the north bank of the Grand in 1831. In 1847 he bought land on the north bank, platted it and named it **Dansville**. In 1851 a post office opened with George K. White as postmaster, named Lowell after the township. The settlement took the name of the post

The Grand River just east of Lowell photographed about 1912. The road in the foreground is M-21, now known as Blue Water Highway.

office when it was replatted in 1854, although an 1855 map still labels it Dansville. It was incorporated as a village in 1861 and is now a city. In 2000 Lowell had a population of 4,013 and an area of 3.1 square miles. For many years a showboat operated in the summer on the Flat River, the retired boat, the Robert E. Lee, is still an attraction. The town is thought to have been named after Lowell, Massachusetts.

69.6 **Segwun** Old maps (some as late as 1978) show a settlement called Segwun in section 11 on the south bank, opposite and slightly west of Lowell. It was platted as a village site in 1863 but never incorporated. At one time the community had a railroad depot which served the area south of the river.

69.6 Bridge. Alden Nash Avenue or Segwun Avenue (M-50, called South Hudson Street in Lowell) crosses the river north-south through Segwun. There is a small park on the northeast corner of the bridge.

69.1 Lee Creek enters from the north.

Between Lowell and Ada the Grand River runs through a flat valley a half to three-quarters of a mile wide with bluffs on the north and south. Several small, unnamed, seasonal streams trickle down to the water.

67.2 Court Drain enters from the south.

67 Drain from north

65.8 Drain from south

65.3 Drain from north past Rolfe Cemetery. Between miles 64 and 65 there are three old roads which come down to the water, indicating that there might have been a settlement around a landing, and, perhaps, a ferry crossing. There is no bridge across the river between Lowell and Ada.

64.7 Enter Cascade Township, Kent County

62.6 Enter Ada Township, Kent County

61.6 Thornapple River enters the river from the south. The Thornapple River begins about 100 miles from its confluence with the Grand in the northwestern part of Eaton County near Potterville, south of Grand Ledge. Before it reaches Ada it has received water from Butternut Creek north of Charlotte, Sharp and Thornapple Drain, Wright Pardee Skinner Drain, Little Thornapple River, Cole Wright Helms Drain, Darken and Boyer Drain, Thompson Creek, Lacey Creek, Stoney Creek and Scipio Creek, all in Eaton County. The river crosses the Barry County line and receives flow from Quaker Brook at Nashville, Mud Creek which has already picked up Hagar Creek and Gravel Brook, High Bank Creek which enters at Thornapple Lake, the outlet from Long Lake, Pratt Creek and Cedar Creek (having already picked up North Branch and Kellie Creek) at Quimby, Butler Creek and Fall Creek which join the Thornapple at Hastings, Bullhead Drain, the outlet from Black Lake near Irving, Hill Creek, Glass Creek, Turner Creek and Bassett Creek upstream from Middleville, and Duncan Creek just before the river passes through Parmelee and enters Kent County. The Thornapple River receives the Coldwater River which gathers water from a three county area including Tyler Creek and Duck Creek upstream from the Labarge dam where the main river widens. It then receives the outlet from Campau Lake near Alaska, Holly Creek, McCords Creek, Whitneyville Creek, and the outlet from Quiggle Lake near Cascade, before flowing into the Grand River at Ada. An old covered bridge has been restored and erected in a park on the Thornapple River a half mile upstream from the junction.

61.5 Bridge. Fulton Street (M-21) crosses the river east-west and enters the community of Ada. At the northwest corner of the bridge, west of the Thornapple River, there is a DNR hard surfaced boat ramp with limited parking. Below the bridge there is a long narrow island in the river.

Ada The business area of Ada is west of the mouth of the Thornapple River. Rix

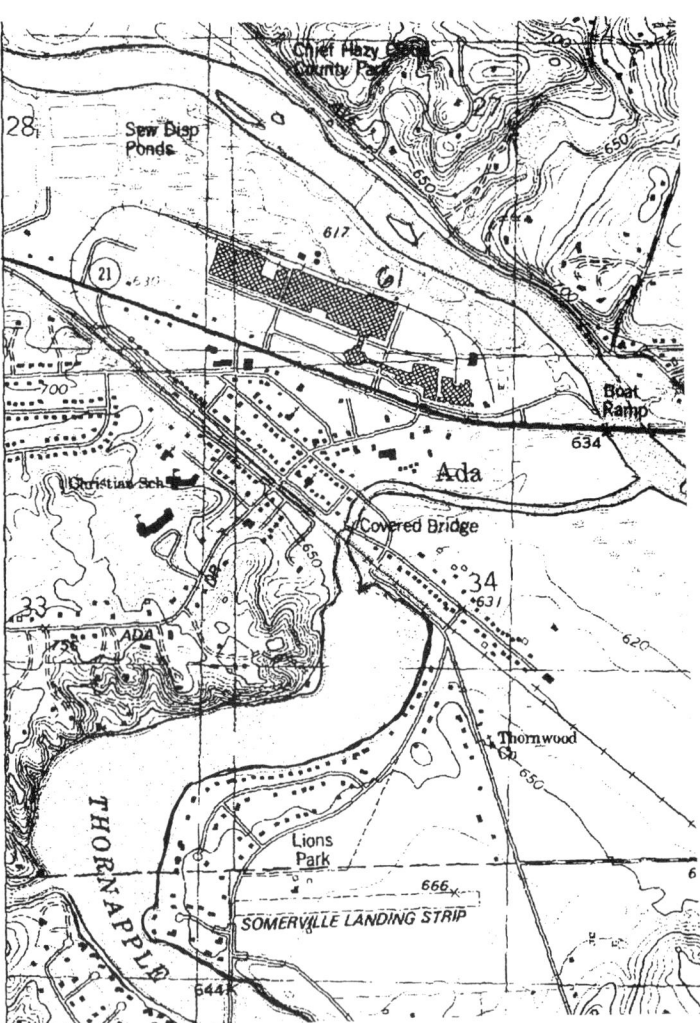

The junction of the Thornapple (bottom left) and Grand (top right) rivers near Ada. Large buildings in the upper center are those of the Alticor (formerly Amway) plant and headquarters.

Robinson established a fur trading post at the mouth of the river in 1821 and purchased land in 1833. The township and post office were named for Ada Smith, daughter of Sidney Smith, who became the first postmaster on January 5, 1837. Although the town was platted in 1857 it was never incorporated and is now part of Ada Charter Township. Amway Corporation, now a subsidiary of Alticor, has a large factory and office complex along the banks of the river. The population of Ada Township in 2000 was 9,882.

61 Honey (or Haney) Creek enters river from the northeast.

60.6 Chief Hazy Cloud County Park on the north bank. This 22.5 acre park was established in 1928 and named for an American Indian chief. It has facilities for picnicking and rest rooms and is reached off Pettis Avenue. In 2007 plans were being considered to greatly enlarge this park.

58.6-57-8 Roselle Park on the west bank, run by Ada Township, was just starting development in 2007. Plans do not include facilities for launching boats, but a small landing area will allow people on the water in canoes and kayaks to land there and look around the natural area.

56.1 Bridge. Knapp Street crosses the river east-west. There is a boat ramp, parking area and toilets off the southeast corner of the bridge.

On some old maps there is a small community named **Groves Ferry**, on section 7 near the Knapp Street bridge, indicating that at one time a ferry was operated here.

A stone marker honoring Ada's first white inhabitant, Rix Robinson. This stone was erected near the junction of the two rivers, where Robinson lived, but later moved closer to town.

55.8 Egypt Creek enters river from the northeast.

55 Sunny Creek enters river from the west.

54.5 Enter Cannon Township, Kent County, on the east side of the river, and Plainfield Township, Kent County, on the west bank of the river

53.3 Leave Cannon Township, the river turns slightly west causing both banks to be in Plainfield Township, Kent County.

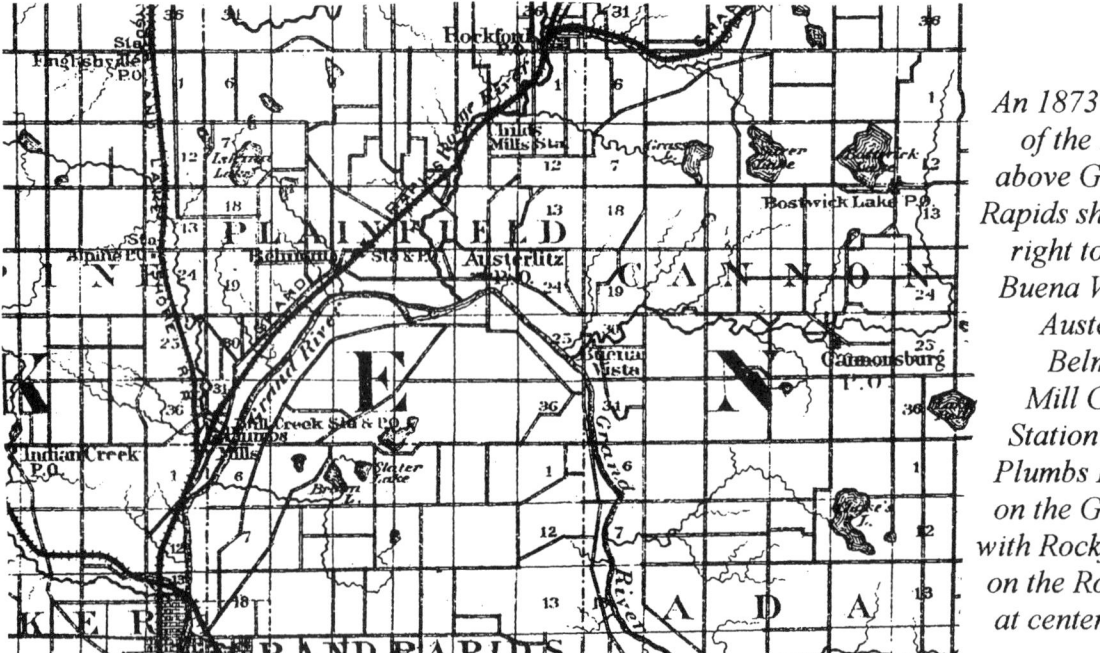

An 1873 map of the river above Grand Rapids shows, right to left, Buena Vista, Austerlitz Belmont, Mill Creek Station and, Plumbs Mills on the Grand with Rockford, on the Rogue, at center top.

53 Bear Creek enters the river from the northeast having picked up Waddell Creek, and other small streams around the hills of Cannon Township. There is a falls at the mouth of Bear Creek, the site of a flouring mill, built in 1848. The mill was destroyed by fire in 1875, and replaced with a new building in 1881 which still stands, and is in use as a private home. A post office opened in December of 1882 just north of Bear Creek called **Chauncey**, after Chauncey Porter, a chief land owner and the first postmaster. The post office closed September 30, 1903, but the community is still labeled on a 1967 survey map. The 1873 Tackabury map puts a community named **Buena Vista** at this site, but most authorities give Buena Vista as an old name for Austerlitz.

Plainfield The area on the north bank of the river in Plainfield Township, near the mouth of the Rogue River was an early Indian gathering place. It grew up as a place where settlers could be ferried across the river and there was a bridge built at the site, at least partially financed by the state, in 1848. It was given a post office as **Austerlitz** on January 30, 1841 which operated until 1910. Some sources indicate that this settlement was also known as **Buena Vista**.. Plainfield Avenue, now a major commercial street of Grand Rapids, is built on the old diagonal road that crossed Plainfield Township.

51.3 Bridge. M-44 or Northland Drive (connects with East Beltline in Grand Rapids) crosses the river north-south.

51.2-50.9 There is a large Plainfield Township park west of the bridge off West River Drive, east of the mouth of the Rogue River. Turn south onto Indian NE. Facilities include soccer fields, rest rooms and a boat launch.

51 Rogue River enters from the north. Legend has it that the river which joins the Grand here, was intended to be called the Rouge (French for red) River. However, mapmakers misspelled the name, and it was decided to retain the misspelling because they was already a larger and better-known Rouge River near Detroit. The Rogue River rises at

Bill's Lake in southern Newaygo County and moves south into Kent County picking up Hickory Creek, Walter Creek which has already received Post Creek, Spring Creek, Duke Creek, Ball Creek, Nash Creek which flows through Sparta, the Cedar Creek system which flows from Cedar Springs, Stegman and Becker creeks from Porter Hollow, Shaw Creek just north of Rockford, and Barkley Creek which enters just north of Childsdale Dam. The Rogue River is approximately 50 miles in length.

50-51 Grand Island Golf Course on the north bank. Nearby, off West River Drive, is a home built in 1852 by Dr. Hyser, the Plainfield village physician, which once served as the Austerlitz post office.

49.6 Bridge. The most recent new crossing over the Grand River carries Jupitor Road, which connects with Belmont Road, across the flow north-south.

48.7 Scott Creek enters from the north

48-47.2 **Daniel J. Lamoreaux Park**, run by the Kent County Parks Department, on the southeast bank of the river, has hiking trails along the river bottom and nature study areas.

The North Park bridge about 1910, with the North Park Pavilion on the far bank.

Rowing on the Grand River about 1910. Soldiers' Home is in the background.

45.5-46.3 Comstock Park Daniel North built a sawmill in 1838 on the west bank of the river near the junction of Mill Creek (or Indian Mill Creek) in the southeast corner of Plainfield Township. The settlement was called **North Park.** On an 1873 map it was labeled **Plumb Mills**. It was a station on both the Grand Rapids & Indiana and the Chicago & West Michigan railroads called **Mill Creek** (or some schedules refer to it as **North Mills Station**). A post office called Mill Creek was opened December 28, 1848. Charles C. Comstock represented this district in Congress 1885-86, and on June 8, 1906, the village and the post office were renamed in his honor. It is an unincorporated community 3.9 square miles in size, with a population in 2000 of 10,675. In 1994 Comstock Park became the home of a Class A, minor league baseball team called the West Michigan Whitecaps, associated with the Detroit Tigers. The ballpark is just off West River Drive.

45.7 Enter Grand Rapids Township, Kent County. South of the old township line the east bank of the river is the City of Grand Rapids, and the west bank is the City of Walker.

45.3 Bridge. North Park Street crosses the river east-west and connects with West River Drive. This bridge, which includes ornamental lights with black lamp posts, was reconstructed in 1991, to replace a 1903 model which had been partially rebuilt in 1933.

Near the bridge York Creek enters the river from the northwest.

45.2 Bridge. Twin bridges carry I-96 (M-37) over the river east-west.

45. In 1886 the **Michigan Soldiers' Home** was erected on a 132-acre tract on the east bank as a residential facility for old soldiers, particularly those from the Civil War. The North Park Street Railway Company began operations in 1889 for the convenience of the veterans and their families. To make North Park a more popular destination Charles C. Comstock and others created the North

Park Pavilion and Resort, a popular place for dances, picnics and reunions, especially military regimental reunions. Activities included fishing, rented rowboats and occasionally boat races on the river. At its peak, about the turn of the century the park had a roller coaster, bear and elk, and frequent hot air balloon ascensions. Now called the Grand Rapids Veterans Facility, the old soldier's home is still active, both as a residential facility and as an out-patient clinic for veterans. With the need for updated medical facilities most of the old buildings were razed in the 1970s. The post store is the only structure that remains of the 19th Century complex, along with an ornate fountain dedicated in 1894. Portions of the grounds have been transferred to Comstock Riverside Park by the Legislature, and the Veterans Facility grounds now cover only about 80 acres.

45 Lamberton Creek, is dammed near its mouth to form two scenic ponds between the veteran's facility and cemetery to the north. There is also has a dock outfitted for handicapped-accessible fishing, before it enters the river from the east.

45 – 43.8 **Comstock Riverside Park** on the east bank, administered by the city of Grand Rapids, located between the North Park bridge and Knapp Street. The 128-acre park includes picnicking facilities, sports fields, rest rooms and three hard-surfaced boat ramps. Lagoons offer fishing and nature study.

At North Park, Grand Rapids, in 1904.

Grand Rapids to Lake Michigan

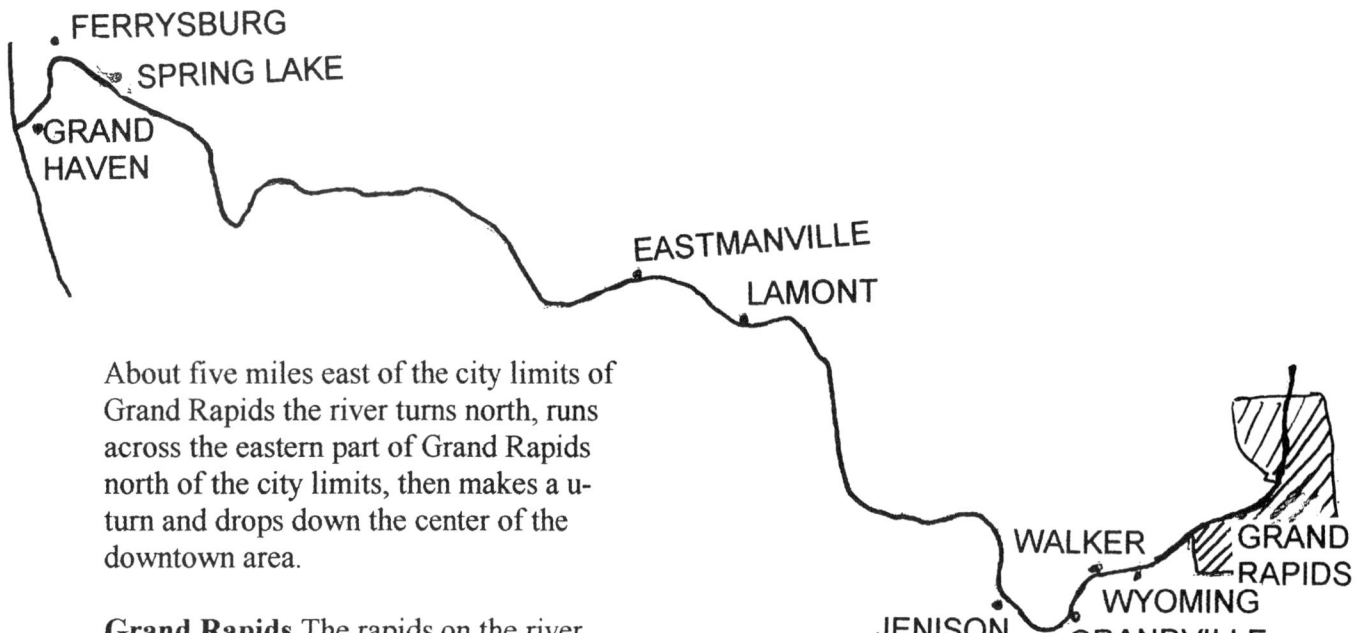

About five miles east of the city limits of Grand Rapids the river turns north, runs across the eastern part of Grand Rapids north of the city limits, then makes a u-turn and drops down the center of the downtown area.

Grand Rapids The rapids on the river formed a natural gathering place for the Native Americans and thus also a natural site for an early trading post. Missionaries were at the rapids as early as 1823 ministering to the Indians, but it was not until June 23, 1833, that the first real settlers arrived, Joel Guild, his wife, Abby, six daughters and a son, Consider Guild, then 18 years old, from Herkimer County, New York. In 1831 fur trader Louis Campau had purchased what would be the site of the future city's downtown for $90, selling a portion of his land to Lucius Lyon in 1835. Campau platted a village named Grand Rapids, Lyon's portion of the land was called Kent (named for the county which was named for Chancellor James Kent, a prominent New York state jurist). The plats were laid out in differing grids, so no streets intersected, causing traffic problems in the city yet today. The first post office which opened in 1836 was called Kent, and the settlement is so designated on some early maps. With abundant water power the village became a manufacturing center moving from lumber to furniture as skilled workmen congregated there. Grand Rapids was also a major railroad center. An 1876 map shows service by the Grand Rapids, Newaygo and Lake Shore Rail Road, the Detroit & Milwaukee Railway, the Grand Rapids, Greenville & Alpena (a connector to the Lansing and Lake Michigan Railroad), the Grand Rapids & Indiana, and the Grand River Valley line. Grand Rapids was incorporated as a village in 1838 and a city in 1850. Population in 2000 was 197,800 with a land area of 45.3 square miles.

43.2 Bridge. Ann Street crosses the river east west. The river was first spanned at Ann Street in 1907.

42.8 Railroad bridge for the old Grand Trunk Western, crosses the river east-west. Nearby stand the sturdy and architecturally interesting buildings of the Grand Rapids Filter Plant, built in 1912, and remodeled in 1923 to filter impurities from the water. In 1963 the facility became largely obsolete when a new filtration plant was built near the Lake Michigan pumping station, There is also a small park on the east side of the river near the railroad bridge.

42.4 Bridge. Leonard Street (BR131) crosses east-west. The first toll bridge here was a wooden one, with stone abutments. It was replaced by a ornate lattice-work model in 1879, which yielded in 1913 to a concrete span.

42.2 Coldbrook Pumping Station is on the east bank. The main source of water for the city of Grand Rapids is a 32-mile long water transmission line to Lake Michigan built in 1938.

42 **Canal Park** on the east bank of the river with rest rooms, playground and a river viewing area.

41.9 Bridge. 6th Street linking with Newberry Street on the east, crosses the river east-west. This bridge was constructed in 1885 and was originally 618 feet long, but it was shortened to 545 feet after the addition of a concrete retaining wall in 1921. It is the second oldest and longest truss bridge in Michigan. In 1976, after a long public protest, the City of Grand Rapids reconsidered plans to demolish the bridge and instead, from 1979 to1980, rehabilitated it..

6th Street Bridge Park just south of the bridge, provides access to the river bank where watching fishermen in waders fish the water below the dam is a major recreation in the fall.

41.7 **Grand Rapids Dam**. Water flowing over the dam once generated

The dam at Grand Rapids about 1910.

The new Bridge Street bridge about 1908, note railroad depot center background.

electric power, but is now used only as a scenic attraction, and a fishing site. On the west bank a fish ladder, designed by artist Joseph Kinnebrew IV as an environmental sculpture as well as a way to provide access upstream for spawning fish, especially salmon, can be visited. The fish ladder also included a sea lamprey barrier. It was dedicated in 1975. **Fish Ladder Park** is reached by road from Front Street.

41.6 Bridge. I-196, a dual highway, crosses east-west

41.5 In 1927 to better control the level of the water in the downtown area four small dams were erected. This is the site of Small Dam 1. The little dams also enhance fishing at most water levels.

41.4 Bridge. Bridge Street, which connects with Michigan Avenue, crosses the river east-west. This was an early crossing, the first bridge was constructed in 1845. It lasted only seven years and was replaced by a lattice-work covered bridge which burned in 1858. The lattice-work bridge was replaced and remained a toll bridge until 1874, when the city purchased it from a private company. It was replaced by an iron bridge in 1884, and in 1906 by a stone span.

41.35 **Ah-Nab-Awen Park**, located just south of the bridge on the west bank, was built to celebrate the nation's bicentennial, the city's sesquicentennial and to honor the area's original inhabitants. Ah-Nab-Awen means "resting place." The Tree of Dates in the park's patio area is constructed of 324 granite paving blocks laid out in the shape of a tree. Each is inscribed with a date beginning in 1776 and there are more than 100 blank blocks symbolizing the future. To the south are three earth mounds symbolic of those the earliest Native Americans built in the area, and also honoring the three tribes, Odawa, Potawatomi and Ojibway, which dwelt here when the first settlers arrived. The park also features an award-winning children's playground.

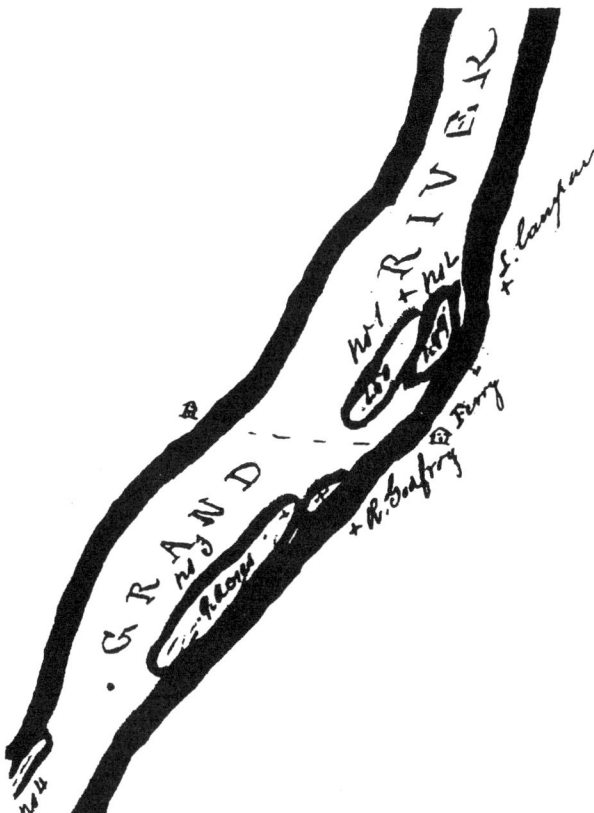

An early map showing the ferry between Islands 2 and 3.

41.32 Small Dam 2.

41.3 Ford Museum, a presidential museum honoring the 38th U. S. President, Gerald R. Ford, Jr., who grew up in Grand Rapids, sits on the west bank. On his death in 2007, Ford was buried on the grounds between the museum and the river.

41.25 Small Dam 3.

41.2 A pedestrian bridge crosses the river east-west permitting people on foot to move freely between the Ford Museum on the west bank, and the DeVos Convention and Exhibition Hall and the rest of downtown Grand Rapids on the east bank. This bridge once carried the electric railway tracks across the river on the way to Kalamazoo. In 1988 it was officially named the Gillett Bridge, honoring Richard M. Gillett and his efforts to make Grand Rapids "the meeting place on the Grand."

41.12 Small Dam 4.

41.1 Bridge. Pearl Street crosses the river east- west. From 1858 to 1886, the river at this point was crossed by a six-span covered bridge. The present concrete bridge was built in 1922 and restored in 1983. A plaque on the downtown side, recalls the old covered bridge and its role in the logjam of 1883.

41.05 A rounded appendage to the Van Andel Museum Center which houses the Public Museum of Grand Rapids extends above the east bank of the river. It contains a 1928 Spillman carousel which offers rides when the museum is open.

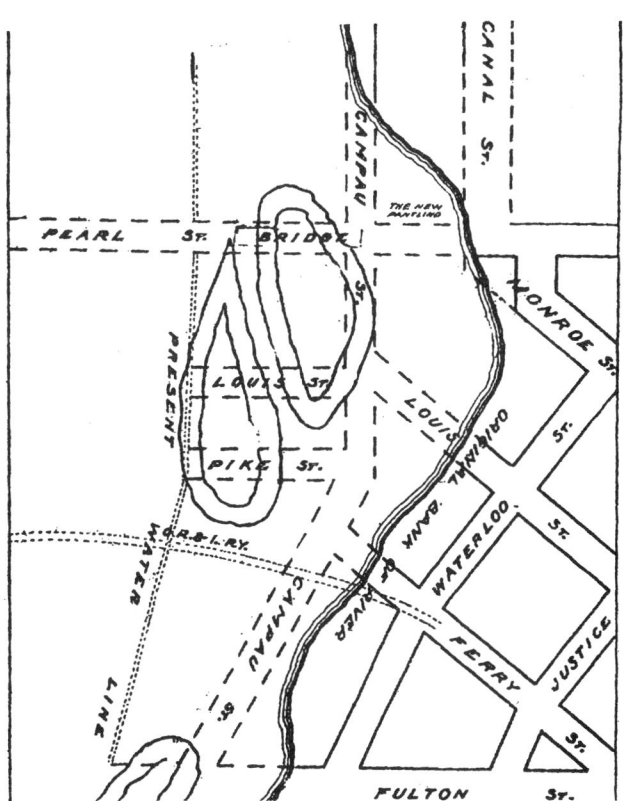

The river around the islands was filled in before 1925.

Pearl Street bridge looking west about 1930. The bridge on the right is the old interurban span, now a pedestrian walkway. Note passenger train on west bank.

41. Pedestrian bridge. A former railroad span, converted to a pedestrian bridge, crosses the river east-west to allow foot traffic from downtown easy access to the Van Andel Museum run by the City of Grand Rapids, and the Pew campus of Grand Valley State University.

Lacks Park, run by Grand Valley State University, is on the west end of the bridge. The area also has a marker relating the history of the Grand Valley Milling Company which operated at this site until 1970. An early ferry was established here between Islands 1 and 2, and Island 3. The area around the island and the canals were later filled in.

40.9 Bridge. Fulton Street crosses the river east-west. An old iron bridge which had been built in 1883, was replaced by a sturdier concrete structure in 1927.

40.8 Bridge. U. S. 131, a dual highway, crosses southeast to northwest.

40.75 On the west bank near the bridge a small park marks the former site of the Converse burial mounds, built by the Hopewellian Indians more than 2000 years ago. The mounds were destroyed by development of the city of Grand Rapids during the late 19th Century. The historical marker also honors members of the Odawa, Ojibwe and Potawatomi tribes which, at various times, lived in communities near the rapids which they called "Baw-wa-ting." The park was established in 2000.

40.5-7 A long thin island stretches down the center of the waterway, with a railroad bridge which carries the Amtrak line across the south end of island.

40.3 Bridge. Wealthy Street crosses the river east-west. The flow of the river, which had been largely northwest begins to turn toward the west, it was first spanned at this point in 1905.

40. Pedestrian bridge. The old C & O and Michigan Northern Railroad bridge crosses the river northwest-southeast.

39.3 Plaster Creek enters from the south

38.7 Bridge. The Gerald R. Ford Freeway, I-196, loops over and crosses the river north-south.

38.6 **Eagle Mills Station** shows on the north bank on an 1873 map. It was a small sawmill settlement on the Lake Shore and Michigan Southern Railroad.

38.4-35 **Millennium Park**, a 1,500 acre park administered by the Kent County Parks Department, includes more than three miles of riverfront on the west bank and, when plans are complete, will touch four cities: Grand Rapids, Walker, Grandville and Wyoming. The first phase opened in 2003, and includes a large swimming area at several inland lakes formed when a major industry of the area was the mining of sand and gravel. Present plans call for bicycle trails and rental, picnic areas, a campground, heritage center, and a boating center on the Grand River with canoes and boats for rent as well as a launching area for canoes and other small, hand-carried craft. Millennium Park is open May 1 to October 31.

38.2 Enter City of Wyoming, on the southeast bank, City of Walker on the northwest bank.

Wyoming When the Township of Wyoming (named for Wyoming County, New York) was established in Kent County in 1848, the only settlement of any note in the township was Grandville, which began in 1832 and was incorporated as a village in 1885 and a city in 1933. As the city of Grand Rapids crept slowly south and east Wyoming Township decided, in 1956, to incorporate all of the township which had not already become part of a city, Grandville or Grand Rapids, as the City of Wyoming. Even after incorporation as a city Wyoming has experienced some loss of territory, but has also annexed some additional land on the east. In 1960 it was given a post office named Wyoming. The population of the city, in 2000, was 69,368 and it had an area of 24.5 square miles. Gypsum was and early important industry, but that production has now ceased.

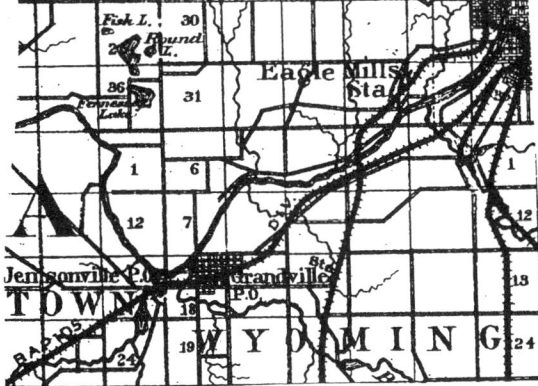

Eagle Mills Station, Grandville and Jenisonville on an 1873 railroad map.

37.7 Pedestrian bridge. An old New York Central Railroad bridge has been converted to a pedestrian span which takes a portion of the Kent County trail system across the river southeast-northwest. This area, south of the river, is part of a public park, but the only facilities are a few benches and areas to picnic or fish.

A Few Idle Days
by Cadette Everett Fitch

Inspired by Mrs. Pennell's account of a trip down the river Thames, with her artistic husband, and reasoning that while all English streams are far away, and correspondingly difficult to reach, and the noble Grand flows majestically, in its course; nearer home, what more natural conclusions than that the outing contemplated should be upon this lovely water, and that every nook and corner should be made familiar by a leisurely survey.

Accordingly three brave spirits M., L. and G. thrusting aside all thought of danger from the molestation of unknown tramps of whom they were sufficiently warned, from accidents upon the water, or disasters that beset the unwary in every condition of life, and especially while traveling through lonely regions – resolutely determined to risk the undertaking, and conduct an expedition of forty miles, with their transporting medium only a rowboat.

The simple preparations were soon concluded and on Sept. 18th 1889 at ten o'clock A.M. a carriage could have been seen wending its way steadily toward the boat landing. This vehicle contained besides its human freight, a lunch basket; satchel; shawl straps encircling cushions and blanket; umbrellas; and three chairs, minus their legs.

Passing over a little neck of ground which connects Island No. 2 with the mainland the boathouse was soon reached . . . The frail boat was loaded and the happy crew pushed off. "Goodbys" were said, and pleasant wishes expressed for those embarking on the raging river, and for the one who preferred the comforts of home.

The channel was, as usual, covered with a green odoriferous scum, mixed with oil from the gas works, and was uninviting to ride through, but this was an unpleasantness of short duration and a few minutes served to leave it behind. Then came the sense of relief and calm enjoyment of the clear, dignified, moving current of the river.

Willows, Elms, Maples and other trees and shrubs, line the banks in rich profusion, and when once accustomed to the motion of the boat and more confident that it was not going over, if reasonable quiet was maintained, all enjoyed, to the utmost, the delicious panorama.

The Plaster bed, with its tall white chimney and quaint buildings, with surrounding verdure was soon in sight, and the reflections in the water were especially charming.

(Below) The plaster operation.

Two or three flocks of geese basked round on islands, and a large drove of cows seemed to have waded out through the shallow channel and were chewing their cud with great satisfaction. One in particular excited our admiration by standing in the river and sprinkling herself with her tail, as it switched in and out of the water in her defence against flies.

On we went, past a few pleasant farm houses, and finally stopped about one mile before reaching Grandville, under a most delightful wide spreading tree. This was evidently a resort for Grandville people as the shade was perfect, and eggs and clam shells, paper, and the like, indicated that parties know a good place . . . for a picnic.

On our way to Grandville we were overtaken by a young Grand Rapids boy who was gliding down the river in a pretty canvas canoe. This boat had a little sail, but, when the wind was unfavorable he used an odd paddle, shaped like the bow of a spoon at each end. This he dipped in the water, first to one side then the other. The trimmings of the little craft were red, all very picturesque. . . While we were lounging after our dinner, the steamer Barrett passed us, dragging a scow loaded with lumber and bushel baskets. One of the men in the pilot-house, paid the young lady of our party the compliment (?) of grabbing a hat from the head of the man standing by him, and waving it. A Hollander passed in a rowboat and announced that he had forty pounds of fish that he was taking to town. Four country girls were rowing about. . . .

We reached Grandville at 5 o'clock, left part of our baggage at the nearest house, after having turned the boat over, and then walked to the hotel, a half a mile away. After bathing and enjoying a good supper – we spent an hour with Mr. Vinklemulden and wife who entertained us with genuine hospitality after true Holland fashion.

Cadette Everett Fitch was the daughter of Franklin Everett, who wrote an early history of the Grand River Valley. The three travelers on this trip were herself, and her teenage children, Louise and George.

The mosquitoes sang their sweetest lullabys during the hot night that followed – two of them will never sing any more to the weary travelers, and one alone remains to bewail the tragic fate of his companion minstrels.

At eight o'clock in the morning we were on our way again. The river and woods were more lovely than ever, and we sang and chattered as merrily as the robins and thrushes from their hiding places in the green foliage.

A shady bank was our next stopping place where we heard the quiet rippling of the passing river or contemplated with never tiring gaze, the cool depths of shadows in the woods and fields farther back. . . The steamer passed while we were taking our midday lunch.

At half past six we reached Lamont and thought some of pushing on to Eastmanville, but it was getting dark and vapor was rising. G. went up the hill to a store to get a lock and chain for the boat, and the merchant advised us to remain there as the hotel at Eastmanville could not be recommended. Lamont had no establishment of this kind but an old lady, Mrs. Rice, some-times opened her house to transients. So we disembarked, left our extra luggage at the ferryman's little office, and sought the residence of the above named lady. A pleasant quiet homestead with a hospitable look was before us. . . The evening was spend in listening to old reminiscences, accounts of the struggles of early settlers and of their dances and good times generally. This lady's home was a favorite resort. We had good beds, and a fair breakfast – biscuits, apple sauce, coffee.

Lamont is built upon hills and is very picturesque owing partly to its numerous houses, mills and barns that are not only deserted, but in a ruined condition. The piers of an old bridge stand, as sentinels in the river, and will probably remain many a year longer before falling, as no one chooses to help time in his destructive work. It was hard to leave this locality as there were many fine points for sketching – we remained until eleven o'clock and the sun was very warm. The ferry boat interested us being drawn across the river with heavy chains running over wheels.

At Eastmanville we visited the stores to replenish our basket and secured lemons, sugar, ginger, cookies and cheese. No bakery – and went to several houses and at last found some bread. In the store we met the hero of the canvas boat and the funny paddle. He was glad to see us and said his camp was only two miles away. We found Eastmanville like Lamont a place of only three or four hundred inhabitants. Enterprising citizens have left, one by one, and those who remain have no hope that the old time prosperity will return.

Our sailor lad's camping place was in some grand old woods. The boys were engaged with various occupations as we passed them a washing hung on a line. It was evidently the work of amateurs and had rather a brown appearance. A flag drooped over the door of the tent, and gave a finishing patriotic bit of color.

A bridge and an island.

Thurs. eve we neared Spoonville where we had promised to make a call upon the owner of the place. The ruins of the bridge there remind one of Roman pillars, aqueducts and the like. We found an entrance to the grounds, going past a boom around a narrow island, and across a channel that may be filled up, in time, to perfect the long slope to the house. We drew up to a boathouse, before which was a finely built family boat capable of seating a dozen people. We crossed a stretch of sawdust and refuse lumber that had been drawn there load by load to fill up the low ground – then we passed over a nicely kept lawn where flowers and trees are interspersed in tasteful profusion. The house was commodious, and fitted up with every luxury needful and its inmates were delightfully cordial and hospitable.

It was hard to leave these genial people, but from experience we knew that an early start was better than long delay, as the sun is quite warm in the middle of the day and our rowing must be done by easy stages. A little time was spent in sketching the ruined bridge, the house and mills then we pushed our boat onward. On, on we go, sometimes singing, or reading aloud, and always noting and speaking of every new object of interest: the glowing sun in its fiery gorgeous setting; fluffy willows, tall waving rice grass, much higher that our heads among which flock myriad birds, looking from a distance like mosquitoes; patches of lily pads; long stretches of piles, which extend for miles to hold secure the logs of our enterprising lumbermen.

We pass under the swing bridge after leaving Spring Lake, and feast our eyes upon the white sand hills in the distance. We notice several ruined boats, great hulks that are mere skeletons; having bravely done their work, their worn out frames are left, exposed to wind and sun and are interesting only to the antiquarian. New boats are being built not far away, one of which is beautiful and symmetrical in its proportions; a yacht of some jaunty sort.

A heavy mist-like cloud, hangs like a veil over the lowland, at our right, as we approach Grand Haven, and at the dock we see the grand steamer "Milwaukie" and our little Barrett, which looks like a pigmy in such aristocratic company. All are loading up for the next trip and we pass them and draw up to the landing. After G. had helped us to firm land, he carried the boat, cushions, blankets &c to the Barrett, and relinquished all guardianship for the present. We expressed much regret that the river was only 40 miles long, from our starting point, and would gladly have continued a trip which had been so full of rich enjoyment.

Grand River at Grandville in 1909.

37.4 **Norton Indian Mounds** on south bank. Left by the Hopewell people who lived in the area more than 2,000 years ago, the Norton group consists of 13 conical-shaped mounds, the largest 15 feet high and 80 feet in diameter. First excavated by the Kent Scientific Institute in 1877, the mounds have been under the protection of the Public Museum of Grand Rapids since 1936. As Millennium Park is developed an advisory council is studying a long-term preservation plan for the mound area.

37 Enter City of Grandville on the southeast bank, City of Walker on the northeast bank.

Walker was settled by Canadians Samuel White and Jesse Smith in 1836, and organized as a township of Kent County in 1838. Historians are uncertain where the name came from, but offer three major possibilities. There was a Walker Tavern built on the Vergennes Road in 1836 by Joseph Walker, or after the Indian Chief Cobmusa, a word that can mean "walker," or perhaps it was Charles I. Walker, an early Indian agent in the area. The settlement was given a post office as **Indian Creek** in 1847 and became a station on the Detroit, Grand Haven & Milwaukee Railway. At one time the community had five saw mills. Gypsum was located on the south edge of the township and was mined beginning in 1852. The post office was renamed Walker in 1884, **North Grand Rapids** in 1891 and closed in 1894. Faced with increasing annexation pressures from the City of Grand Rapids, a portion of Walker Township incorporated as the City of Walker on November 8, 1962. On April 1, 1963, the remainder of Walker Township, annexed to the new city. The population of Walker in 2000 was 21,842, with a land area of 25.4 square miles.

35.8 A creek, called Tallman Creek on some maps, enters the river from the north.

35 The west end of **Millennium Park** joins **Henry Johnson Park**, established by the City of Walker. There is a boat ramp and parking area off Butterworth Street on the north bank. the park also includes picnicking facilities, playgrounds, and a sledding hill for wintertime sport.

34.5 Bridge. M-11 crosses northwest-southeast. On the northwest bank of the river the road is called Wilson Avenue and enters Walker, on the southeast bank the bridge connects with 28th Street and enters Grandville. West of the bridge on the south bank there is a boat ramp in shallow water, run by the city of Walker with a small parking area. It is west of Wilson Avenue.

Grandville Luther Lincoln, Amos Gordon, Robert Howlett and Stephen Tucker arrived at the river landing in Grandville in 1832 with five yoke of oxen. Lincoln was drawn to the agricultural promise of the area because of the Indian cornfields near the river. The settlement was given a post office in 1834 with William B. Godwin as its first postmaster. According to some sources it was first known as **Byron**, then **Little Prairie**, and finally platted in 1835 as Grandville. Industry included wagon makers, two whiffle-tree manufactures, and three plaster mills which refined gypsum from nearby mines. The community was a stop on the Detroit and Milwaukee Railway in 1858 and later on the Lake Michigan Rapid Railway Company's line to Holland. Grandville was incorporated as a village in 1885 and became a city in 1933. The land mass of the city was increased. between 1948 and 1956, by the annexation of the communities of **Carleton Park** and **Wyoming Ranches**, and more than six square miles of Wyoming Township. The settlement of **Ivanrest** still shows on old maps on the northeast corner of Grandville. The population of Grandville in 2000 was 16,263 with a land area of 7.6 square miles.

34.3 Landing Dock. The **Grand Lady** a stern paddle wheel excursion boat which offers dinner cruises on the river, has a floating dock, with a parking area for passengers on the west bank off Indian Mounds Drive..

33.8 Buck Creek enters from the south

33.6 Enter Georgetown Township (on the south bank) and Tallmadge Township (on the north bank), Ottawa County. The river serves as the township boundary.

33.5 Rush Creek enters from the southwest, nearly on the township line.

33.6 **Jenison** near the mouth of Rush Creek was founded by Lemuel Jenison and the first sawmill was built in the area in 1834. In 1837 Lemuel was killed by a falling limb and the work continued by his three sons, Hiram, and the twins, Luman and Lucius. It was a station on the Chicago & West Michigan Railway. A post office opened in 1872 named **Jenisonville**, but the name was changed to Jenison in 1887. Jenison never incorporated as a village or city, and is now an unincorporated community and school district, in Georgetown Charter Township. In the early 1900s there was a ferry which ran between Tallmadge Township on the north bank and Jenison to make it easier for residents of the north bank to reach market with their farm produce, have access to a post office and other needed services.

29.4 **Harris Landing** was located on the north bank of the river where a road down to the river appears on an 1876 map and is designated "Harris Landing." Both the road and the structure on the early map have disappeared.

29.3 **Haire Landing**, on the south bank of the river, was begun by John Haire in 1851. He built a steam sawmill in 1856. The 1864 Ottawa County map shows 13 buildings including a steam sawmill, store, blacksmith shop, school and cemetery. He later built a large cement house overlooking the river. Today the area has been considerably altered by gravel mining operations and the only sign of past settlement is an occasional dock piling sticking out of the bank.

28.9 Sand Creek enters the river from the north. Before settlement there was an Indian village on the north bank just west of the creek. At the mouth of Sand Creek there was a settlement by T. B. Woodbury as early as 1835 with a small trail down to the river. The area had a post office called **Tallmadge,** beginning in 1839, which moved around the map, depending on the residence of the postmaster. The settlement at this location was also known as **Sand Creek** and the Sand Creek school still stands on the river road east of the town. **Sand Creek Landing** was a regular stopping place for steamboats from Grand Rapids in the 1850s and 1860s.

28.5 The outlet from Grand Lake enters the river from the south. **Grand River Park**, a 162-acre facility, includes Grand Lake, a five-acre lake. The park has picnic facilities, playground and also a warming shed for winter sports around

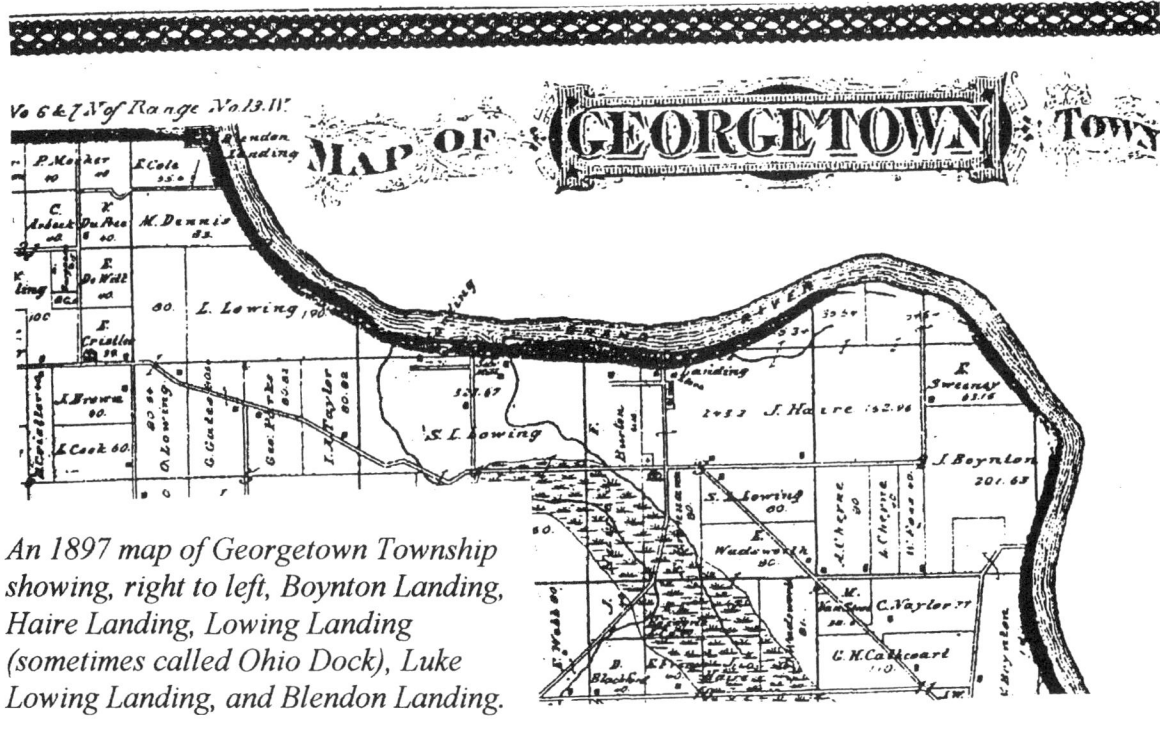

An 1897 map of Georgetown Township showing, right to left, Boynton Landing, Haire Landing, Lowing Landing (sometimes called Ohio Dock), Luke Lowing Landing, and Blendon Landing.

the lake. On the Grand River there is a hard-surfaced boat ramp with fishing docks, and a river overlook. This landing was once part of the Ohio Dock operation, and an early sawmill was located nearby. The park is reached by taking 28th Avenue north from Fillmore Street. It is administered by Ottawa County.

28 A small creek enters the river from the south. Some old maps show this as the location of **Ohio Dock** or sometimes **Lowing Landing**, after Stephen L. Lowing who owned land nearby. The 1864 map of Ottawa County shows a dock with a "lumber railroad" running down to the river.

27.5 **Luke Lowing Landing** near another small creek. Luke was a brother of Stephen L. Lowing of Ohio Dock He came to Ottawa County in 1844. Later a family named Hubbard lived there. In old accounts it is sometimes called **Hubbard's Landing**.

26.6 Enter Allendale Township on the south (west) bank. Tallmadge Township continues on the north (east) bank.

26. **Blendon Landing** A village existed from 1854 to about 1880 on a bluff overlooking the Grand River. It existed before the Civil War largely because of the lumbering activities of the Blendon Lumber Company which constructed a steam railroad to carry logs from the pine forests to the landing for shipment. The sawmill burned in 1864 and the entire settlement was deserted by 1912. Its site, now located on the campus of Grand Valley State University, is sometimes used as a teaching laboratory by the archeology department. According to an early resident wild blackberries grew rampant on Blendon Hills and it was a favorite place for people from Grand Rapids to visit, picking berries and sometimes "putting up tubs and jars of blackberry jam" over the campfire.[5]

24.7 **Grand Valley State University** crew dock. Grand Valley College (since elevated to the status of a university) opened in 1963. Since it was founded on the banks of a major river one of the first sports organized was a rowing team. The tradition continues..

25.4 Bridge. Lake Michigan Drive, or M-45 crosses the river east-west. In 1883 a triangular section of land in Range 13 North, but south of the river, sometimes called "The Gore" because of its shape, was removed from Georgetown Township and became part of Allendale Township which promised to build a bridge over the Grand River which would connect with Bridge Street in Grand Rapids. Prior to the construction of the first bridge in 1926, there was a ferry across the river at this point for 45 years. The bridge was built with a

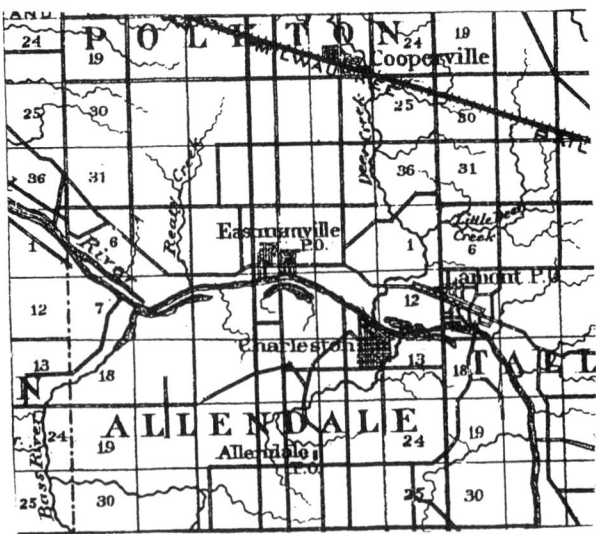

Lamont, Charleston and Eastmanville from an 1873 map.

Steamer Grand at Lamont about 1907.

swing span, but it was never opened. Lake Michigan Drive from Grand Rapids to the bridge, was constructed by a private company and was operated as a toll road from 1887 to 1908 when the circuit court ruled that the highway should be free because it was not being adequately maintained. There are many small islands in the river at this point. Just east of the bridge a post office named **Elgin** opened on August 20, 1886 with John Rose as the first postmaster. Elgin disappeared after the post office closed in 1902, but a small modern community, slightly east and south of old Elgin, is now known as **Grand Valley**.

25.2 Ottawa Creek enters the river from the southwest.

23.1 Lamont The first name for the settlement at this point may have been **Cedar Springs**. In 1833 Harry and Zine Steele settled on the north bank of the Grand River and the area became known as **Steele's Landing**, also the name of a post office that opened on January 9, 1851, with Reuben Reynolds as its first postmaster. Later that year Thomas Woodby platted the area as a village which he called **Middleville,** because it was halfway between Grand Haven and Grand Rapids, but the post office remained Steele's Landing. In 1855 Lamont Chubb of Grand Rapids offered a road scraper in exchange for renaming the village for him, and the offer was accepted. The village and its post office were named Lamont on July 2, 1856. The village's boulevard main street, is an extension of Leonard Street in Grand Rapids, the old Lake Michigan Road. In earlier days there was a toll bridge across the Grand at Lamont, but the structure was gone by the 1880s. The river landing is over a bluff and the river itself can only occasionally be glimpsed from the village, especially in the summer. Commercial Street, which leads diagonally down to the river from downtown Lamont, was the landing for steamboat traffic until 1920. Today a medical rehabilitation facility is the only structure on the riverbank.

The farm residence of Richard Roberts at Charleston Landing. Note ferry crossing the river on a chain and the small steamer Barrett going by.

22.2 Enter Polkton Township, Ottawa County on the north bank. Polkton Township was named for President James K. Polk. Allendale Township continues on the south bank.

22 Charleston About 1810 Pierre Constant, a Frenchman employed by the British Fur Company established a post on Traders Creek. A town called Charleston was platted near the remains of the old trading post and recorded March 12, 1836. The 1864 Ottawa County map shows a settlement just west of the juncture of Traders Creek and the Grand in section 10 and 11. Charleston was another contender for county seat and land owned by Galen Eastman is labeled "Proposed site for the County seat" on an early map. At its height the settlement included a steam sawmill, a blacksmith shop, a carpenter's shop and a large warehouse on the river. When the sawmill was removed in 1872 the village began to decline and little is left now to mark the spot.. Traders Creek itself has largely disappeared. For many years there was a chain-driven ferry across the Grand River at this spot, run by the Cooley family.

22-20.8 Ripps Bayou A new 160-acre park under development on the north bank which officials hope some day to connect up with Deer Creek Park (see below). It is now accessible only from the river. Ripps Bayou is a long narrow bayou parallel to the main river.

20.7 Deer Creek enters the river from the north having already incorporated Little Deer Creek and Beaver Creek. The city of Coopersville is located four miles upstream on Deer Creek. **Deer Creek County Park** is just west of the mouth of the creek, and includes a gravel-surfaced boat ramp for carry-down boats only, and a small picnic and parking area and a toilet. The park is at the foot of 60th Avenue, off Leonard Street.

Eastmanville and Newburg from an 1876 Ottawa County atlas.

20.6 Charleston Landing or **Charleston River Landing** on the south bank of the river across from, and slightly west, of Deer Creek. Here Richard Roberts built a house down by the water which was later used as a stopping place for river traffic because it was about halfway between Grand Haven and Grandville. By 1876 Roberts had built himself a large home on the top of the bluff. An engraving of this house along with a ferry crossing the river is included in the 1876 Ottawa County atlas.

20.5 Newburg (sometimes wrongly spelled Newbury). A settlement platted in section 11, Polkton Township, on the north bank of the river a half mile east of Eastmanville by Jacob DeHaan in 1857. At its height the settlement contained a spoke factory and a small boarding house.

20.4-19.8 Eastmanville Bayou Park An 80-acre park is being planned on the south bank of the river east of the bridge, incorporating the Eastmanville Bayou.

19.8 Bridge. A two-part bridge carries 68th Avenue across the river north-south. A bridge was first built at this site in 1917. It was a swing bridge designed to open to allow river traffic to pass. In 1969 it was replaced, and further rebuilt in 1998. It is the only Grand River crossing between Grand Haven to the west, and M-45, east of Allendale, to the east. In the early days there was a cross-river ferry at this point. Originally it was a poled scow, it later ran on a chain, and, after 1900, was powered with a gasoline engine.

19.6-19.9 Eastmanville The area on the north bank of the river, in section 3,

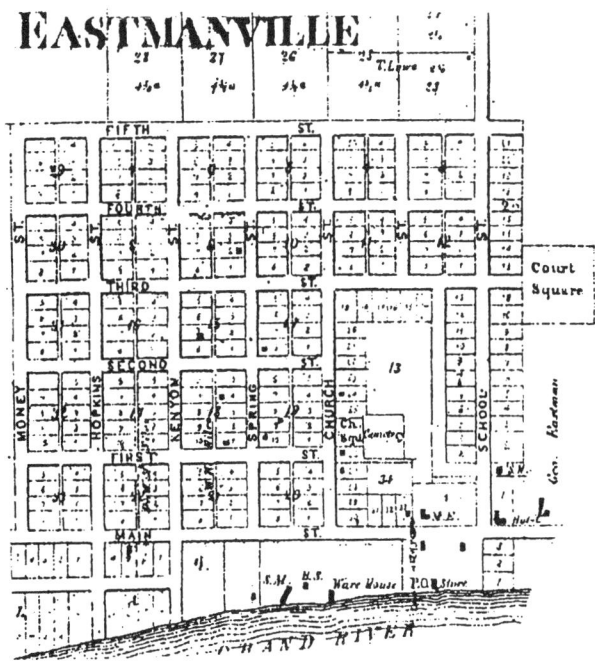

Plat of Eastmanville on an 1864 map. Note Court Square, at right, in anticipation of moving the county seat from Grand Haven..

Polkton Township, was first settled by Dr. George W. Scranton in 1835. A post office called **Scranton** was opened on July 11, 1838, but closed in 1842. Maine native Dr. Timothy Eastman arrived in 1842 and on May 28, 1846, he became the first postmaster of Polkton, named for the newly-organized township. Eastman and two of his sons, Galen and Mason, platted a village in 1855 called Eastmanville. In 1857 the settlement was officially named the county seat of Ottawa County, but the government remained at Grand Haven even though period maps show an area set aside for the court house at Eastmanville. It was the site of the County Poor House with a working farm. This facility continued to operate as a residential care facility for impaired adults into the 21th Century.

19.3-191 West Eastmanville Bayou Park West of the 68th Avenue bridge another piece of park property, just under 50 acres, will become West Eastmanville Bayou Park. A small canal provides access from the river to the West Eastmanville Bayou. These riverside parks are one of the few places that Virginia Bluebells grow in Michigan.

18.4-18.2 Community Haven A 229 acre former farm, with one-quarter mile of riverfront on the north bank, is being developed by Ottawa County as a "farm park" to allow the city children of today to get a glimpse of farm life. A large barn on the property will be refurbished into a teaching venue and there may be areas for equestrian activities.

17.2 Bass Creek (on some maps called Bass River) enters from the south having picked up Little Bass Creek and Bear Creek. The stream is nearly 15 miles long and begins in Georgetown Township, north of Hudsonville.

16.5 Bur Oak Landing Open Space, a 86-acre undeveloped park with an open meadow, but no additional facilities, on the north bank. It is located at the foot of 90th Avenue, off Leonard Street. More land purchase is anticipated. The landing at this point was the north bank terminus of the Bass River cross-river ferry.

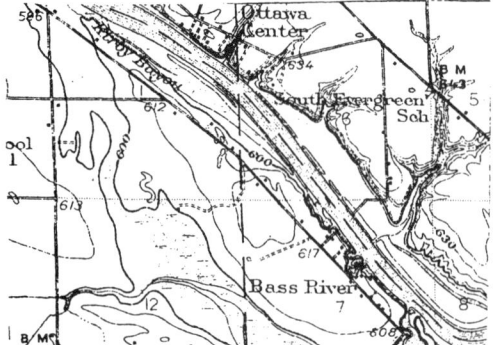

Ottawa Center and Bass River are both shown on this 1936 survey map.

16.4 Bass River A settlement in section 7, with a landing on the south bank of the Grand River, was given a post office July 18, 1882, with Andrew J. White as its first postmaster. The office closed in 1910, but the site is still marked on a 1936 survey map. This was also the location of a cross-river ferry. The Bass River delta was the center of a rich gravel deposit and about 1920 Construction Aggregates Company of Chicago began buying up land and buildings. Today the buildings of the former town have been replaced by a series of gravel pits and the river is nearly half a mile wide at this point. The **Bass River State Recreation Area** includes 1,650 acres and three miles of riverfront.

16 **Warren City** A projected town called Warren City was platted in 1837 on the south bank just west of the mouth of the Bass River in Robinson Township, section 1. The Ottawa County Commission voted in 1840 to relocate the county seat to that point, but the vote was never acted upon.

15.4 Enter Robinson Township, Ottawa County, on the south and Crockery Township, Ottawa County, on the north.

15.2 **Ottawa Center** (or Ottawa Centre, on some maps just Center) The community of Ottawa Center was founded in an effort to lure the county seat away from Grand Haven to the "center" of the county. A post office opened July 11, 1853, with Benjamin Smith as the first post mater, and the town plat was recorded in 1855. It was chosen as county seat in 1856, but the decision was later put to a vote of the people and the change in county seat was rejected. At its height the settlement

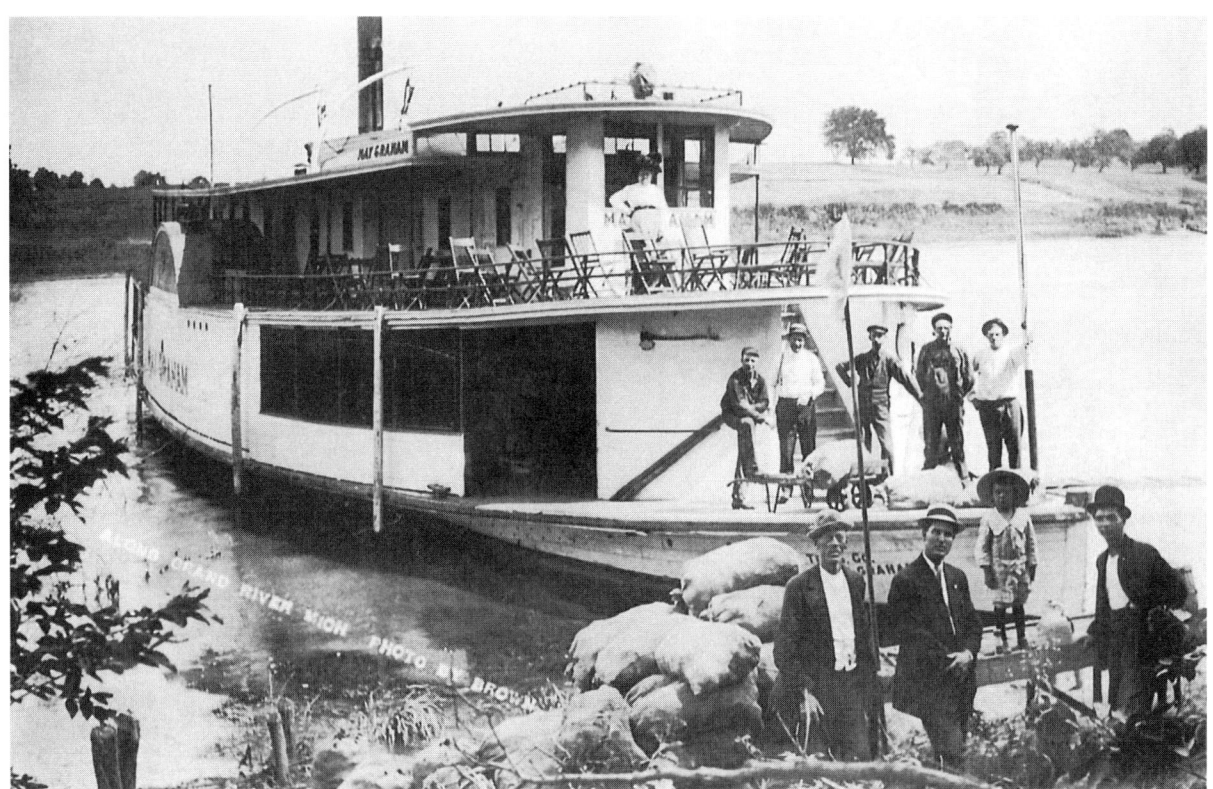

The May Graham on the lower river.

contained two general stores, a boarding house, saloon, wagon shop, blacksmith shop, a stream saw mill and a river boat landing. The post office closed in 1862, and by 1910 all businesses were gone, but the site is still labeled on a 1972 topographic map at Oriole Drive and 96th Avenue. The road no longer goes to the river and the site on the bluff is occupied by a campground. The only easily identifiable part of Ottawa Center viable today is the cemetery on Oriole Drive.

14.8 **Riverside County Park** on the south bank in Robinson Township with 4,300 feet of waterfront along the Grand River. There is a boat launching ramp here, at the foot of Cedar Drive with a fee to launch. The park also includes picnicking facilities, rest rooms and fishing. A long body of water within the park is called Kirby Bayou on early maps.

13.1 – 14.2 Jubb Bayou, parallels the Grand River on the north bank for more than a mile, but has no direct access to the main channel. Off Oriole Drive, east of 104th Avenue, the 97-acre **Jubb Bayou Open Space** offers public pedestrian access to the riverbank and bayou, but no facilities.

12.4 Crockery Creek enters from the north having already picked up Ovid Lake Creek, Lawrence, Sanford and DeVries drains and Brandy Creek. Crockery Creek begins at the northern boundary of Muskegon County south of Grant. It was an important camping area for Native Americans and early writings and maps record a large village near its mouth at the Grand. The Ottawa County Parks department owns 306 acres on the east side of the creek, with one half mile of river frontage and two miles up the creek including a farmstead. It is in the process of development.

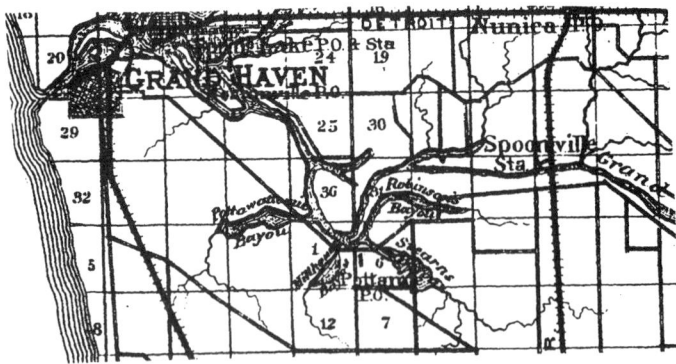

The river east of Grand Haven has many bayous. At right is Spoonville Station. This 1876 map shows Chicago & Michigan Lake Shore tracks at that point The line was redundant when the Chicago & West Michigan Railway Company bought up several other lines and they were removed in 1881.

12.3 **Robinson Township Park** on the south side of the river, across and just west of Crockery Creek. It has a boat ramp, toilets and a 58-space parking area reached by 118th Avenue off North Cedar Drive.

12 **Spoonville** John Spoon arrived from New York and settled on the north bank in 1856, later joined by his younger brother, Don. Vroman Becker came the same year and the area was earlier known as **Beckerville**. In 1857 Becker sold his interest and when the settlement was given a station on the Chicago & Michigan Lake Shore Rail Road in 1870 it was called Spoonville. A hand-operated chain ferry crossed the Grand River at this point, now the foot of 120th Avenue (earlier called the Spoonville Road), before the building of the railroad bridge. The railroad at this point was short-lived. In 1881 the Chicago and West Michigan Railway company purchased two routes to Muskegon, and chose to eliminate the one through Spoonville. They started wrecking operations in the middle of the night, and by dawn it was too late to get an injunction to stop them. The mill was dismantled in 1890. The site, today, is occupied by a waterfront RV park and a private marina. There is a sloping bank at the old landing where small hand-carried boats might be launched.

10.8 Connor Bayou on the south has a tenuous connection to the main river. The Ottawa County Parks Department owns 140 acres, one mile of Grand River frontage, on and west of the bayou under development as **Connor Bayou Park**. The property includes a large log home. Some form of camping is being considered for the site. On land it is reached from 128th Avenue and North Cedar Drive.

10.5-5 **Grand Haven State Game Area** Beginning at Bruce's Bayou on the north the Grand Haven State Game Area administers many acres of property along the river, including several islands.

9.8 Bruce's Bayou flows into the river from the north. It is fed from the north by Black Creek. The bayou is a mile and a half in length and has two public access areas which can be reached from Leonard Street. Bruce's Bayou East is off 132nd Avenue and Bruce's Bayou West is approached on 138th Avenue

8.6 East entrance to Indian Channel. There is a boat ramp, parking area and toilets on the northwest bank of the river, reached from the foot of 144th Avenue

8.5 Stearns Bayou flows into the river from the south. The bayou itself is mostly in Robinson Township and is a favorite fishing venue especially known for its bass fishing.

8.4 Enter Grand Haven Township (on the south bank) and Spring Lake Township (on the north bank), Ottawa County. At this point the river passes into low lying land and from here to the mouth there are several large bayous and swampy islands.

8.4 A small community called **Clark Corners** is shown on the 1936 and 1972 survey maps on Mercury Drive and 144th Avenue.

8.35 **Odawa/Battle Point Launch**, run by Grand Haven Charter Township is located at the head of 144th Avenue on the south bank. It has rest rooms and a hard-surfaced boat ramp.

8.2 **Pottamie** From January 28, 1870 to April 10, 1873, a rural post office operated between Stearns and Millhouse bayous on the south bank. The first postmaster was Alonzo Carter.

8. **Battle Point** The point protruding from the north into the river's course is known as Battle Point, now an island as the result of Indian Channel.. It was the site of an early Odawa Indian settlement. According to legend it was at this place that Shiawassee tried to induce men of the village to rise up in rebellion against the settlers. Reverend Ferry at Grand Haven had sent a friendly Indian to monitor proceedings but it was Bay-vhos-a-key, a young brave, who spoke so convincingly against the arguments of Shiawassee that "Shiawassee pulled his blanket over his head and, with his followers, retreated to their canoes."[6] The next day they left for Canada. The legend gets muddled, but it would appear that the name, Battle Point, is not connected to its Native American inhabitants, but to two early settlers fighting over land boundaries or, some say, rivermen from a passing boat. As early as 1855 there was an Indian school

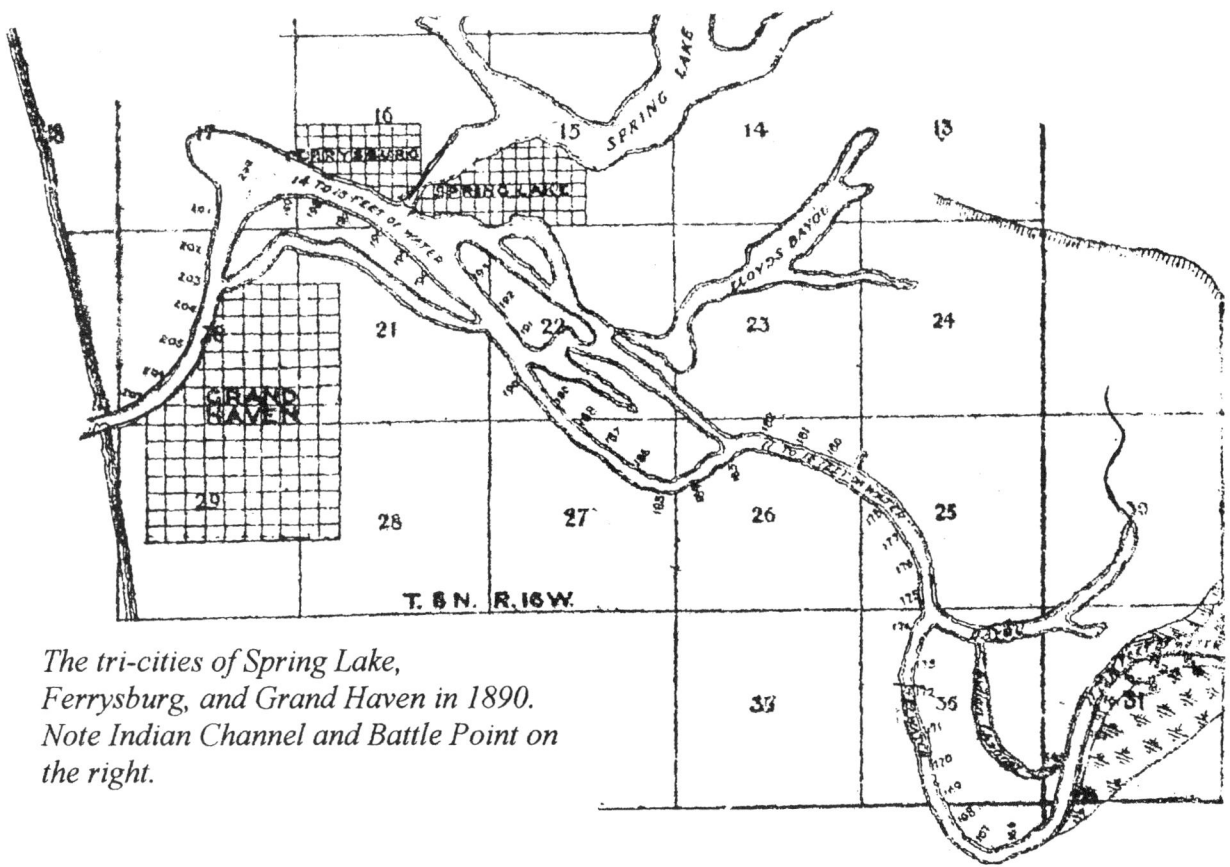

The tri-cities of Spring Lake, Ferrysburg, and Grand Haven in 1890. Note Indian Channel and Battle Point on the right.

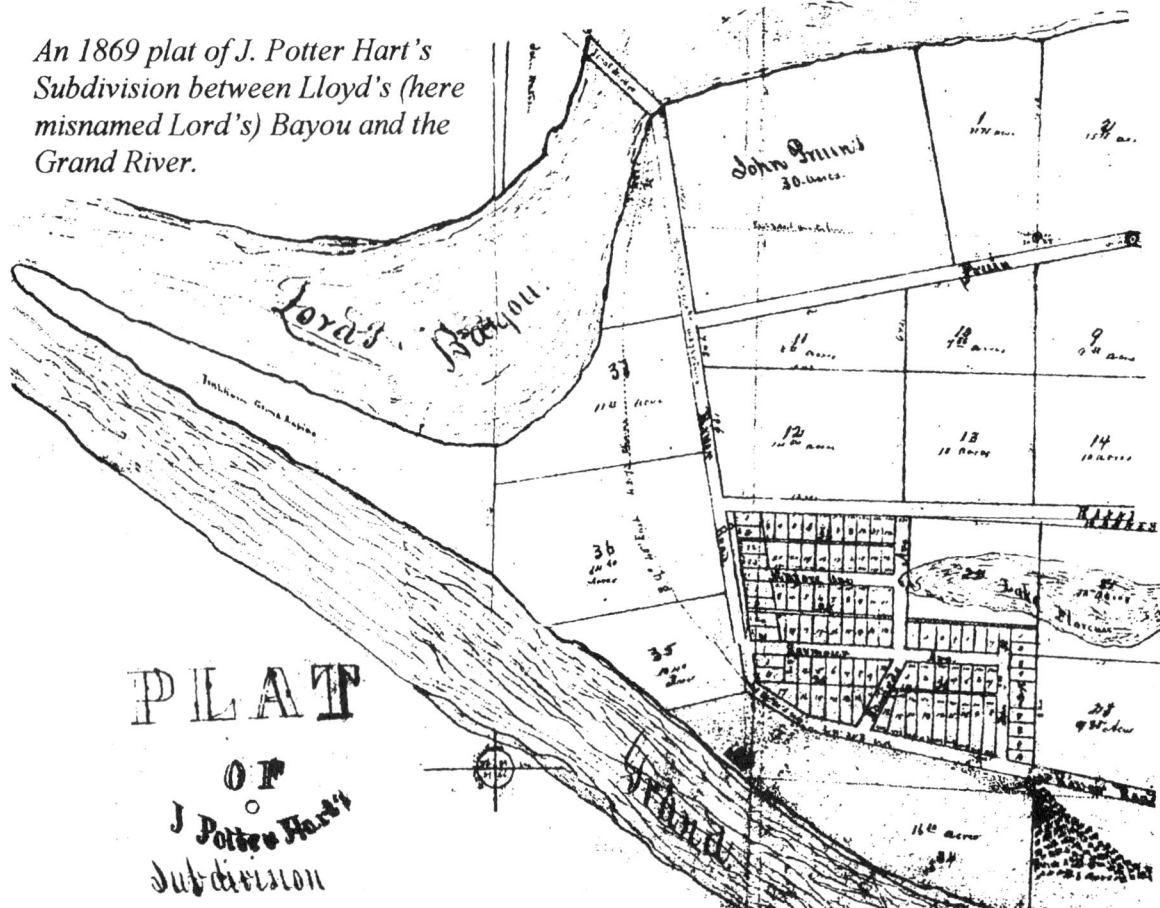

An 1869 plat of J. Potter Hart's Subdivision between Lloyd's (here misnamed Lord's) Bayou and the Grand River.

nearby, founded by the Methodist circuit rider. There is a boat ramp near the southern end of the point, on Indian Channel.

8.7-6.4 Poel Island. South of Battle Point, between the outlets of Stearns Bayou and that of Dermo Bayou, there is a long curving island in the river called Poel Island. Battle Point and much of the north bank of the river is part of the Grand Haven State Game Area, with Poel Island being further designated as a nature sanctuary.

8 Millhouse Bayou enters from the southwest.

7.5 Pottawattomie Bayou flows into the river from the west. The bayou is nearly two miles in length and includes several residential areas and a community called **Snug Harbor** on the north bank. **Pottawattomie Park** is located on the north shore of the bayou with a playground, restrooms, picnicking facilities and a floating fishing dock. It is reached by land off Comstock Road, just west of Mercury Drive.

6.5 Dermo Bayou flows into the river from the northeast. From 1871 to about 1946 there was a floating bridge across the bayou. A partially manmade connection just under a mile long called Indian Channel connects the Grand River in section 31, Crockery Township to the bayou and thence into the river in section 25, Spring Lake Township.

6.5–4.8 Dermo Island A large low island, south of the main channel. Some accounts and maps (including the U. S. Survey maps) spell the name Deremo.

5. – 3.8 Martinique Island. A large low island, south of the main channel, separated from Dermo Island by a shallow channel. During World War II some areas of these islands were used for Victory Gardens by the residents of Grand Haven and Spring Lake. Children remember the fun they had tending a garden they had to reach by boat.

4.5 Lloyd Bayou flows into the river from the north. A second entrance, at 3.7 is more dependable during low water. There is a boat launch at **Oak Point** on the northeast end of the bayou, off Cleveland Road. In June of 1869 J. Potter Hart and his wife, Nancy, platted a 93-lot subdivision between the Grand River and Lloyd's Bayou called simply, **J. Potter Hart's Subdivision**.

4.4 Gigley Bayou enters the south channel from the south.

4. **East Grand River Park** on the south bank of what is sometimes called "Lost Channel," the waterway that runs south of the islands near the wastewater treatment plant. Facilities include rest rooms, a picnic area, playground and the Scott A. Flahive Memorial Boat launch, and loading pier for boats under 20 feet, with parking nearby. Flahive was a policeman who died on duty in 1984.

*The Spring Lake ferry **Fanny M. Rose** getting ready to land in Grand Haven probably about 1907.*

The message on the back of the postcard reads, "This is how you are going to get to Fruitport."

4.6 - 3.5 Spring Lake In 1837 a mill was built on the point of land between Big Bayou, later renamed Spring Lake, and the Grand River by Canadian settler Benjamin Hopkins and the area was known as **Hopkins Mill**. When the plat was recorded in 1849 it was called **Mill Point** and received a post office by that name in 1851 with LeMoyne M. S. Smith as the first postmaster. In 1867 the name of the office was changed to Spring Lake, and, in 1869, it became a stop on the Detroit, Grand Haven & Milwaukee Railway. Spring Lake incorporated as a village March 24, 1869. The population in 2000 was 2,513, with a land area of 1.1 square miles.

Nortonville on the north bank in 1882.

3.8 Nortonville On the south bank of the river shows on an 1873 map. The settlement was founded in 1837 when Colonel A. N. Norton built a sawmill at this point. In 1846 he became the first postmaster. The office closed in 1859, but was reopened from April 22, 1872 to July 31, 1876. When the place became a station on the Chicago & West Michigan Railway it was called **Norton**. An 1882 history shows Nortonville on the north side of the river where there was still a Nortonville Chapel on a 1976 map.

3.8-.8 Grand Haven. Rix Robinson built a trading post near the mouth of the Grand River in 1833, and the following year, with Reverend William M. Ferry, Robert Stuart and Nathan M White, formed the New Haven Company. The first post office was opened May 2, 1835, and named **Stuart** to honor Robert Stuart. The name of the post office was changed to Grand Haven in August of 1835. The 1838 gazetteer by John T. Blois noted, "Steamboats and vessels from Chicago to Detroit touch here on their passage. The river forms the best harbor on this side of the Peninsula. It is 65 rods wide, bold shore, with a depth of from 15 to 30 feet water, and at its entrance on the bar at the mouth, never less than 12 feet. There is a light-house erecting at its mouth. The location of this village, in point of natural advantages has no superior on the west of the Peninsula." [7] Grand Haven was incorporated as a city in 1867. Since 1924 Grand Haven has held an annual event in August celebrating the presence of the U.S. Coast Guard in their community and honoring those who serve. In 1998 the commandant issued an official proclamation naming Grand Haven "Coast Guard City USA." The population of Grand Haven in 2000 was 11,168 with an area of 7.4 square miles.

3.7 Lloyd Bayou flows into the river from the north. Water from the bayou reaches the main river at two different places, but this entrance is the most dependable at low water.

3.2–3.6 Eastmans Island, named for the Eastman family, is north of the main channel in the river. South of Eastmans island is a channel though a number of unnamed swampy islands which provides access to Lloyd Bayou.

3. **Mill Point Park,** with a boat ramp and 64 car parking lot, is located at the

Landing for pleasure boats at the foot of Washington Street in Grand Haven. Note the railroad depot at left.

Dewey Hill across from downtown Grand Haven after 1920. The hill is now the site of the "World's Largest Musical Fountain."

Ferrysburg, on this 1864 map, had many platted lots, but few buildings.

end of School Street in Spring Lake on the north side of the river. The park has a playground, shelter, and rest rooms. There is a fee to use this ramp.

2.9-3.2 Dornbos Island, an oval shaped island between the larger Harbor Island and the entrance to Spring Lake.

2.8. Entrance to Spring Lake. Spring Lake is a large bayou more than five miles in length and nearly a half mile wide in some places which flows into the river from the north. Rhymer Creek, Norris Creek, Vincent Creek and Stevens Creek flow into the bayou from the north. Within the lake there are several named bayous: Stahl, Jerusalem and Smith Bayous on the west side, and Pettys Bayou on the east. The area has supported a cottage community since the early 1900s. The Village of Spring Lake is located on the southeast edge of the lake.

2.6 Bridge. There was a ferry at this point early in settlement. The first bridge was slightly to the west from the end of 7th Street, later replaced by a toll bridge, then in 1924 by a swing span. The lift bridge which takes U.S. 31 across the river at Grand Haven was dedicated in the summer of 1955. It is the only Grand River crossing in the area, the next being at Eastmanville, 17 miles upriver. When large freighters, or even sailboats, need to get past the highway the bridge must be opened, disrupting traffic. There have also been mechanical difficulties with the mechanism, which makes a long detour necessary just to travel between Grand Haven and Spring Lake. The State Highway Department has tried for many years to extend U.S. 31 and build a new bridge, but a swampy and complex river bed, and resistance from agricultural interests, fishermen and environmentalists to condemning the farmland needed has delayed the work.

2.5 Railroad bridge. The old C & O (earlier Grand Trunk Western Railroad) tracks cross both the south channel and the main river north-south on a bridge built in the late 1800s. The portion over the main channel swings open to allow boats to pass.

3.3 -1.2 Harbor Island. Just north of Grand Haven the river is nearly three-quarters of a mile wide, and includes a large island known as Harbor Island, with **Rix Robinson Park,** and several marinas and other service businesses. The Grand Haven Municipal Boat Launch is near the west end of Harbor Island. Also a dock for unloading supplies and passengers. There is an exit from U.S. 31 to the island, after the highway bridge crosses the south channel but before it reaches the draw portion of the bridge. The island can also be reached by bridge from Grand Haven from the north end of 3rd Street.

2.6 Ferrysburg, between the north bank of the river and Spring Lake, was earlier called **Ottawa Point** and **Ferry Point**, because it was the place where early settlers crossed the wide Grand River by ferry. In 1857 it was platted and recorded by Colonel William Montague Ferry Jr. and Thomas White Ferry and named for their father, Reverend William M. Ferry, founder of Grand Haven. A post office opened in August of 1859. Ferrysburg was incorporated as a home rule city in 1963. Its major industries over the years has been the Johnston Boiler Works which provided boilers for most of the boats built in Western Michigan and Construction Aggregates, a Chicago firm which opened a facility in Ferrysburg in 1923 to process gravel mined near Bass River. The Bass River operation is closed but large lake-going vessels, many in excess of 500 feet in length, continue to call at the plant and can be viewed from Harbor Island. The population of Ferrysburg in 2000 was 3,040 with a land area of 3.56 square miles.

1.8 The Sag, a circular bayou on the north side of the river, which was used as a turning basin for early boat traffic.

1. **Dewey Hill**. Although it had no name until 1898 "the big sand hill" across from the railroad depot was considered a Grand Haven landmark, and the site of an annual Fourth of July celebration that included a mock battle, usually complete with an attack by water. The attacking vessel was often crudely built just for this purpose and set on fire as part of the pageant. In 1898 the naval victory of Admiral George Dewey at Manila, during the Spanish-American War, was celebrated with great bonfires on the hill and the elevation was named for him. In 1963 the city of Grand Haven erected a musical fountain which gives nightly sound, light and water shows during the summer, best viewed from downtown Grand Haven across the river. As a wintertime attraction the city created a giant nativity pageant using large cutouts to tell the Christmas story. On a 1972 survey map the elevation of Dewey Hill is given as 650 feet above sea level.

1. The **Grand Haven Municipal Marina** is located off Harbor Drive almost directly across the river from Dewey Hill. Charter fishing boats also dock here. Facilities include a playground, grills, restrooms, a statue honoring the Boy Scouts of American, and a fish cleaning station. The area is called Chinook Pier and is the beginning of a riverbank walk that extends to the harbor piers.

.9 **Tri-Cities Historical Museum**, on the south bank, is housed in the old Grand Trunk Western railroad depot which served as a passenger station until 1955. A brass replica of the Grand River, embedded in the pavement just south of the museum, was donated by employees of the Grand Haven Brass Foundry in 1985. The area is part of

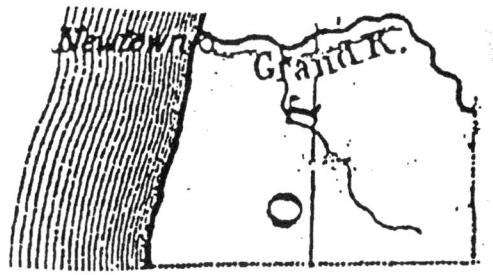

Grand Haven, called Newtown, in 1844.

William M. Ferry Landing Park at the foot of Washington Street.

.9 A modern sculpture called "Starboard Tack", designed by Terry Westra and manufactured by the Bastian-Blessing Company of Grand Haven is part of **Bicentennial Park** on the south bank. There is also a river overlook along Harbor Drive.

.8 The U.S. Army Corps of Engineers, Grand Haven area offices on the south..

.6 A U.S. Coast Guard station and offices. In 1989 new buildings near the park replaced the old station on the north shore, just inside the mouth. The sector field office is located nearby, across Harbor Drive.

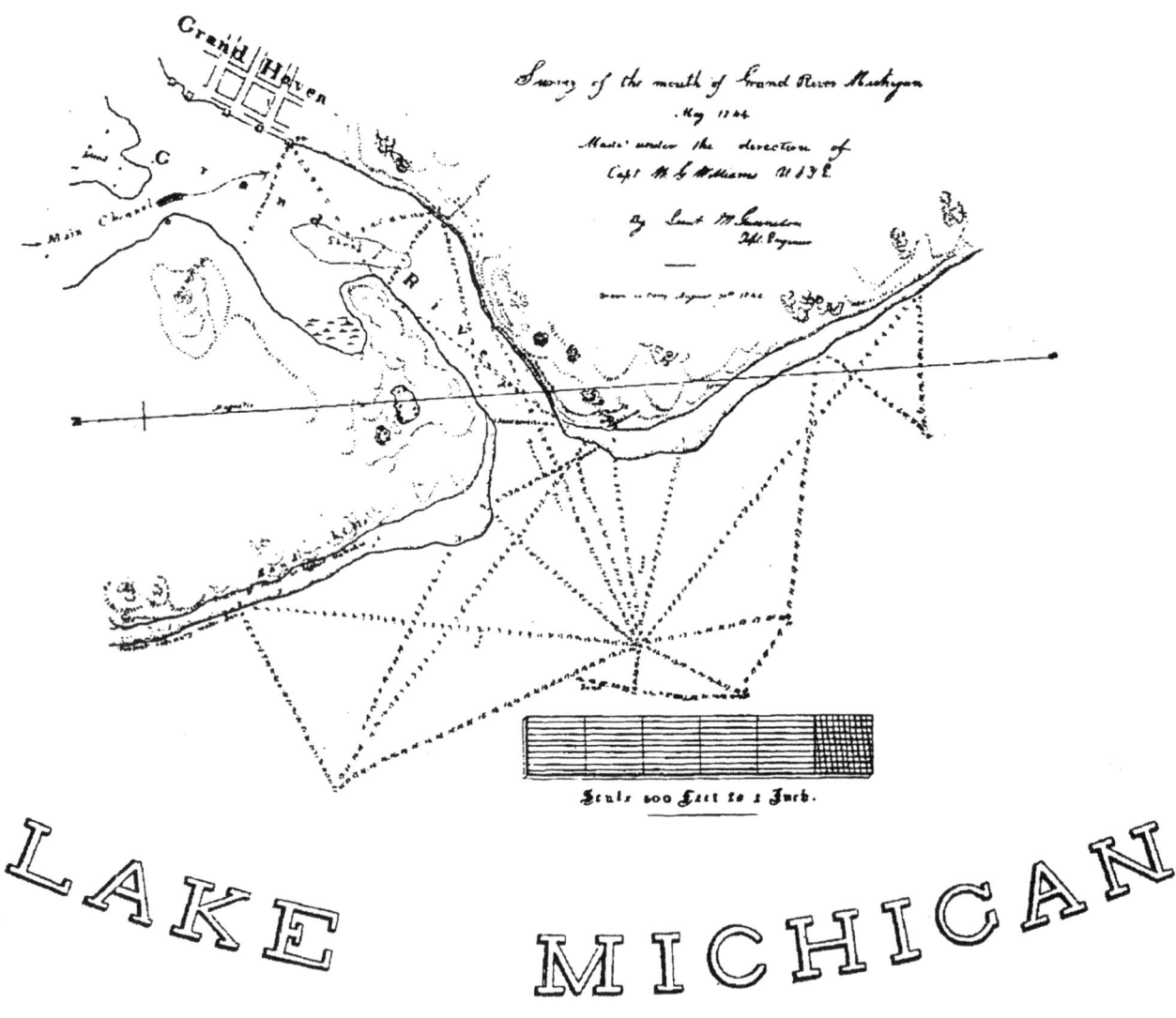

A U.S. Army Corps of Engineers map drawn in 1844 of the mouth of the Grand River. Note in river at the west end of the island on the south bank there is a small structure that is partially in the river and is labeled "Warehouse fallen." This was said to have been Louis Campau's trading post, built about 1821.

5 **Escanaba Park**, a flat area on the south bank was constructed from swampy shores and material left from dredging and dedicated as **Kelly Park** in 1933. Following the sinking of the U.S.S. Escanaba on duty off Greenland in 1943, the mast of the Escanaba which had been removed before its World War II service, was erected at a memorial and the park rededicated as Escanaba Park. The Escanaba, an ice-breaking cutter, had been stationed at the Grand Haven Coast Guard station since shortly after its launch in 1932. The area also contains several other Coast Guard-related memorials. The dock at Escanaba Park is used by Great Lakes cruise ships when they visit Grand Haven.

.4 Lower Diggings. Near the mouth of the Grand River Louis Campau established a trading post before 1821, but the river bank was not stable and water began to undermine the building. An 1844 Corps of Engineers map shows a structure on the south bank, actually within the water of the river, with the notation "warehouse fallen." This area was later flooded by the river and known as Government Pond. According to legend, somewhere nearby was the site of an early treasure hunt. In October of 1826 the schooner Andrew was driven ashore near the mouth of the river. There were 20 barrels of whiskey on board which were salvaged by Rix Robinson and buried in the sand nearby until he had time to retrieve them. When he returned the shifting sands had obliterated his landmarks and the barrels were never located.

Harbor, Grand Haven, Mich.

A tug heads into the harbor about 1918, with the life-saving station at upper right.

Weekly life-saving drill at the station on the north bank of the river near its mouth.

2 A Life-Saving Service Station was established on the north bank in 1877 and manned by volunteers, later men were hired on a seasonal or year-round basis. Grand Haven also served as headquarters of the 11th District which covered Lake Michigan. In 1915 the Life-Saving Service and the Revenue Cutter Service were combined as a military operation known as the U.S. Coast Guard, now under the U.S. Department of Homeland Securities. The station on the north bank was closed in 1989 when they moved to the new complex across the river, but the old boat house, with rails for the lifeboats was still standing as late as 2007.

.2 – 0 **Grand Haven State Park** The original Grand River lighthouse was constructed here in 1839 at beach level on an acre of land on the south bank of the river. It succumbed to stormy waters in 1852 and was replaced by a stone tower high up on the bluff nearby. In 1920 the city of Grand Haven purchased 22 acres between Harbor Avenue and Lake Michigan and deeded it to the State of Michigan to develop as a State Park. The "lighthouse acre" was contributed in 1936 by the federal government and another 4.2 acres was purchased. The WPA leveled the area and the enlarged park was dedicated at the Second Annual Coast Guard Festival in August of 1938. A boardwalk connects the end of the south pier at the State Park with downtown Grand Haven. Facilities include picnicking, a con-cession stand, public restrooms, pier fishing, and a playground area. A user fee is required for entrance. At the end of Harbor Drive there is a parking lot operated by the Michigan Department of Natural Resources especially for cars of those who want to fish from the south pier. A similar facility exists on the north bank.

.1 According to an 1857 report to Congress written by Lieutenant Colonel J. D. Graham summarizing the harbors of Lake Michigan the first work to be done at the harbor at Grand Haven had already been approved and was described as making some effort to defend the channel "from the abrasion of the current which impinges against it."[8] The 1857 report recommends that the next step be to construct two parallel piers "to project out into the lake in prolongation of the direction of the river channel."[9] These piers were eventually built, beginning in 1857 and added to in increments until 1894 where they reached the length they are today. Additional work was done before World War I to shore up the north bank. There are two red structures on the south pier, a lighthouse shaped tower and a fog signal house with a flashing red light. On the north pier there is a flashing green light atop a 36-foot cylindrical tower.

Enter Lake Michigan

1772—PIER IN STORM, GRAND HAVEN, MICH.

Sourcenotes

[1] *History of Jackson County, Michigan* (Interstate Publishing Co.: Chicago) 1881.

[2] Ingersoll, Mrs. E. S. "Early Settlement of Delta" *MPHC*, Vol. 1, p. 157-158.

[3] *Grand Ledge Independent*, April 21, 1922.

[4] Bishop, Levi "Recollections," *MPHC*, Vol. I, p. 514-515.

[5] Belknap, Charles *The Yesterdays of Grand Rapids* (The Dean-Hicks Company: Grand Rapids) 1922, p. 158.

[6] Lillie, Leo C. *Historic Grand Haven and Ottawa County* (n.p.:Grand Haven) 1931.

[7] Blois, John T. *Gazetteer of the State of Michigan (Sydney L. Rood & Co.: Detroit) 1838*, p. 291.

[8] *Letter from the Secretary of War communicating the last annual report of Lieutenant Colonel J. D. Graham on the harbors of Lake Michigan, January 6, 1857* 35th Congress, 1st Session, House of Representatives Ex. Doc. No. 23, p. 90.

[9] *Letter from the Secretary of War. .* p. 91.

Bibliography

Adams, Carl Lorrin *River Landings and the People Who Made Them* n.p. n.d

Allendale Township: 150 Years (Allendale Historical Society) 1998.

Bartholomew, Harland *The Lansing Plan: A Comprehensive City Plan Report for Lansing, Michigan, submitted to the City Council, April 4, 1922.*

Baxter, Albert *History of the City of Grand Rapids Michigan* (Munsell & Company: New York and Grand Rapids) 1891.

Baxter, Albert "Some Fragments of Beginnings in the Grand River Valley," *MPHC* Vol 17, (Robert Smith & Co.: Lansing) 1892, p. 325-331.

Bedford, Jim and Ton Pagliei *Grand River, Michigan: River Journal Series* (Frank Amato Publication, Inc.: Portland, Oregon) 2002.

Belknap, Charles E. *The Yesterdays of Grand Rapids* (The Dean-Hicks Company: Grand Rapids) 1922.

Bennett, Orlie Lewis *Shipping in the Port of Grand Haven, 1820-1940* n.d. n.p.

Blois, John T. *Gazetteer of the State of Michigan* (Sydney L. rood & Co.: Detroit) 1838.

Branch, Rev. E. E. *History of Ionia County* (B. F. Bowen & Co.: Indianapolis) 1916.

Bratt, James d. and Christopher H. Meehan *Gathered at the River: Grand Rapids, Michigan, and Its People of Faith* (William B. Eerdmans Publishing Co.: Grand Rapids) 1993).

Bush, George *Future Builders: The Story of Consumers Power Company* (McGraw-Hill Book Company: New York) 1973.

Cascade Chronicles (Cascade Historical Commission) 1987.

Chrysler, Don *The Story of the Grand River: A Bicentennial History* (n.p.) 1975.

Cleland, Charles E. *A Brief History of Michigan Indians* (Michigan History Division) 1975,

Cleland, Charles E. *Rites of Conquest: The History and Culture of Michigan's Native Americans* (University of Michigan Press: Ann Arbor) 1992.

Crockery Collection, The: A History of Crockery Township (The Crockery History Group, Spring Lake Public Schools) 1994.

Darling, Birt *City in the Forest: The Story of Lansing* (Stratford House: New York) 1950.

Eckert, Kathryn Bishop *Buildings of Michigan* (Oxford University Press: New York) 1993.

Etten, William J., ed. *A Citizens' History of Grand Rapids, Michigan* (A, P, Johnson Company) 1926

Everett, Franklin *Memorials of the Grand River Valley* (The Chicago Legal News Company: Chicago) 1878.

Ewing, Wallace K. *A Chronological Directory of Industries, Businesses and Other Organizations in Northwest Ottawa County* (Tri-Cities Historical Museum: Grand Haven) 1999.

Fisher, Ernest B., ed. *Grand Rapids and Kent County Michigan* Vol. I (Robert O. Law Company: Chicago) 1918.

Fitting, James E. *Archaeology in Michigan: Present Knowledge & Prospects* (Michigan Department of State: Lansing) 1973.

Flood on Grand River Area of Grand Rapids, Michigan (Grand River Watershed Council, by the U. S. Army Corps of Engineers) 1960.

Gibbons, Bill *Grand Ledge M-100 Bridge Replacement.* 1991.

Grand Ledge Remembered (Grand Ledge Area Historical Society) 1976.

Hager, Dan "When Mighty Grand River Filled These Hills" *Grand Rapids Press*, November 24, 1968.

Hamilton, Claude T. *Western Michigan History: Colonial Period* (Merchants Life Insurance Company: Des Moines, Iowa) 1927 [?]

Hinshaw, Candace and Jane Henderson *Enjoying Grand Rapids and Surrounding Environs* (Etheridge Company: Grand Rapids) 1981.

Historic Tour of Kent County, Michigan (Kent County Library Staff) 1975.

Historical and Business Compendium of Ottawa Co. 1892-3 (Potts & Conger: Grand Haven) 1892.

History of the Grand Haven State Park, 1921-1983 (State Park Committee) [1983?]

History of Jackson County, Michigan (Interstate Publishing Co.: Chicago) 1881.

History of Ottawa County, Michigan, with Illustrations and Biographical Sketches (H.. R. Page & Co.: Chicago) 1882.

Hyde, Charles K. *Historic Highway Bridges of Michigan* (Wayne University Press; Detroit) 1993.

Kent County Library Staff *An Historic Tour of Kent County* n.p. [1976?]

Kent, Timothy J. *Paddling Across the Peninsula: An Important Cross-Michigan Canoe Route During the French Regime* (Silver Fox Enterprises: Ossineke, Michigan) 2003.

Kuiper, Ronald E. *Crisis on the Grand: The Log Jam of 1883* (River Road Publications, Inc.: Spring Lake) 1983.

Lane, Kit *Lucius Lyon: An Eminently Useful Citizen* (Pavilion Press: Douglas, Michigan) 1991.

Leach, Hugh "Dimondale dam comes down," *Lansing State Journal* October 1, 2006, p.1B, 4B.

Letter from the Secretary of War communicating the last annual report of Lieutenant Colonel J. D. Graham on the harbors of Lake Michigan, January 6, 1857 35th Congress, 1st Session, House of Representatives Ex. Doc. No. 23.

Linebaugh, Donald W. *Nineteeth-Century River Landing Settlements in the Grand River Valley, Ottawa County, Michigan* (Published by the author) 1990.

Lydens, Z. Z. *The Story of Grand Rapids* (Kregel Publications: Grand Rapids) 1966.

Lyons/Muir, Michigan n.p. n.d.

Michigan and Its Resources (Robert Smith & Co., State Printers: Lansing) 1893.

McGee, John W., ed. *Bend in the River: The Story of Grandville and Jenison, Michigan 1832-1972* (William B. Eerdmans Publishing Company: Grand Rapids) 1973.

Munn, W. Scott *The Only Eaton Rapids on Earth* (Edward Brothers, Inc.: Ann Arbor) [1952?].

Newnom, Clyde L. *Michigan's Thirty-Seven Million Acres of Diamonds* (The Book of Michigan Company: Detroit) 1927.

Past and Present of Eaton County, Michigan (Michigan Historical Publishing Assn.: Lansing) [1915?]

Romig, Walter *Michigan Place Names* (Wayne University Press: Detroit) 1986

Santer, Richard A. *Michigan: Heart of the Great Lakes* (Kendall/Hunt Publishing Company: Dubuque, Iowa) 1977.

Saranac Area Centennial, 1869-1969 (Centennial Book Committee) 1969.

Squires, Clara and Jan Kline *Island City: Pictorial History, 1835-1986.* n.p., n.d.

Thorpe, Patrick A. *The Identification of Heavy Metals, Their Movement and Their Impact on Life in the Lower Grand River, Michigan* (Grand Valley State University Water Resources Institution) 1994.

U. S. Army Corps of Engineers. *Preliminary Feasibility Report on Shallow Draft Navigation, Grand Rapids, Michigan* January 1978.

-- *Flood Plain Information for the Grand River, Ionia, Michigan* (Corps of Engineers, Detroit District) 1975.

Vaughan, Charles and Dorothy Simon *The City of Wyoming: A History* (The Wyoming Historical and Cultural Commission, Inc.: Wyoming, Michigan) 1984.

Versluis, Warren, ed. *Echoes of the Past: A Bicentennial History of the City of Walker, Michigan* (City of Walker) 1976.

Voice of the River, The: A History of Eastmanville (n.p.) 1951.

White, George H. "Sketch of the Life of Hon. Rix Robinson; A Pioneer of Western Michigan," *MPHC*, Vol. 11, p. 186-200 (Thorp & Godfrey: Lansing) 1888.

Winslow, Charles Dale *A Nation of Might* (Wm. B. Eerdmans Publishing Co.: Grand Rapids) 1945.

Woodruff, James C. *LaSalle and Michigan's History: About the Adventures of Rene Robert Cavelier, Sieur de LaSalle in and around Michigan 1679-1683* (Published by author) 1999.

Woodruff, Jim *Across Lower Michigan by Canoe, 1790* (Published by author) 2004.

-- *Locating Michigan's Old Canoe Portages* (Published by author) n.d.

MPHC=Michigan Pioneer and Historical Collections

Index

3rd Street 139
4th Street 63,64
5th Street 65
6th Street 35,114
6th Street Bridge Park 114
6th Street Dam 39,54
7th Street 138
28th Street 34,124
68th Avenue 129,130
90th Avenue 130
96th Avenue 131
104th Avenue 131
120th Avenue 132
128th Avenue 132
144th Avenue 132,133

Abbot Drain 77
Ackerson Lake 64
Ada 5, 9,11,16, 18.21,37,102, 107,108-109,108
Ada Charter Township 109
Ada Township 16,108
Adams Street 68
Ah-Nab-Awen Park 116
Airline Drive 64
Alaska 108
Albrau Creek 70
Albrow Creek 70
Alden Nash Avenue 107
Algomah 29
Allen Lake 69
Allendale 6,129
Allendale Township 14,126, 128
Allendorf, John 65
Allouez, Claude 17
Alticor 108,109
American Energy Co, 72
American Fur Co. 14
Amtrak 118
Amway 108,109
Andrew 141
Ann Arbor 8
Ann Street 114
Appleton, Wisconsin 36
Arland 70
Arland Road 70
Arnold, G. W. 102
Arnold, Oliver 102
Askin, John 14
Aurelius and Delhi Drain 77
Aurelius Township 76
Austerlitz 9, 21,110,111
Avenue A 63
Ayer Road 62

Bad River 7-8,7,23
Bad River Canal 23
Badgley Boulevard 63
Bailey Road 78
Baker Creek 100
Balderson Drain 96
Baldwin Park 71
Ball Creek 111
Ball, John 29
Bannister 100
Banta Drain 84
Baraga, Frederic 18
Barrett 121,122
Barry County 18,108
Bartholomew, Harland 54
Bass Creek 130
Bass River 31,130,130,139
Bass River landing 30
Bass River State Recreation Area 130
Bassett Creek 108
Bastian-Blessing Company 140
Battle Point 11,30,133,133
Baw-wa-ting 118
Baxter, Albert 17
Bay-vhos-a-key 133
Bear Creek 7,7,53,110,130
Beaver Creek 128
Becker Creek 111
Becker, Vroman 132
Beckerville 132
Belknap, Charles E. 30
Bellamy Creek 104
Bellin, Jacques Nicola 7
Belmont 110
Belmont Road 111
Bend Area Mine Reclamation Project 55
Bentley Drain 76
Benton Road 92
Berry Bridge 69,69
Berry Lake 70
Berry Road 69
Berryville 9,69,70
Bicentennial Park 140
Biddle City 21,22,84,84
Biddle, John 84
Big Grand Lake 60
Big Rapids 37
Bill's Lake 111
Bivens, Jesse 61
Black Creek 106,132
Black Lake 23,108
Black River 6,23
Blackman Township 68

Blackman, Horace 21,66
Blackskin 18
Blackstone Street 68
Blakeslee Drain 77
Blendon hills 30
Blendon Landing 125,126
Blendon Lumber Co. 126
Blois, John T 5,136
Blue Ridge 62
Blue Water Highway 103,107
Bogue Flats 95
Bogue Flats Recreation Area 96
Booth Drain 64,75
Booth, Oliver 22,71
Boston 21,104
Boston Township 104
Bower Drain 100
Boyce Creek 100
Boyer, Joshua 94
Boynton Landing 125
BR-U.S.-131 114
Bradley Drain 100
Brandy Creek 131
Braxee Lake 58,59,59,61
Brenke Fish Passage 86
Brenke, William 86
Bridge Highway 78
Bridge Street 18,42,89,94,106,116,126
Brill Lake 69
Brimmer Creek 106
British Fur Company 14
British Museum 12
Brock County Park 104
Brooklyn Road 64
Brown Lake 59,63,64
Browns Lake Road 63
Bruce Bayou 54,132
Bruce Bayou East 132
Bruce Bayou West 132
Buck Creek 124
Buckland, Warren B. 71
Buena Vista 110,111
Bullhead Drain 108
Bulls Creek 89
Bunday Hill 59,61
Bunker Highway 76
Bunker Road Lansing 76
Bur Oak Landing Open Space 130
Burchard John W. 86
Burke Highway 77
Bush, George 36
Butler Creek 108
Butternut Creek 108

149

Butterworth Street 124
Button Drain 84
Byron 124

C & O RR 96,101,106, 119,138
Cady Road 64
Cahogan Creek 69
Calhoun County 11
Cameron Gas and Electric 39
Campau Lake 108
Campau, Jacques 16
Campau, Louis 15,16,18,19, 21,100,114,140,141
Campau, Toussaint 16
Canal Park 114
Canal Street 44,46
Cannon Township 109
Carlton Park 124
Carpenter, Mr. 43
Carrier Creek 87,89
Carson City 100
Cascade 108
Cascade Township 107
Cass, Lewis 93
Cedar Creek 108,111
Cedar Drive 131
Cedar Lake 84
Cedar Springs 111,127
Center Lake *59*,65
Centerline Road 96
Charleston 9,14,*126*,128
Charleston Landing 128,*128*,129
Charlotte 108
Charlotte Highway 93
Chauncey 110
Chicago & Lake Michigan RR 94
Chicago & Michigan Lake Shore RR 132
Chicago & Milwaukee RR 41
Chicago & West Michigan Ry 124,132,136
Chicago 31,32,49,70,130,136
Chicago Road 60
Chief Hazy Cloud County Park *108*,109
Child's Mill 37
Childsdale Dam 111
Chinook Pier 34
Chippewa 11,93,98
Chubb, Lamont 21,127
Churchill Road 70
Cincinnati Northern RR 64
Cincinnati, Jackson &
 Mackinaw RR 62
City of Grand Rapids (1967) 33,*33*
City of Grand Rapids 31
City of Two Rivers 94
clamming 51-52
Clark Corners 133
Clark Lake 62
Clarke Lake 59
Clear Creek 106
Cleveland Street 101
Clinton and Ionia Drain 97
Clinton County 92,96
Clinton River 23
Clise Drain 94
Coast Guard City USA 136
Cobmusa, Chief 123
Coffinberry, Wright L. 10
Coldbrook Pumping Station 114
Coldwater river 108
Cole Wright Helms Drain 108
Collier Creek 100
Collings, Robert 30
Collins 96,*96*
Columbia 59,77
Columbia Creek 76,77,*77*
Columbia Highway 77
Columbia Township 62
Columbia, Lake 62
Commercial Street 127
Commonwealth Power Co. 36,37,*38*,39,97
Community Haven 130
Comstock Park 9,112
Comstock Riverside Park 113
Comstock Road 134
Comstock, Charles C. 112, 113
Connor Bayou 132
Connor Bayou Park 132
Conrail 71
Constant, Louisa "Lisette" 14
Constant, Pierre 14
Construction Aggregate Co. 32,130,139
Consumers Energy 37,97
Consumers Power 37,47,97, 98,99,105,106
Converse burial mounds 10, 118
Cook Drain 97
Cooley family 128
Coon Creek 84
Cooper Road 69

Cooper Street 67
Coopers Creek 106
Coopersville 37,128
Corunna 99
County Line Drain 76
Court Drain 107
Court Street 11
Cove Lake *59*,64
Cox Drain 100
Creeping Bear 33
Crietz Road 79
Crockery Creek 10,11,54,131
Crockery Township 130,134
Crooked Creek 104
Crosby Street 46
Cryderman Lake Drain 93
Culver Road 62
Cutter Drain 94

Dailey, Jim 30
Danby *21*
Danby Township 92-93
Daniel Ball 28
Daniel J. Lamoreaux Park 111
Dansville 8,16,106,107
Darken and Boyer Drain 108
Darling, C. C. 22,73
David Highway 96
Deepdale Memorial Gardens 80
Deer Creek 84,128
Deer Creek County Park 128-129
DeHaan, Jacob 129
Delhi Township 77
Delta 87
Delta Center 89
Delta Charter Township 87
Delta Mills 9,13,22,40,87
Delta Mills Park 89
Delta Township 89
Department of Natural Resources (DNR) 52,72,92, 97,101
Deremo Island 134
Dermo Bayou 134
Dermo Island 134,135
Detroit & Milwaukee Ry 114,124
Detroit 8,12,17,66.86,87, 101,106,136
Detroit Free Press 81
Detroit River 12
Detroit Tigers 112
Detroit, Grand Haven &

Milwaukee Ry 31,41,123
Detroit, Grand Rapids &
   Western RR 91,100
Detroit, Lansing & Lake
   Michigan RR 87
*Detroit, le 9,*9
DeVos Convention and
   Exhibition Hall 117
DeVries Drain 131
Dewey Hill *137,*139
Dewey, George 139
Dewitt 96
DeWitt Road 86
Dexter Street 102, 103,*103*
Dexter, Samuel 21,102
Diamondale 78
Dickerson Creek 106
Dimond, Isaac M. 78
Dimondale 9,22,37,*77,*78,*78*
Dimondale Mill 79,*79*
Dixon road 70
Dixon's Creek 37
Doan Creek 8
Dodge, Frank 87
Dollar Lake 65
Dornbos Island 138
Draper Road 62
Duck Creek 108,111
DuJaunay, Fr. 8
Duncan Creek 108
Duplain and Ovid Drain 100

E. S. Pierce clothing store 35
Eagle Leather Co. 50
Eagle Township 92
Earll, William 71
East Grand River Park 135
East Michigan Avenue 67
East Washington Street 67
Eastman family 22
Eastman, Galen 128,129
Eastman, Mason 129
Eastman, Timothy 129
Eastmans Island 136
Eastmanville 9,22,30,31,*114,*
   121,122,*126,128,*129,*129,*138
Eastmanville Bayou Park 129
Eaton County 22,37,71-76,
   77-79,87-92,108
Eaton County Battalion 74
Eaton Rapids 9,*21,*22,35,39,
   45,46,*66,*72-76,*73*
Eaton Rapids Township 76
Eaton, John H. 73
Edison Light and Fuel Co. 37
Edison, Thomas Alva 36

Edwards Drain 87
Egypt Creek 109
Elgin 127
Ella Sharp Park 63
Elm Street 84
Elsie 100
Empire 29
Enterprise 29
Erie Canal 23
Escanaba Park 141

Faiver Drain 94
Falahes Road 65
Fall Creek 108
Fanny M. Rose *135*
Farewell Lake 61
Federal Energy Resource
   Commission (FERC) 38,85
Ferdon Creek 100
Ferris State College 55
Ferry Point 139
Ferry, William M..21,133,
   136,139
Ferry, William M. Jr. 139
Ferrysburg 9,10,32,33,*114,*
   *133,*138,*138,*139
Field, Eugene 83
Fillmore Street 126
Finlayson, J. 8
Fish Creek 7,8,54,100
Fish Ladder Park 116
fishing 51-54
Fitch, Abel F. 65
Fitch, Cadette Everett 120-
   122
Fitzgerald Dam 91-92
Fitzgerald Park 91
Fitzgerald, Frank D. 91
Flat River 5,16,18,22,28,37,
   41,47,54,94,106,107
Flat Rock 8
Ford Museum 117
Ford, Gerald R. Jr. 117,47
Ford, Jerry and William 84
Fowlerville 84
Frances Park 82
Francis Road 64,67
Franklin Street 40
Frayer Creek 92
Friend Brook 96
Front Street 35,116
Frost Corners 93
Frost Road 93
Fruitport 135
Fulton Street 43,46,108,118

G.A.R. Park 74
Gabaguoache 9
Gale Road 71
Ganson Street 68
Gardner and Hiar Drain 93
Gates Road 62
Gaulty, Mr. 12
Gazetteer of the State of
   Michigan 5
Generaux Road 100
Generauxville 100-101
Genereauville, Louis 100
Genereauville, Louis Jr. 100
George P. Savidge *31*
Georgetown Charter
   Township 124
Georgetown Township 124
Gerald R. Ford Freeway 119
Gigley Bayou 135
Gilbert Drain 78
Gillett Bridge 117
Gillett, Richard M. 117
Gillette Road 62
Glass Creek 108
Goodrich Transit Line 32
Goodwin Road 96
Goose Creek 97
Gordon, Amos 124
Gov. Mason 27,28
Graham, J. D. 143
Grand 31,127
Grand Avenue 85
Grand Haven 5,6,8,9,16,18,
   21,,22,,25,27,28,29,30,31,
   49,50,52,59,61,85,87,*114,*
   129,132,*133,136,137,*136-
   143,26
Grand Haven Brass Foundry
   139
Grand Haven Charter Town-
   ship 133
Grand Haven Municipal Boat
   Launch 138
Grand Haven Municipal
   Marina 139
Grand Haven Municipal Pier
   34
Grand Haven State Game
   Area 132,134
Grand Haven State Park 142
Grand Haven Township 133
Grand Lady 34,124
Grand Lake 58,*58,59,*59,60,
   125,127
Grand Ledge 9,13, *21,*32,
   33,37,46,*81,*88-92,*88,89,*

*90,91,*108
Grand Ledge Spiritualist Camp Association 91
Grand Point 60
Grand Rapids 5,6,9,10,14-15, 19,20,*20,21,*21,22,14-15, 26,27-31,35-37,39,42-48,*45,*49-52,54,66,86, *102,*112-119,*114-118,*119, 123,127
Grand Rapids & Indiana 114
Grand Rapids and Lake Michigan Transportation Co. 31
Grand Rapids Boom Co. 41
Grand Rapids Dam *114,*114
Grand Rapids Edison Co. 37
Grand Rapids Electric Light and Power Co. 35,37
Grand Rapids Evening Press 49
Grand Rapids Filter Plant 114
Grand Rapids Herald 42-43, 45,46
Grand Rapids Press 52,53
Grand Rapids Telegram Herald 23-24
Grand Rapids Township 112
Grand Rapids Veterans Facility 113
Grand Rapids Watershed Council 47
Grand Rapids, Greenville & Alpena 114
Grand Rapids, Newaygo and Lake Shore RR 114
Grand Rapids-Musekgon Power Co. 37
Grand River Avenue 86,87, 94
Grand River City 87
Grand River Greenway 55
Grand River Market 68
Grand River Mini-Game Area 101
Grand River Navigation Company 28
Grand River Park 82,125-126
Grand River Power Co. 39, 72,75
Grand River Transportation Company 31
Grand River Valley Line 114
Grand Trunk Railway car ferries 32
Grand Trunk RR 44,46, 68,101
Grand Trunk Western RR 84,103,106,114,138
Grand Valley 127
Grand Valley Milling Co.118
Grand Valley State University 10,118,126
Grande Riviere, la 6,7
Grandville 9,11,*21,*30.34. 37.40,44,*114,,119,*119, 121,123,129
Granger and Ball 29
Grass Lake Drain 65
Gratiot County 23
Gravel Brook 108
Great Spring 60
Great Western 29
Green View Point 33,98
Green, Fred W, 98
Greenville 106
Griffon 11-12
Grovenburg Drain 77
Grovenburg Road 77
Groves Ferry 109
Guild cabin *19*
Guild, Abby 114
Guild, Consider 114
Guild, Joel 21,114
Guinan Drain 92
Gun Lake 18

H.M. S. Felicity 12
Hackett Motor Car Co. 67
Hagar Creek 108
Hague Avenue 62
Haire Landing 30,125,*125*
Haire, John 125
Halterman Creek 100
Hamlin Street 74
Hamlin Township 71-72
Hamlin Township Park 72
Hamlin, Samuel 22,73
Hammer Lake 62
Hanse, Andrew 99
Harbor Drive 140,142
Harbor Island 138,139
Harbor Steamer 34
Harper's Weekly 42
Harris Drain 76
Harris Landing 125
Hart, Nancy 135
Harvey, Hosey 78
Hastings 108
Hawley Road 106
Hazel Devote Park 99

Heath 31
Hemmingway Lake 106
Hennepin, Louis 17
Henry Johnson Park 124
Henry, Patrick 61
Herkimer County, NY 21,114
Heward, Hugh 13
Heyden, W. C. 29
Hickory Creek 111
High Bank Creek 108
High Street 66
Hill Creek 108
Hillsdale County 5,58,59,60, 61
Hinkley Road 63
Historical and Business Compendium of Ottawa County 28
Hobart Drain 75
Holland 23,24,25,49
Holland City News 25
Holly Creek 108
Holly Drain 89
Holton Dam 66-67,*67*
Honey Creek 109
Hopkins Mill 136
Hopkins, Benjamin 136
Horner Brothers Woolen Mills 45,75,76
Horsebrook School 87
Hovey's plaster mill 30
Howard Drain 77,94
Hubbard's Landing 126
Hubbardston 37,100
Hudson River 23
Hudson Street 107
Hudsonville 6,24,130
Hugh Heward Challenge 13
Huhn Mill 104
Huhn, Daniel G. 106
Hummingbird 28
Hunters Orchard Park 89
Huntoon Creek 22,70
Hurd Marvin Drain 59
Huron River *4,*8,12,13
Husted and Landenburg Drain 94,96
Hyser, Dr. 111

I-94 68,89,93,112
I-196 119
I-496 84
Illinois Canal 29
Illinois River 6
Impression 5 Science Center 85

152

Indian Channel 132,134
Indian Creek 123
Indian Line 4
Ingersoll Station *87*
Ingersoll, Erastus 87
Ingersoll's Station 89
Ingham County 13,22,37,70,
  76-77,79-87
Ingham County Parks Dept.
  77
Ionia 9,11,*21*,37,*81*,101,
  102,102-103,*103*
Ionia County 22,92-106
Ionia Free Fair 102
Ionia Rivertrail 101
Ionia State Recreation Area
  104
Ionia Township 100
Irving 108
Island Avenue 83
Island House Summer Resort
  90
Island Park 74,*74*
Island Queen 33
Ithaca 23
Ivanrest 124

J & K Steamboat Line 34,82
J. Potter Hart's Subdivision
  134,135
Jackson 9,12,18,*21*,28,37,48,
  51,52,*59*,59,60,66-68,*66*
Jackson County 5,8,11,12,37,
  59,60-70
Jackson County Fairgrounds
  68
Jackson prison 68
Jackson, Andrew 66,73
Jacksonapolis 66
Jacksonburgh 66
Jaycees Park 89
Jefferson Road 62
Jefferson Street 91
Jeness Hotel 44
Jenison 9,24,40,44,*114*,
  124-125
Jenison, Hiram 124
Jenison, Lemuel 124
Jenison, Lucius 124
Jenison, Luman 124
Jenute 16
Jerusalem Bayou 138
Jesuits 17
John Almy 28
Johnston Boiler Works 139
Jones Road 92

Jones, Whitney 87
Jubb Bayou 131
Jubb Bayou Open Space 131
Jupitor Road 111

Kalamazoo County 11
Kalamazoo River 5,9,12,16,
  23,34,55,61
Kalamazoo Street 44,84,85
Kalamink Creek 84
Kansas 29
Kellie Creek 108
Kellogg Drain 94
Kelly Park 141
Kent 114
Kent County 22,24,37,55,
  106-124.
Kent County Red Cross
  Disaster and Preparedness
  Committee 47
Kent Scientific Institute 10,
  123
Kent Street 93
Kent, James 114
Kettler and Norris Drain 71
Kewaycooshcum 18
Kimball Road 98
King Street 42
Kinnebrew, Joseph E. IV 86,
  116
Kinneville 9,71
Kinney, Stephen Van 71
Kinnieville 22
Kirby Bayou 131
Knapp Street 109
Knight Street 39,74,113
Knight, Benjamin 73
Kossuth 96,*96*
Kossuth, Lajos 96
Kruger, Verlen 60

L.G. Mason 28
la Framboise, Joseph 14
la Framboise, Madeline 14
la Richarde, D. 8
La Salle, Robert Cavelier,
  Sieur de 11-12
Labarge Dam 108
Lacey Creek 108
Lacks Park 118
Laingsburg 96
Lake Chicago 6
Lake Creek 104,*104,105*,106
Lake Erie 4,8,23,62
Lake Huron 6,7,23

Lake Lansing 84
Lake Michigan 5,8,11,23,24,
  51,53,54,143
Lake Michigan Drive 126,
  127
Lake Michigan lobe 6
Lake Michigan Rapid Ry 124
Lake Shore and Michigan
  Southern RR 78
Lamberton Creek 113
Lamont 9,21,24,28,31,
  114,121,122,*126*
Lamson, Edmund L. 89
Lanes Lake 70
Langlade, Charles 13,14
Lanota 32,33,*32*
Lansing 5,7,8,*21*,22,32,35,
  37,40,44-46,48,50,54,70,
  78,81-87,*81*,99,101
Lansing and Lake Michigan
  RR 114
Lansing Board of Water and
  Light 38,78,83,85,86
Lansing Center 85
Lansing City Council 54
Lansing City Electric
  Railroad Company 80
Lansing Lugnuts 86
Lansing Township 81
Lansing, John 81
Lawrence Drain 131
Le Ann, Lake 58,*58,59*,60
Leadley Park 80
Leadley, Gottleib 80
Lee Creek 107
Leonard Street 46,114,127,
  130,132
Leonard, Henry A. 99
Leoni 37,65
Leoni Township 64,65,66
Leslie 11,70
Lewis Street 66
Liberty 37,*59*
Liberty Dam 61,*61*
Liberty Mill 61,*61*
Liberty Road 62
Liberty Township 59,60,62
Libhart family 22
Libhart, H. V. 98
Life-Saving Service 142
Lime Lake *58*,60
Lincoln Brick Park 92
Lincoln Lake 106
Lincoln, Luther 21,124
Lions Park 68
Little Bass Creek 130

153

Little Creek 106
Little Deer Creek 128
Little Grand Lake 60
Little Olcott Lake *59*,64,65
Little Prairie 124
Little Thornapple River 108
Little Traverse Bay 17
Little Wolf Lake *59*,64
Little Wolf Lake County Park 64
Livingston County 84,94
Lloyd Bayou 136
Lloyd, Zena 96
Lloyd's Bayou 134,*134*,135
Logan Street 44,82
Logan Street dock 80
London 49
Long Lake 108
Looking Glass River 5,8,37, 94-96
Loomis Road 62
Loomis Steam Ferries Co. 32
Loomis, A. P. 32
Losey Street 66
Louis Glick Highway 67
Lowe Lake 8
Lowell 5,9,11,18,*21*,22, 37,41,47,*102*.106-07,*106, 107*
Lowell State Game Area 106
Lowell Township 106
Lowell, Mass. 107
Lowing Landing *125*,126
Lowing, Stephen L. 126
Luke Lowing Landing *125*, 126
Lyon, Edmund 27
Lyon, Lucius 22,27,99
Lyon, Truman H. 98
Lyons 9,11,22,27,33,35,37, 39,42,*42*,54,*81*,98-99
Lyons Dam 99
Lyons Herald 42
Lyons Township 37,96
Lyons Water Power Co. 99

M-11 124
M-16 86
M-21 107,108
M-37 112
M-45 126,129
M-50 74
M-99 76,78,83
M-106 69
M-150 64
M-188 74

Mackinac Island 14,17,75
Main Street 47,82
Manistee River 53
Manufacturer's Beltline Railroad 87
Maple 96-97,*96*
Maple Rapids 100
Maple River 5,6,7,8,*7*,22,23, 33,41,43,94,98,99-100,*101*
Maple Road 97
Marameg 9
Marker Lake *104*,106
Market Street 46
Marquette, Jacques 17
Marsac, Daniel 16,106
Martin Luther King Jr. Boulevard 86
Martin Luther King Jr. Highway 78
Martinique Island 135
Mascouten 12
Mason 77
Mason, Stevens T. 23
Maumee River 4
May Graham 31,131
McArthur River Park 73
McArthur Road 106
McCausey Branch 96
McCords Creek 108
McCoy, Isaac 17,26
McKay Brook 70
McNamara Landing 77
Mechanic Street 67,68
Memorial Auditorium 72
Menominee Indians 98
Mercedes Lake 62
Mercury Drive 133,134
Meridian Road 62,64
Michigan 29
Michigan and Its Resources 51
Michigan Avenue 40,44,67, 68,82,85,86,116
Michigan Center 37,*59*,65
Michigan Central RR 70,71, 86
Michigan Department of Environmental Quality 50
Michigan Fish Consumption Advisory 53
Michigan Health Department 49
Michigan, Heart of the Great Lakes 55
Michigan Northern RR 119
Michigan Power Co. 83,85

Michigan Princess 34,82
Michigan Road 78
Michigan Soldiers' Home 112,*112*,113
Michigan State Holiness Camp Meeting Ground 72
Michigan State Penitentiary 68
Michigan State Reformatory 103,*103*
Michigan State Supreme Court 49
Michigan Territory *4*
Michigan Veterans Memorial Bridge 85
Michigan, Michigan 81
Middle Branch 84
Middleville 108,127
Mill Creek 112
Mill Creek Station *110*
Mill Point 136
Mill Point Park 136-137
Mill Street 99
Millennium Park 55,119,123, 124
Miller Creek 89
Millett 79
Millett, S. E. 79
Millett's Station *77*
Milletts 79
Millhouse Bayou *132*,133, 134
Mills & Lacey's Drug Store 35
Milwaukee 32
Milwaukie 122
Mineral Wells bridge 40
Mineral Wells Hotel 32
Minnie Case 32
Mirror Lake 58,*58*,*59*,60
Mississippi River 6,17
Mix Dam 39,72,75-76,*76*
Monroe 62
Monroe Street *19*,68,44
Montcalm County 100,106
Montgomery 61
Montreal 16
Montrose Station 100
Montrose, NY 100
Moon Lake 65
Moon Lake Road 65
Moon, Darius 87
Moore Island 97
Moores Park 82-83
Moores Park Dam 38,39,44, 83

Moores River Drive 82,83
Morrell Street 66
Morrison Lake *104*,106
Morrison Lake Road 105,106
Morrison, Jefferson 104
Mt. Hope Cemetery 45
Mud Creek 84,94,108
Mud Drain 94
Mud Lake *59*,64
Mud Lake Drain 84
Mudge, J. S. 90,92
Mudge's Folly 90,91,*91*
Muir 5,7,22,33,43,98,100
Muir, H. K. 100
Murray Lake 106
Museum Drive 85
Museum of Surveying 85
Muskegon 27,32,37,51
Muskegon River 12,16,35,37

Napoleon Road 64
Napoleon Township 64
Nash Creek 111
Nashville 108
Nawbeck 29
Nawequageezhig 18
Nevelson, Lourse 67
New Haven Company 21,136
New York Central RR 66,119
New York City 36
Newaygo County 111
Newberry Street 114
Newburg *128*,129
Newman, Elisha 94
Newsome Creek 100
Newtown 139,*139*
Niagara County, New York 60
Nichols Road 77
Niles 17
Nolan, J. B. 7
Noonday, Chief 18,19
Norris Creek 138
North Branch 64-65,108
North Cedar Drive 132
North Grand Rapids 123
North Lansing 13
North Lansing Dam 38,39,86
North Logan Street 86
North Mills Station 112
North Muskegon River 5
North Onondaga Drain 71
North Park 112,*113*
North Park Pavilion 111,*111*, 113
North Park Street 112

North Park Street Railway Co. 113
North Shade Drain 100
North Street 68
North, Daniel 112
North, Joseph H. Jr. 81
Norton 136
Norton Indian Mounds 10, 11,34,123
Norton, Amos N. 136
Norton, Anson N. 10
Nortonville 136,*136*
Nortonville Chapel 136
Nova Scotia 71

Oak Grove 87,*87*
Oak Lane 64
Oak Park 91
Oak Point *59*,64,135
Oakland Avenue 85,86
Odawa 11,16-19,102,116,118
Odawa/Battle Point Launch 133
Odd Fellow 29
Odel Drain 76
Ogimaans 93
Ohio Dock 126
Ojibway 11,19,116,118
Okemos 93
Olcott Lake *59*,64,65
Old Clinton Road 70
Old Lansing Road 79
Olds plant 87
Olds, Ransom E. 81
Oldsmobile 81,82
Oldsmobile Park 86
Olive Branch 28,30
Oneida County, New York 21
Onondaga 9,13, 22,37,*66*, 71,*71*
Onondaga County, NY 71
Onondaga Township 70-71
Operlander Drain 94
Orchid Creek 69
Oriole Drive 130
Osborn Creek 94
Ottawa 11
Ottawa Center 9,*21,130*, 130-131
Ottawa County 24,54, 124-144
Ottawa County Boom Co. 41
Ottawa County Parks Dept. 54
Ottawa County Poor House 129
Ottawa Creek 127
Ottawa Point 28,139
Ottawa Street 85
Ottawa Street Power Station 38,85,86
Otto E. Eckert plant 38,83
Ovid 100
Ovid Lake Creek 131
Owashtanong 8,28

Page Creek 106
Palisades 88
Park Drive 64
Parks, J. B. 29
Parks, Robert S. 29
Parmelee 108
Parnall Road 52,69
Patronage 29
Paulson Creek 106
Peacock Ditch 104
Peake Road 93
Pearl Street 35,48,117,118, *118*
Pearl Street bridge 41,*41*
Peck Lake 106
Peckins Road 97
Pee-miss-a-quot-o-quay 16
Peninsula and Northern Navigation Co. 32
Peninsula Light Power and Heat Co. 37
Penn Central 69,70
Perch Lake *58*
Pere Marquette RR 43,44,94
Perry Creek 70
Perry Drain 94
Perry Lake 70
Peter F. Hurst Planetarium 63-64
Peter White Lake 62
Petrieville 9,76
Petrieville Highway 76
Pettis Avenue 109
Pettys Bayou 138
Phelps, Orange 71
Piatt powerhouse 44
Pickett Drain 69
Pickwick 32
Pierce Drain 94
Pierce, Benjamin K. 14
Pierce, Franklin 14,61
Pine Creek 100
Pine Mud Lake Drain 84
Pine River *7*,8
Plainfield 110

Plainfield Avenue 49,110
Plainfield Township 109
Plains Highway 74
Planet Walk 85
Plaster Creek 119
Platte River 53
Plumbs Mills *110*,112
Poel Island 134
Pohl Road 93
Polk, James K. 128
Polkton 22
Polkton Township 128
polycholorinate biphenyls (PCB) 54
Pontiac 29
Portage Creek 8
Portage Lake 8
Portage River 5,8,13,69
portages 7-8
Porter, Chauncey 110
Portland 5,8,9,11,*21*,36, 37,39,46-47,*46,81*,94-95
Portland Municipal Dam *95*,96
Portland River Trail *94*,94,96
Portland State Game Area 92,93
Post Creek 111
Potawatomi 11,17,19,98,116, 118
Pottamie 9,133
Pottawatomie Bayou 54,134
Pottawattomie Park 134
Potterville 108
Powers' Opera House 35-36
Prairie *102*,101
Prairie Creek 37,54,*102*,94,101
Prairie Street 99
Pratt Creek 108
A. Preusser's Jewelry Store 35
Price Lake 65
Princess Laura 34,82
Probert Road 63
Public Museum of Grand Rapids 117
Puddleford Bridge 69
Putney Millpond 61

Quaker Brook 108
Quiggle Lake 108
Quimby 108

R. E. Olds Transportation Museum 85
Raisin River 62
Ramsey Drain 93
Rapids 31
Recollet order 17
Red Cedar River 5,8,22, 40,48,81,*84*,84
Red Creek 14
Reed Road 62
Remey Chandler Drain 94
Revolutionary War 13
Reynolds Drain 87
Reynolds, Reuben 127
Rhymer Creek 138
Rice, Mrs. 121
Richard, Gabriel 17
Ripps Bayou 128
River Bend 92,*92*
River Drive 82
River Front Park 86
River Road 84
River Street 73,89
River Street Park 84
River Styx 100
River Trail 83,85
River Trail Walk 86
Riverbend Natural Area 77
Riverfront Plaza 85
Riverside County Park 131
Riverside Drive 102
Riverside Park 54,82
Riverwalk Theatre 85
Rives Junction 70
Rives-Eaton Road 70
Rix Robinson Park 138
Robbins, Tom 30
Robert E. Lee (boat) 107)
Roberts, Richard 128,129
Robinson Township 130,132
Robinson, Andrew 100
Robinson, Rix 14,16,18,21, 108,109,136,141
Rockford 22,*110*
Rogue River 5,22,37,54, 110,*110*,111
Rolfe Cemetery 107
Rose, John 127
Roselle Park 109
Rouge Drain 94
Rouge River 110,111
Round Lake 65
Royal Shore 60
Royston Drain 70
Rush Creek 124
Russell, John W. 89

S.S. Escanaba 141
Sag, The 139
Sagana 13
Saginaw Bay 4,6,7
Saginaw Bay lobe 6
Saginaw County 23
Saginaw River 5,7,8,23,25
Saginaw Street 40,86
Sand Creek 30,125
Sand Creek Landing 125
Sand Creek School 30
Sandstone Creek 70,91
Sanford Drain 131
Santer, Richard A. 55
Saranac 9,21,22,*102,104*, 104-106
Saranac Nature Center 106
Saugatuck 34
Sault Ste. Marie 17
School Street 138
Schumacker, Martin 65
Scipio Creek 108
Scott A. Flahive Memorial Boat Launch 135
Scott Creek 111
Scott Park 84
Scranton 22,129
Scranton, George W. 129
Searbird 32
Sebawa Creek 93
Se-be-quay 16
Seely Creek 106
Segwun *106*,107
Segwun Avenue 107
Seneca Falls Power Co. 39
Sessions Creek 104
Seven Islands Resort 32,33, 90
Seymour Street 40
Shaddock drain 94
Sharon Township 5
Sharp and Thornapple Drain 108
Sharp Creek 62
Sharp Lake *59*,64
Sharp, Ella (Merriman) 63
Shaw Branch 70
Shiawassee 133
Shiawassee County 94,99
Shiawassee River 7-8,23
Shiawassee Street 40,86
Shimnecon 93
Silver Creek 78
Six Lakes 106
Skiff Lake 62
Skinner Extension Drain 77

Slater, Leonard 18
Sligh, Charles 25
Sloan Creek 84
Sloan, Bradley 78
Smith Bayou 138
Smith Drain 94
Smith, Abraham 89
Smith, Ada 109
Smith, Benjamin 130
Smith, Lemoyne M. S. 136
Smith, Sidney 109
Smithville 71
Smithville Dam 39,71,*71*,75
Smithville Road 72
Snug Harbor 134
Somerset Center *58*,60
Somerset Township 60,61
Somerset, NY 60
Soule, Robinson & Co.100
South Branch 84
South Bridge Street 99
South Division Street 106
South Ionia 102,*102*
South Jackson Road 61
South Lakeside Street 65
South Street 64
Southern Michigan State Prison 69
Sowanquesake 16
Sparta 111
Spicer Creek 76
Spicer, Amos 22,73
Spicer, Pierpoint E. 22,73
Spicerville Dam 45
Spillman carousel 117
Spoon, Don 132
Spoon, John 132
Spoonville 9,10,122,*132*,132
Spoonville Road
Spring & Co. Dry Goods Store 35
Spring Brook 45,73-76
Spring Creek 111
Spring Lake 9,11,22,31,33, 34,*114*,122,*133*,135,136, *136*,138
Spring Lake Township 133, 134
St. Charles 23
St. Joseph River 10,11,17,31
St. Louis, Missouri 54
Stahl Bayou 138
Star Clothing House 35
Starboard Tack 140
State Prison Farm 69
State Road 92,102,103

State Street 70,74
State Street Dam 39
Stearns Bayou 41,132,*132*, 133
Stebbinsville Station 96,*96*
Steele, Harry and Zine 21, 127
Steele, Henry 28
Steele's Landing 21,127
Stegman Creek 111
Stevens Creek 138
Stiffler Drain 93
Stone Coal Creek 92
Stonewall Road 63
Stoney Creek 108
Straits of Mackinac 6.18
Stuart 136
Stuart, Robert 21,136
Sturgis Drain 100
Sulpican order 17
Summer Night Tree 67
Summers Drain 94
Summit 37
Summit Township 62-63
Sunny Creek 109
Sweeney's Landing 84
Sweet's Hotel 35
Sycamore Creek 84

Tallmadge 9,10,125
Tallmadge Township 124
Tallman Street 82
Talmadge Drain 84
Taylor, David 89
Tecumseh Park 87
Tecumseh River Drive 87
Thomas Mission 17
Thompson Creek 108
Thornapple 37
Thornapple Creek 69
Thornapple Lake 108
Thornapple River 16,22,72,108
Three Bridge 77,*77*
Timberland Creek 104
Tittabawassee River 8
Tobin-Wheeler-Snyder Drain 69
Todd, Robert T. 70
Toledo 4
Toles Creek 106
Tomahawk Power and Pulp 39
Tomkins 70
Tompkins Center 70
Tompkins County, NY 81

Tompkins Road 70
Tompkins Township 70
Tompkins, Daniel D. 70
Towner Road Park 93
Townley, Richard 70
Towslee, Orange 78
Toxic Substances Control Act 50
Trader's Creek 14,128
Treaty of 1783 13
Treaty of Chicago 18
Treaty of Detroit 18
Treaty of Saginaw 18
Treaty of Washington 18
Trestle Bridge Park 70
Tucker, Stephen 124
Turkey Creek Drain 94
Turner Creek 108
Turner Road 92
Turner, James 87
Turner-Dodge House 86-87
Tuthill, Moses 61
Twin Lakes Creek 69
Tyler Creek 108

US-31 138
US-127 64,65,70
U. S. Army Corps of Engineers 25,57,59,31,140
U.S. Coast Guard 126,140, 141,142

Van Andel Museum Center 117,118
Van Buren County 11
Van Schelven, G. 25
Vandercook Lake (village) *59*,62
Vandercook Lake *59*,62-63, *63*,64
Vandercook Lake County Park 63
Vandercook, Henry H. 62
Vermilion Creek 96
Vernon 99
VFW National Home 71
Vicary Road 60
Vincent Creek 138
Vinklemulden, Mr. 121

Wabasis Creek 106
Wacousta 96
Waddell Creek 110
Wagar Dam 97-98,*98*
Wagar, H. R. 37,97

157

Wait Drain 100
Walker 9,112,*114*,119,123
Walker, Charles I. 123
Walker, Joseph 123
Walter Creek 111
Warren City 130
Washington Avenue 84
Washington Street 137,140
Washtenaw County 5,11
Washtenong 5
Waters Drain 100
Waterville Mill 104,105
Waverly Park 9,79-80,*79,80*
Waverly Road 71,87
Wayne County 8
Wealthy Street 37,46,119
Wealthy Street dock 29
Webber Dam 35,*36*,38,39, 97,*97*
Webber Dam Boat Access 97
Webber Road 97
Webberville 84
Webster Road 87
Welland Canal 53
Wells, Franklin P. 79
Welsh Civic Auditorium 48
West Eastmanville Bayou Park 130
West Michigan Whitecaps 112
West River Drive 111,112

West Town Drain 78
Western Creek 70
Wheatland 5
White, Andrew J. 130
White, George K. 106
White, Nathan M. 21,136
Whitneyville Creek 108
Wildcat Creek 69
Wiley Creek 84
William D. Monroe Bridge 68
William M. Burchfield Park 77
William M. Ferry Landing Park 140
William Toan Park 94
Williams Lake *59*.63
Williamston 8,84
Willing 97
Willow Creek 64,71,84
Wilson Avenue 34,124
Winchell and Union Drain 93
Windsor 77,*77*,78
Windsor Township 77
Windsor, Vermont 78
Winfield 71,*71*
Wisconsin and Michigan Transportation Co. 32
Wise Creek 100
Wm. H. Barrett 24,29
Woldumar Nature Center 79

Wolf Creek 106
Wolf Lake *59*,64,*65*
Wolf Lake Casino *65*
Wolf Lake Road 64
Wolverine Chair Factory 35
Woodbridge, William 15
Woodbury, T. B. 125
Woodby, Thomas 127
Woodruff, James 60
Wright Pardee Skinner Drain 108
Wyoming 9,*114*,119
Wyoming County, NY 119
Wyoming Ranches 124
Wyoming Township 124

Yeomans, Erastus 102
York Creek 112
Young & Delleker 8
Youth Haven Recreation Area 70
Ypsilanti 8

Zeeland 24

Photo Credits and Acknowledgments

p. 13 Drawing by Cadette Everett Fitch, from "A Few Idle Days," Grand Rapids History & Special Collections, Archives, Grand Rapids Public Library, Grand Rapids, Michigan.

p. 17, 19, 20 from Albert Baxter's, *History of Grand Rapids Michigan*, published 1891.

p. 30 "A Day on the Olive Branch," from *The Yesterdays of Grand Rapids* by Charles E. Belknap.

p. cover (bottom), 29, 36(top), 75(top) ,98, 127, 131, 143 from the collection of William and Robin Kemperman, Saugatuck

p.38 Map of the Commonwealth Power Company system from a 1908 promotional brochure.

p. 41 "Logjam at the Pearl Street Bridge, July, 1883," from photo collection at Grand Rapids History & Special Collections, Archives, Grand Rapids Public Library, Grand Rapids, Michigan.

p. 60 map from "A New Map of Michigan with its Canals, Roads & Distances" published by Thomas, Cowperthwait & Co.,Philadelphia. Copy courtesy Jim Woodruff.

p. 93 Drawing by artist Ann Gray of Ganges Township, Allegan County.

p.177 Early map from map file at Grand Rapids History & Special Collections, Archives, Grand Rapids Public Library.

p. 120-122 "A Few Idle Days" by Cadette Everett Fitch, condensed from an illustrated manuscript in Grand Rapids History & Special Collections, Archives, Grand Rapids Public Library, Grand Rapids, Michigan. Drawings by Cadette Everett Fitch.

All other illustrations from the collection of the author.

The author would like to recognize the assistance of many people along the course of the Grand River including Doug Schlappi, Dave Haueter in Grand Ledge, Connie Bos in Saranac, Jim Woodruff in Delta Mills, the DNR office, Portland State Game Area personnel, county park workers and administrators, city park directors, and the ever patient librarians in Grand Haven, Portland, Saranac, Lansing, Jackson, Grand Ledge, Eaton Rapids, Ionia, Lyons, and Spring Lake, and especially Rebecca Mayne of the Grand Rapids Public Library archives. Also the captain and crew of the Grand Lady from Grandville and the Michigan Princess in Lansing.

And Jack Sheridan of the Saugatuck-Douglas Historical Society for technical assistance.

Rivers of Michigan Series

The Kalamazoo

The Kalamazoo River of southern Michigan rises in the Irish Hills south of Jackson in Hillsdale County and flows gently westerly until it exits into Lake Michigan near Saugatuck nearly 200 miles later. On the way it passes through two of Michigan's middle-sized manufacturing cities, Battle Creek and Kalamazoo, and many smaller towns with big histories, Homer, Albion, Marshall, Concord, Ceresco, Galesburg, Allegan, Otsego and Plainwell. A few places that were once important stops on the river, Singapore, Sheridan, Bath Mills, and Harmonia, no longer exist at all. There was a time, too, when hydroelectric dams on the Kalamazoo River furnished most of the electricity for southern Michigan.

In this volume there are chapters on the meaning of "Kalamazoo," information on the almost annual flooding and environmental concerns that once caused the Kalamazoo River to be known as the "sewer of West Michigan." A mile by mile trip down the river tells the history and present-day status of the settlements along its banks.

978-1-877703-40-9   128 pp, illustrated, indexed, 2006

The Grand

The Grand River was the superhighway of early Michigan. It connected with the Saginaw River, or the Huron River, to cross the peninsula. On its way from the Irish Hills to Grand Haven on Lake Michigan, it passes through three major cities, Jackson, Lansing and Grand Rapids, and many small settlements begun with great hope. Several areas of rapids furnished power for grinding wheat and turning furniture. Steamboats carried a steady traffic into the 20th Century, but today the smoke-belching giants have been replaced by excursion boats taking tourists on scenic trips. Canoes, kayaks and motorized pleasure boats share the ripples.

In this volume the plans to create a cross-peninsula canal are discussed, along with the difficulties caused by floods, ice buildup, and log jams. Read how fishing has actually improved in the last 50 years. Profusely illustrated with maps, old postcard views and photographs.

978-1-87773-39-3   160 pp. illustrated, indexed, 2007

Future projected volumes:

>   The Raisin
>   The St. Joseph